Black Plays: Three

Boy with Beer Paul Boakye, **Munda Negra** Bonnie Greer, **Scrape off the Black** Tunde Ikoli, **Talking in Tongues** Winsome Pinnock, **A Jamaican Airman Foresees His Death** Fred D'Aguiar

Boy with Beer 'Boakye's writing is brash and excitingly fresh . . . *Boy with Beer* has cutting edge.' *Independent*

A Jamaican Airman Foresees His Death 'A tough, warm, and thrillingly individual play full of live-wire humour and athletic assurance . . . The writing is reckless but controlled, the humour dark, ribald and dangerous . . . Simply bursts with that fiery energy of which true theatre is made.' John Peter, *Sunday Times*

Munda Negra Bonnie Greer's plays have been hailed for their 'gently expressed but complex insights' and 'the precision and near-poetic beauty of the writing . . . finely-wrought, penetrating and very moving.' *Guardian*

Scrape off the Black 'Ikoli's play is funny, wry and at times positively searing.' Jim Hiley, *Listener*

Talking in Tongues 'Winsome Pinnock, a writer of extraordinary promise, is here expressing with guile and tenacity, many unsayable things about sexual and social miscegenation . . . She writes with enormous verve.' Michael Coveney, *Observer*

Black Plays: 'A pathfinding anthology; one of political as well as theatrical significance, signalling the weight and authority of black cultural achievement in Britain.' *African Times*

Volume Three in Methuen's series of *Black Plays* provides another wide-ranging selection by theatre director Yvonne Brewster: Paul Boakye's *Boy with Beer* reveals a funny and sexy story of a *Guardian*-reading gay photographer who finds his fantasy 'African Prince'; poet and novelist Fred D'Aguiar's *A Jamaican Airman* is a rhapsody on a colonial theme set in WW2 Scotland; novelist Bonnie Greer's *Munda Negra* examines the heart of darkness in Western civilisation; Tunde Ikoli's much-revived *Scrape Off The Black* is an East End mixed-race family drama; and Winsome Pinnock's wonderfully atmospheric *Talking in Tongues* explores the tangled racial and sexual issues in modern-day Britain.

Yvonne Brewster has worked extensively in theatre, film, television and radio both as an actress and director. In 1965 she began her career as a director by co-founding The Barn, Jamaica's first professional theatre, with Trevor Rhone. She is a founder member and the current Artistic Director of Talawa Theatre Company, based at the Cochrane Theatre, London. Her theatre career spans work with numerous companies and includes *Two Can Play* by Trevor Rhone at the Bristol Old Vic, *Abigail's Party* by Mike Leigh (Cambridge Theatre Company), Lorca's *Blood Wedding* at the Royal National Theatre and *The Dragon Can't Dance* by Earl Lovelace at Theatre Royal Stratford East. Her productions with Talawa include *The Road* by Wole Soyinka, *The Love Space Demands* by Ntozake Shange, *Resurrections* by Biyi Bandele Thomas, as well as *The Importance of Being Earnest*, *Anthony and Cleopatra*, and *King Lear*. She is a Fellow of the Royal Society of Arts and was awarded an OBE in 1993.

in series with

Frontline Intelligence 1 – New Plays for the Nineties (ed. Pamela Edwardes)
April De Angelis, *Hush*; Declan Hughes, *Digging for Fire*; Judith Johnson, *Somewhere*; Edward Thomas, *East from the Gantry*

Frontline Intelligence 2 – New Plays for the Nineties (ed. Pamela Edwardes)
Karen Hope, *Foreign Lands*; Sarah Kane, *Blasted*; David Spencer, *Hurricane Roses*; Rod Williams, *The Life Of The World To Come*

Gay Plays: Four (ed. Michael Wilcox)
Neil Bartlett, *A Vision of Love Revealed in Sleep*; Eric Bentley, *Round 2*; Gerald Killingworth, *Days of Cavafy*; Joe Pintauro, *Wild Blue*

Gay Plays: Five (ed. Michael Wilcox)
Rod Dungate, *Playing by the Rules*; Noel Greig, *Plague of Innocence*; Jonathan Harvey, *Beautiful Thing*; Joe Pintauro, *Snow Orchid*

Made in Scotland – An Anthology of new Scottish plays (eds. Ian Brown & Mark Fisher)
Mike Cullen, *The Cut*; Simon Donald, *The Life of Stuff*; Sue Glover, *Bondagers*; Duncan McLean, *Julie Allardyce*

New Woman Plays (eds. Linda Fitzsimmons & Viv Gardner)
Elizabeth Robins, *Alan's Wife*; Cicely Hamilton, *Diana of Dobson's*; Elizabeth Baker, *Chains*; Githa Sowerby, *Rutherford and Son*

Plays by Women: Seven (ed. Mary Remnant)
Kay Adshead, *Thatcher's Women*; Claire Dowie, *Adult Child/Dead Child*; Lisa Evans, *Stamping, Shouting and Singing Home*; Marie Laberge, *Night*; Valerie Windsor, *Effie's Burning*

Plays by Women: Nine (ed. Annie Castledine)
Marieluise Fleisser, *Purgatory in Ingolstadt, Pioneers in Ingolstadt, Avant-Garde, Early Encounter* and *I Wasn't Aware of the Explosive*; Maureen Lawrence, *Tokens of Affection*; Sheila Yeger, *Variations on a Theme by Clara Schumann*

Plays by Women: Ten (ed. Annie Castledine)
Simone de Beauvoir, *The Woman Destroyed* (adapted by Diana Quick); Elfriede Jelinek, *What Happened After Nora Left Her Husband*; Claire Luckham, *The Choice*; Phyllis Nagy, *Weldon Rising*

Walks on Water – an anthology of work by leading experimental artists (ed. Deborah Levy)
Rose English, *Walks on Water*; David Gale, *Slips*; Guillermo Gómez-Peña, *1992*; Claire MacDonald, *Storm from Paradise*; Deborah Levy, *The B File*

Black Plays: Three

Boy with Beer
Paul Boakye

Munda Negra
Bonnie Greer

Scrape off the Black
Tunde Ikoli

Talking in Tongues
Winsome Pinnock

A Jamaican Airman Foresees His Death
Fred D'Aguiar

Selected and Introduced by Yvonne Brewster

Methuen Drama

Methuen New Theatrescripts

This collection first published in Great Britain in 1995
by Methuen Drama
an imprint of Reed Consumer Books Ltd
Michelin House, 81 Fulham Road, London SW3 6RB
and Auckland, Melbourne, Singapore and Toronto
and distributed in the United States of America
by Heinemann, a division of Reed Elsevier Inc.
361 Hanover Street, Portsmouth, New Hampshire NH 03801 3959

Reprinted 1995, 1996

ISBN 0–413–69130–6

A CIP catalogue record for this book is available at the British Library

The front cover photograph of Ella Wilder as Irma in *Talking in Tongues* is by Simon Annand

Typeset by Wilmaset Ltd, Birkenhead, Wirral
Printed in England by Clays Ltd, St Ives plc

Caution
All rights whatsoever in these plays are strictly reserved. Applications for performance, including professional, amateur, recitation, lecturing, public reading, broadcasting, television and the rights of translation into foreign languages, should be addressed as follows:

Boy with Beer: Alan Brodie, International Creative Management Ltd, 76 Oxford Street, London W1N 0AX
Munda Negra and *A Jamaican Airman Forsees His Death*: Curtis Brown Group, Fourth Floor, Haymarket House, 28/29 Haymarket, London SW1Y 4SP
Scrape off the Black: Theatre Royal Stratford East, Gerry Raffles Square, Newham, London E15 1BN
Talking in Tongues: Lemon, Unna & Durbridge, 24 Pottery Lane, Holland Park, London W11 4LZ

Contents

Introduction

It is six years since the publication of the second volume in this series. During this time there has been a proliferation of revivals of North American classics such as James Baldwin's *Blues for Mister Charlie*, Alice Childress's *Trouble in Mind* and Ralph Ellison's *Invisible Man*. More contemporary American work has also been produced quite widely, from writers such as August Wilson at the Royal National Theatre and the Tricycle, Ntozake Shange and Endesha Ida Mae Holland produced by Talawa Theatre Company. George C. Wolfe's *The Coloured Museum* and *Spunk* added to the productions from the American stable, along with Anne Deavere Smith's one-woman show *Fires in the Mirror* produced by the Royal Court Theatre. However, black plays from South Africa have been less in the forefront than in the 1980s. While Wole Soyinka remains virtually the only produced West African writer, Derek Walcott continues to be the established voice of the Caribbean.

Happily, the younger black British voices during this period have not been silent. These include Trish Cooke, (*Back Street Mammy, Running Dream*) Zindika (*Paper and Stone, Leonora's Dance*), Biyi Bandele Thomas (*Marching for Fausa, Two Horsemen* and *Resurrections*) and those whose work has been chosen for this anthology.

The playwrights in this volume reflect clearly the realities of black life in the British dimension and do not imagine from anecdote, through rose-coloured spectacles, the life and times of recent ancestors. This is a trend which should be encouraged in the hope that fewer playwrights will feel impelled to succumb to the populist need to be sentimental, exotic and naïve. These writers have not presented us with characters who continually cry 'who are we, what are we' but have given us real people in all their complexities.

In all these plays, black people are inextricably bound up in the being of Britain. They seek their place within society or within institutions in our society. In *Scrape off the Black* that institution is The Family, in its obvious and immediate sense. In *Talking in Tongues, Boy with Beer* and *Munda Negra* it is the family in the wider sense of society as a whole. In *A Jamaican Airman Foresees His Death* it is a desire for a place in the history of the nation for which the characters were prepared to offer up their lives.

Spanning the decades from the forties to today, an underlying thread that binds these stories is the theme of lost youth. Our starting-point is Fred D'Aguiar's *A Jamaican Airman Foresees His Death*. Working on the familiar theme of young Jamaicans with a powerful image of England as their mother country, he usurps the cliché by exposing the vulnerability of brave young men who perceive their worth and duty in going to fight for a country to which they have never been. Three young Jamaican men join the Royal Air Force during the Second World War. A strong bond of friendship and memories of home accompany them on their way to the mother country. All Alvin wants to do is regain his prehistoric wings and fly. When he achieves his ambition, one mistake leads to his wings being clipped.

Fred D'Aguiar is better known as a poet. The language of his play has strong lyrical overtones and evokes powerful and emotional images.

We stay with a theme of idealistic youth in Tunde Ikoli's *Scrape off the Black*. I have included it as I regard it as a modern classic of the black British stage and was astonished to find that it was not available in print. It is a play that dragged us kicking and screaming into the late sixties and seventies. Ikoli's uncompromising presentation of characters and the issues that preoccupy them results in a play with a disquieting impact, full of the people and language of the East End. Arguably you could not get more English than this play. This is perhaps the most poignant piece with regard to a character's desire to belong.

Winsome Pinnock's work finds its way once again into this series. Since her *A Rock in Water* was published in the last anthology, Winsome has been awarded the George Devine Award for a body of work. Both Winsome and Tunde are British born and bred, yet they speak with vastly different voices.

Talking in Tongues begins at a New Year's party, with Leela, Curly and Claudette hiding amongst the coats, away from the crowd and the noise of the celebration. Claudette bemoans what she sees as the betrayal of black womankind: the tendency of black men to venerate the attentions and attractions of white women over those of black women. Her friends may have heard it all before but when they inadvertently witness Leela's husband having sex with white Fran, Claudette's words become sharply focused. Only when Leela breaks away and takes a holiday in Jamaica, can she begin to come to terms with her own feelings. The depth of those feelings are ameliorated by the unknown energy which dwells on a section of the beach, enabling women to express their innermost feelings and purge themselves by 'talking in tongues'.

Paul Boakye is a young playwright of immense promise, who chooses to deal with hitherto taboo subjects including homosexual love and, in his recent commissioned piece *No Mean Street*, AIDS. Some black writers have stopped short of touching such subjects for fear of upsetting 'their own'. In *Boy with Beer*, Paul rises above the temptation to self-censor with an uncompromising representation of subject and character. One of the strengths of this honest and moving play, about a black gay relationship, is that it is non-sensational; it is issue-based but not constrained by the issue. Boakye manages to create an almost tangible atmosphere, in which he envelops his characters and immerses his audience in their passion.

American-born Bonnie Greer is perhaps the most prolific and unusual writer on the scene at the moment. She is a writer, director, novelist and theatre critic, and was joint winner of the 1992 Verity Bargate Award for her play *In the Country of the Young*. In the play in this volume, *Munda Negra*, Anna, a black American art lecturer now living in England, opens with an impassioned plea to a group of teachers to re-examine the art of the great Masters, with respect to their representation of black people. Anna is full of brilliance and angst for past wrongs done to her. She has a great deal to say about others but is less earnest when talking about herself and her feelings. Just when the play begins to weigh heavy on the anguish side, the Pope makes a cameo appearance. There is both depth and much humour in this tale of a woman who has achieved so much and yet is unfulfilled.

Bonnie could not be accused of sticking to tired conventions or hackneyed representations of reality. Like Paul and the other contributors to this anthology, she produces work that is original. Black British plays are pushing the boundaries of style and content. There is no one view or one 'thing' that is the sum total of us as black people. We are everything and everyone, and it is only by exposing what we truly are that we can explode the myths and show our diversity, individuality and humanity.

I would like to thank young black British playwright Yazmine Judd for all her invaluable help and advice in the choice of the plays in this volume.

Yvonne Brewster
Talawa, London 1994

Boy with Beer

A Stage Play in Three Acts

Paul Boakye

Characters

Karl, *African, aged 27*
Donovan, *Afro-Caribbean, aged 21*

Boy with Beer was first presented by HOB Productions, in association with This is Now Theatre Company, at The Man in the Moon Theatre, London, from 14 January to 1 February 1992 with the following cast:

Karl   Clive Wedderburn
Donovan   Tunde Oba

Directed by Steven Luckie
Designed by John Lynch
Lighting by Nicola Stammers
Sound by Jimmy Mackness
Produced by Paul Boakye and Steven Luckie

The action takes place in a London flat on two levels.

Act One

A kitchen–dining-room. **Karl** *frantically prepares dinner for two. He sets the table, lights an incense stick, and puts on 'Loving Pauper' by Gregory Isaacs. The doorbell rings, he panics and runs to the door.*

Karl Donovan? Hi! Come in.

Donovan This place is hard to find.

Karl Come in. It's not numbered properly.

Donovan Went right past it at first.

Karl It says thirty-five upstairs. People don't notice there's a thirty-five A down here. Pass your coat. Ta. Go in. Grab a seat.

Donovan So that's what you look like.

Karl And that's what you look like. (*Silence.*) What's in the bag?

Donovan I got some beer on the way.

Karl Cheers. Do you want one a these now?

Donovan Might as well. (*Silence.*) What's that smell? Have you cooked? You haven't cooked, have you? I couldn't eat a thing.

Karl No problem. (*Clearly disappointed, he removes cutlery from the table.*) Did you have a nice Christmas?

Donovan Christmas is boring, man.

Karl Let's hope the New Year gets better.

Donovan I'm looking forward to summer this year, though, man. People are bubbling in the summer.

Silence. **Donovan** *coughs.*

Karl What do you do? You said you were phoning from work. What do you do?

Donovan I wasn't phoning from work. I was phoning from round some girl's.

Karl No. The first time. You said you were phoning from work.

Donovan Oh, then.

Karl What do you do?

Donovan I drive.

Karl Minicabs?

Donovan I drive a van for this building firm.

Karl Right.

Donovan So you live here on your own, do you?

Karl Yeah. What about you?

Donovan I live with a friend. Not too far from here.

Karl What sort of friend?

Donovan A good friend.

Karl How good is good? I mean, do you . . .

Donovan What, sex? Sometimes. Depends on the mood. Nothing much these days cos she's going through a bad patch.

Karl So you're living with a woman?

Donovan I'm with her, yeah, cos she's going through a bad patch.

Karl Well that's a shame.

Donovan I been there a year. She kinda needs me, y'know.

Karl We all need someone.

Donovan That's it, ennit. But it's petering out now our relationship, petering out. There's always a weak one, ain't there, you just gotta hold them up. That's what I'm doing. She's very good-looking. That's what all my mates say anyway.

Karl They're the ones you got to watch.

Donovan You'd like her.

Karl You should have invited her round, Donovan.

Donovan I can ring her if you want.

Karl *gives him a 'you're very funny' look.* **Donovan** *walks round the room – like a burglar casing the joint.*

Donovan This is a nice place you got here.

Karl It's not bad. (*Opens a beer.*) Do you want this in the can or a glass?

Donovan You could have some raves here, man.

Karl Raves?

Donovan Yeah, you could have some wicked parties here.

Karl I'm thinking of having a party.

Donovan Do you do Hardcore?

Karl The porno or the music?

Donovan Parties, man, parties.

Karl Not lately.

Donovan They still have 'em, you know. Contortions, Rumours, and all them. Don't you go to none a them?

Karl Never heard of them.

Donovan They still have 'em, man. Sussex, Surrey, Aldershot . . . them kinda places.

Karl They move about?

Donovan Every time.

Karl Sounds like too much hard work to me.

Donovan Madness, ennit. There's this place up in Dalston. Reggae place called Scandals. Doesn't open till seven in the morning. What you do is you go out to other places first. Get home for about five. Get a couple hours sleep. Get up, have a shower, something to eat, and get down there before the queues start up. That's a nice place, Scandals. But you get tired, though, man. (*Coughs, takes a swig.*) That club last night . . . I was buzzing, you know, in that club last night.

Karl Me too.

Donovan I got this chest infection, right, so I don't smoke. That Bluenote Club, man, it was hot and sweaty and full-up a ganja smoke. It was giving me a buzz but it was getting in my eyes. I couldn't breath. The club never had no air-conditioning. They should do something about that.

Karl How many clubs have air-conditioning?

Donovan Some have holes in the roof.

Karl I'll take your word for it.

Silence. **Donovan** *drinks and watches Dame Edna on the television.*

Donovan She's good ain't she. What's her name again? Possum?

Karl You're into Dame Edna?

Donovan I wanna see this later. Saw it last week. She's good, man. She's a man, ain't she?

Karl Probably.

Donovan In twenty minutes. Okay. I wanna watch that. (*Drinks.*) What did my friend say to you last night?

Karl He asked if the guy I was with was my boyfriend, as he put it. I said, 'No, he's a friend.' He said that his friend liked me and his friend wanted to know if he could talk to me. I told him I talk to anyone.

Donovan He's out of order, man.

Karl Why, wasn't he following your instructions?

Donovan I never said nothing to him.

Karl I thought you two were a regular double act.

Donovan Naw, man. Sometimes. Sometimes when I'm shy.

Karl   You, shy?

Donovan   Yeah, man.

Karl   You don't seem shy to me.

Donovan   And sometimes we mess about – chat people up for fun.

Karl   For fun?

Donovan   Yeah, you know, flirting.

Karl   So you're a big flirt, are you?

Donovan   Yeah.

Karl   Do you flirt at your parties? Your Hardcore parties?

Donovan   I flirt with everyone, man. It's packed ennit. You have to flirt with them jus' to get 'em out've your way. Hardcore's brilliant. You're just dancing there. Everybody doing their own thing. Moving their arms about like this. Wild, man, wild. The girls are just tripping and wriggling their arms in fronta your face like inviting you for a fuck. Then there's the boys. I love white boys at Hardcore, man. They'll do anything for you. Share their joints . . . their E's . . . their girls . . . even give you a lift right back to your own front door. Man, I mean, them white boys are so fucking good – I just love 'em. Step on a black guy's toe, you could be dead within seconds, step on a white geeza's foot, he'll want to buy you a drink.

Karl *laughs.*

Donovan   No, serious! The other night, right, I was pushing through this crowd. Where was I? – can't remember – anyway, I was pushing through this crowd. Spilt beer all down this white guy's shirt. I mean, all the beer, all over him. The guy turned round, smiled, 'Don't worry about a thing, mate, naw it's awright. It's wet enuf in 'ere as it is.' Big grin across his face like this. Brushed it off. Just carried on dancing. I couldn't believe it. I wouldn't a done that, would you? I woulda brushed it off, but I wouldn't a smiled about it. I woulda said, 'That's awright, mate, just make fucking sure you don't do it again, awright cunt!?'

Karl *looks at him disapprovingly.*

Donovan   Well? What would you a done? Tell me something about yourself. I'm well and truly tired, man, but I'm a good listener.Come on then?

Karl   I'm twenty-seven. I smoke a lot. I take photographs and I live here.

Donovan   Did you tell me about you took photographs last night?

Karl   We didn't get that deep.

Donovan   I can't remember what I said to you, you know. I'm so fucking tired as well. I feel like shit crawling. I was fresh before I got here. (*Yawns, sits down on a piece of paper, pulls it from under him and reads it.*) What's this, is this a love letter?

Karl   No, give it here, that's private.

Donovan   No, wait a minute, man, what's this? 'We are not a people of yesterday. Ask when first a Brother's lips kissed a Brother's mouth.' What's this? 'We are not a people of the destroyer's world, our roots return to Anoa.'

Karl   So you can read.

Donovan   I ain't an idiot, you know. 'There by the banks of the sacred Pra we met. Before Ghana became just a distant memory. Before the desert became desert.' Wait, wait a minute, man! 'In that fabulous Black time when Poets among us still sang songs of praise to the spirit of Brotherhood holding our people together.'

Karl   You're taking the piss.

Donovan   No, I'm not. Let me finish. 'Under the shade of a young Nim tree we slept, while the Prophet Densua pictured a time: The destroyers would come; hurl our soul to humiliation and our benevolent ways into defeat and obscurity; where now in dream or awake, I think of you.' What's this? You don't write poetry, do you?

Karl   What do you think?

Karl *snatches the poem.* **Donovan** *laughs and swigs beer.*

Donovan   Naw, man, you should try writing songs. Then you could chat a thing or two about Africa.

Karl   And you know all about Africa?

Donovan   Did I say that? I didn't say that, did I? I know a thing or two about Rastas, but I didn't say I know anything about Africa, did I? Are you African?

Karl   Ghanaian.

Donovan   What?

Karl   I was born in Ghana, West Africa. I came here nine years ago to study.

Donovan   I thought you was African.

Karl   Is that a problem?

Donovan   No, man, no, why?

Karl   Only Africans and West Indians . . .

Donovan   Ain't s'pose to get on. I know, that's what people say.

Karl   Doesn't mean it has to be that way.

Donovan (*flinches, changes the subject*)   There's a party tonight.

Karl   Oh, yeah?

Donovan   There was a guy last night giving out invitations. Didn't he give you one?

Karl   All I've got is this.

Donovan   It was on a small piece of white paper.

Karl   Unless it's in my coat pocket. Look, are you staying or going?

Donovan   I'm s'pose to page my friend. I'm so tired, though, man. I wanna relax a bit. Aaaaahhhhhh. Had two hours sleep last night. Woke up at five this morning. Driving some stuff up town. You get really worked up with the roads so full.

Silence. **Donovan** *suddenly laughs out loud.*

Donovan   You was doing some really weird dancing last night in that club.

Karl   Stoned outta my head and enjoying the music.

Donovan   You was doing some really weird weird dancing, man. Your legs look like the Rubber Band Man's. (*Giggles.*) Bending down you were. Way, way down as well. You was dancing right in fronta me.

Karl   I didn't see you.

Donovan   I was watching you. I said to myself . . . aaah . . . yeah, man . . . that's nice! Then all of a sudden you just grab your drink and went. I thought: he'll come back.

Karl   I didn't notice you.

Donovan   I was right behind you.

Karl   I didn't see you until you said hello.

Donovan   That guy you were with?

Karl   Mark?

Donovan   He was clinging.

Karl   Mark's my good mate. I like Mark a lot. He has his faults. Don't we all. He's white . . . yeah . . . but he's a better friend to me than many black guys have been.

Donovan   (*takes a swig*)   So what's happenin'?

Karl   What do you mean?

Donovan   What's happenin' now?

Karl   Nothing, by the looks of it.

Donovan   Are you fit?

Karl   (*on edge*)   What kind of question is that?

Donovan   Are you fit?

Karl   Fit enough.

Donovan   How fit are you?

Karl   Right now? About as fit as I need to be.

Donovan   D'you reckon?

Karl   Have you got something in mind?

Donovan   I like to be blunt about these things.

Karl   Go ahead.

Donovan   Are you gonna give it to me tonight?

Karl Is that what you want?

Donovan Yeah.

Karl Are you going somewhere special in a hurry? You've bought all this beer. We've got all night. What's the hurry?

Donovan I didn't mean right right now.

Karl But you'd like to hit the sack soon?

Donovan No, no, not at all now.

Karl Have another beer. Wait for Dame Edna.

Donovan Might as well.

Karl Nothing better to do.

Donovan *goes to the fridge and takes another beer, crosses to the window and looks out at the rain.*

Donovan You remind me of that singer.

Karl What singer?

Donovan Cockroach.

Karl Roachford.

Donovan (*laughing*) I said, Cockroach, didn't I?

Karl Similar.

Donovan Roachford.

Karl I'm sexier than he is, though.

Donovan You're what?

Karl Sexier than he is.

Donovan How do you work that one out?

Karl I don't think he's sexy. He tries to be. But he could learn a thing or two from Seal.

Donovan You think Seal's sexy?

Karl Linford Christie is sexy.

Donovan Would you admit to another black man that you thought he was sexy?

Karl Why not?

Donovan No, man! (*Laughs.*) You go out with a lot of white guys, don't you?

Karl I have white friends.

Donovan And your boyfriend now – he's white?

Karl   No. I've slept with white men, if that's what you want to know. But I want relationships with black men.

Donovan   Yeah?

Karl   Yeah.

Donovan   I don't check for white people at all.

Karl   Your girlfriend is black?

Donovan   Susan? Your colour.

Karl   That's good.

Donovan   She's a little joker Susan is. She makes me laugh.

Karl   That's nice to hear.

Donovan   She ain't too well right now.

Karl   What's wrong with her?

Donovan   Just woman problems, I s'pose, I dunno. I mean, she's fit an' everything. It's jus' if it ain't one thing with her it's the other.

Karl   So does she know about you?

Donovan   No way, man. You joking! You couldn't tell a girl that you go with men. Unless the girl was a lesbian.

Karl   Some couples work it out.

Donovan   Some white couples work it out.

Karl   But not you and your Susan?

Donovan   I don't see how the relationship could work.

Karl   So you lie to Susan instead?

Donovan   I tell her what she needs to know. What else you gonna do? You ain't exactly gonna go up to her, 'Excuse me, babes, but I fuck men – hope you don't mind.'

Karl   Is that what you do?

Donovan   All the time.

Karl   There's a problem.

Donovan   What's that?

Karl   I want to make love to you too.

Donovan   (*shakes his head*)   Uh-huh, man! Not possible!

Karl   That's a big problem then.

Donovan   That's why two bulls can't get laid.

Karl   Sorry?

Donovan   Why two men can't get it together.

Karl So what are the men you fuck?

Donovan Don't get me wrong . . .

Karl No! I think I know exactly where you're coming from. Don't get me wrong! I enjoy a good fuck and I give as good as I get. What makes you think that the men you fuck are any less than other men? And what would you know about it anyway?

Donovan I didn't mean it like that. I don't know why I said it. Do you think I'm out of order? I'm out of order, en' I? I know I am. So what are you saying?

Karl I'm saying I don't sleep with men who have a problem turning over.

Donovan So what are you saying?

Karl I want your arse too.

Donovan What – in the same night?

Karl No big deal!

Donovan We'll see how it goes.

Karl We'll see how it goes before you fall asleep.

Donovan Who's gonna fall asleep? (*Swigs.*) Do you take Poppers?

Karl I don't have any.

Donovan Good thing I brought some then.

Karl You've got a bottle with you?

Donovan In my jacket pocket.

Karl Whatever turns you on.

Donovan Drink some more wine. (*Pours* **Karl** *a glass of red wine.*) Red wine is good for you, anyway. Lots of iron.

Karl Red is my favourite.

Donovan I've never developed a taste for red wine. Can't stand the stuff really. Champagne is nice, though. You can get dead pissed on champagne. No headaches, no hangovers, no nothing. I used to work in this off-licence in Peckham. Me and the landlady used to get pissed all the time on champagne. Then she'd tempt me round the back with a fiver in her bra. I was only a kid, but she'd get me to give her one on the cold stone floor. Sometimes if I was really good at it she'd give me a tenner.

Karl (*teasing him*) Are you any good at it then?

Donovan I think I am.

Karl There's a big difference . . .

Donovan What – thinking?

Karl   Between being good at it and thinking you're good at it. They're not always the same thing.

Donovan   There's only one way to find out. Try it!

Karl (*flirting*)   Is that a challenge or a boast?

Donovan   There's only one way to find out.

Karl   The bed's upstairs.

Donovan   What kind of bed is it? Is it a comfortable bed?

Karl   There's only one way to find out.

Donovan   Maybe I should go up and test the bed. Bounce on it a bit. What do you think?

Karl *leads the way to the bedroom. Hanging from the walls are several black and white photographs of black men in various stages of undress.*

Donovan   This is a nice bed. This is a nice room, man. Don't tell me, you're into wood. Are you a *yuppie*?

Karl   Are you stupid?

Donovan   Don't call me stupid! (*Testing bed.*) This is a nice bed. Let's have a look at your pictures. Is this your boyfriend?

Karl   Was.

Donovan (*looking at photos*)   He's nice. He looks very . . . hhmmm . . . This is nice.

Karl   That guy has got a beautiful arse.

Donovan   I'm gonna have forty winks. Do you mind?

Karl   I thought you wanted to watch Dame Edna?

Donovan   That's in twenty minutes, man. I'll just rest for twenty minutes. Wake me up. Is there a TV up here?

Karl   The television's downstairs.

Donovan   I'm tired, you know.

Karl   Take your clothes off.

Donovan   If I take my clothes off I'll only want to make love to you. You take yours off.

Karl   If I take my clothes off, I'll only want to make love to you.

Donovan   You're being silly. You're being very silly now.

Karl I think we both are. (*Removes* **Donovan***'s shoes*.) Shall I turn the television off downstairs and bring everything up?

Donovan Might as well.

Karl Well, don't sound too eager. You might ruin your street cred!

Donovan I'm tired.

Karl You must have known that before you got here?

Donovan I know.

Karl (*annoyed*) I'm going downstairs to roll another joint. I forget you don't smoke.

Donovan Look in my jacket pocket, bring the Poppers up, will you.

Donovan *closes his eyes and begins to snore.* **Karl** *enters and sits on the bed to roll a joint. He leans forward and kisses* **Donovan** *hard on the mouth.*

Donovan What's happenin'?

Karl You were about to take your clothes off.

Donovan *jumps up, undresses and gets back into bed in his underpants. He fumbles under the covers, removes his underpants, throws them out on to the floor.*

Karl Progress! How much more of that can you handle in one night?

Donovan *sucks his teeth.* **Karl** *removes condoms from a bowl and throws a few at* **Donovan***, who fumbles under the covers again as* **Karl** *strips and gets into bed naked.*

Donovan Lights off! Lights off! Hit the lights, man!

Karl *turns out the light. Silence.*

Karl Well?

Donovan *jumps on top of* **Karl** *and starts gyrating like a mad dog on heat.*

Karl Easy! Easy! Wait a minute! Ain't you ever heard of foreplay? Huh! . . . Awright . . . awright . . . Huh!

Donovan (*moaning and groaning*) I'm gonna cum!

Karl What!?

Donovan I'm gonna cum!

Karl Don't cum now!

Donovan I wanna cum.

Karl Don't cum! Save it!

Donovan I have to!

Karl You'll fall asleep.

Donovan I won't!

Karl You will.

Donovan   I'll cum again.

Karl   How long?

Donovan   Half an hour.

Karl   I don't believe that!

Donovan   How long do you think?

Karl   Two . . . three hours . . . if you wake up at all.

Donovan   Uh! Let me cum. I'm gonna cum. I can cum again!

Karl *switches on the light and sits on the edge of the bed.*

Donovan   What you doing?

Karl   Let's go back downstairs.

Donovan   What you doing, man? What you let me out for? Turn over.

Karl   I ain't your woman.

Donovan   Let me go back in.

Karl   Let go of my arm.

Donovan   You can't do this to me, no, man, please.

Karl   What's the rush? Got some pussy to see to up town? Why hurry? We've got all night.

Donovan   I couldn't be bothered now.

Karl   You couldn't be bothered?

Donovan   I couldn't be bothered.

Karl   Just as well then. (*Rising.*) Let's get up.

Donovan (*grabs* **Karl***'s shoulder*)   What's that? Is that bone? (*Giggles.*) I could break every bone in your body if I wan'ed (*Giggles.*) Why are you so skinny?

Karl   Who's skinny?

Donovan   That's bone, man. Never mind! I thought I was skinny. Have you got Aids?

Karl   Why? Have you?

Donovan   Serious. Do you always use a condom?

Karl   I always use a condom.

Donovan   And this bloke last night, you gave it to him, yeah?

Karl   What are you getting at?

Donovan   You sleep with a lot of white guys, don't you?

Karl   We've had this conversation.

Donovan   Tell me the truth. You sleep with a lot of white men?

Karl None of your business! And if I do, it's probably because I keep meeting jerks like you. Big, dumb, vulnerable black men with no sense of love for themselves let alone anybody else.

Donovan You think I'm out of order, don't you?

Karl I think you're childish, selfish, emotionally immature, sexually retarded and confused.

Donovan Ah, ah, ah, ah . . .

Karl And if on top of that you're trying to say that Aids is a white man's disease, then you're more stupid than I thought.

Donovan Don't call me stupid.

Karl White-man-made disease or not, black people are dying of Aids all over the fucking place – so don't talk crap!

Donovan Have you got Aids?

Karl If you're so afraid of Aids, use a condom like the rest of us, or don't have sex. It obviously wouldn't be a great loss to the world.

Donovan I'm out of order, en' I?

Karl I know enough black men living with HIV and Aids. None to my knowledge have ever slept with white men.

Donovan Yeah? How old are they?

Karl None of your damn business!

Donovan I'd betta go now, you know. What time is it? Shit! I've forgotten the number. I was s'pose to page my friend, but I've forgotten the number. I'd betta get up. Can I use your phone. (*Gets out of bed, grabs a nearby towel and wraps it around his waist. He dials a telephone number.*) Do you think I'm out of order?

Karl (*making bed*) Don't worry about it.

Donovan No, man, I just couldn't be bothered now.

Karl Because you didn't cum or because you think I've got Aids?

Donovan I feel all funny now. (*Hangs up phone.*) I'll just go to the bathroom. Wash my hands. Make sure I have a bath when I get home. Where's the bathroom? Is there one up here?

Karl Straight ahead.

Donovan Nice. (*Exits, smelling his hands. We hear running water as he washes his hands in the bathroom. There is a loud crash as he drops the soap.*) Shit!

Karl What's that?

Donovan I dropped the Simple soap.

Karl *makes the bed and dresses as* **Donovan** *enters, smelling his hands.*

Karl Clean now?

Donovan Safe!

Donovan *dresses in silence.* **Karl** *leads the way downstairs where they sit as before.*

Donovan   I s'pose I'd betta finish my drink.

Karl   Take the rest with you.

Donovan   No, no, man. You have them. I nicked them, anyway.

Karl   It wouldn't surprise me.

Donovan   I used to go to school near here. I know all this area really well.

Karl   What school was that?

Donovan   Why?

Karl   Just asking.

Donovan   I went to Dick Shepherd's.

Karl   I know Dick Shepherd's.

Donovan   Not really. I went to Forest Hill Boys. Do you know it?

Karl   I've heard of it.

Donovan   What do you think of it?

Karl   It's a school like any other school.

Donovan   Useless bunch a bastards, en' they? I left when I was fifteen.

Karl   Did you leave or were you asked not to come back?

Donovan (*laughing*)   No, man. Nothing like that. The teachers didn't like us. We used to mess about. Enjoy ourselves. You know how kids are.

Karl *looks at him.*

Donovan   No, not really. I was expelled when I was fifteen. Hitting a teacher. Busting his nose. That was two years ago. I'm seventeen now.

Karl *looks at him hard, disbelieving.*

Donovan   Don't look it do I? It's cos I'm tired. Sometimes I look a sweet and innocent seventeen. Girls are always coming up to me in clubs and saying . . . 'How old are you? You're really cute aren't you?' Why? How old do I look to you?

Karl   Twenty-one.

Donovan   I am twenty-one. I look it, don't I?

Karl   Twenty-one isn't a bad age. Some people think I'm an old man.

Donovan   You?

Karl   In my shirt and tie, I'm a mature thirty-five.

Donovan   And I'm immature, right?

Karl   You'd better watch yourself. You might be getting a bit drunk.

Donovan   Are my eyes red?

Karl   Red as blood.

Donovan Shit!

Karl I think you should go.

Donovan I used to have really clear eyes once. But that's before I started enjoying myself. I was fifteen at the time. (*Long, deep swig.*) My parents spent the night with this black minister. We're Pentecostals, and his son – a right rude bwai, but very good looking – shared my bedroom. Separate beds, of course. The son was twenty-one. In the night he strip back his top sheet and lay in white Y-fronts wanking away right at me. I pretended to sleep but watched it all. He took fifteen minutes to cum. Squirting cream towards me in my bed. Next morning I found him wanking off all over my jeans and he stained the front pure white. He never seem to mind whether I saw him or not, and the room was light enough for me to see him in. He never said a word about it next day at church and I never mentioned it either. But it was very sexy to watch, believe me. (*Swigs.*) About a week later, my mate Sticks, who was sixteen, spent the night by me on the put-you-up bed. I thought I'd try the same on him. Just after he said 'good night' I pulled back my quilt and face towards him in his bed. I could see him watching, but he never said a word, breathing heavy, making me think he was asleep.

In the silence, **Donovan** *coughs.*

Karl Is that it?

Donovan I know it might sound funny to you, me telling it like this, but it turned me on something rotten that I did it whenever I stayed, or friends stayed, overnight.

Karl Same room of course.

Donovan Try it sometime. See what enjoyment you get, or give, to the one who's watching.

Karl I think you should go.

Donovan What? What for? I don't know why I told you, you know.

Karl I like it. It's a good story. Pity you couldn't muster up some of that imagination upstairs.

Donovan I just couldn't be bothered, man. I couldn't be bothered.

Karl Hey, my brother, no problem. But what are you still doing sitting here?

Donovan I don't know, you know. You ask a lotta questions.

Karl *looks up at him.*

Donovan Where's my Poppers?

Karl Left-hand pocket.

Donovan Oh, yeah! Look . . . what's your name again?

Karl What's my name?

Donovan I've got your number, haven't I? It's on that piece of paper. Shall I give you a call?

Karl If you want.

Donovan See you around, then.

Karl See you around.

Donovan (*off*)   You forgot to lock the security gate. You'll lock it now, though?

Karl   Don't worry!

Donovan (*off*)   Ouch! It's cold out here.

Karl *enters and sits as before. Dim lights to blackness.*

Act Two

One month later. **Karl** *is sorting his washing when the doorbell rings. He goes to the door.*

Karl Who is it?

Donovan (*off*) Me.

Karl Who's me?

Donovan (*off*) Me-me.

Karl There are many me's. Who is it?

Donovan (*off*) Me.

Karl Michael? . . .

Donovan (*off*) Don't you know?

Karl Look, Michael . . .

Donovan (*off*) Why do you keep saying Michael, is he one of your men?

Karl Look, whoever it is, if you're knocking on my door to talk sensibly to me, then let's talk, okay. If not . . .

Donovan (*off*) It's Donovan.

Karl Who?

Donovan (*off*) Donovan from the garage.

Karl What garage?

Donovan (*off*) It's raining out here, man. Can I come in?

Karl *opens the door.* **Donovan** *enters.*

Donovan What's up?

Karl You all right?

Donovan I ain't too bad, y'nuh. What's been happening with you?

Karl Nothing much.

Donovan I was just passing.

Karl Come in, if you're coming.

Donovan I saw your lights on, so I . . .

Karl Come in.

Donovan Cheers, man.

Karl Hey, wait a minute. What've you done to your hand?

Donovan I had a fight jus' now with this bloke outside the toilets.

Karl Stay there. Don't come in yet. I'll get you something to wrap on it. Don't drip blood on my carpet. (*Grabs a towel, runs to the door.*) Does it hurt?

Donovan Yeah, I can't move my thumb.

They enter. **Donovan** *has the towel wrapped round his hand.*

Karl Wait there a minute. (*Exits.*)

Donovan *looks round.* **Karl** *returns with a first-aid kit, disinfectant, cotton wool, plasters and bandages.*

Karl So you cut up your hand?

Donovan (*sucks his teeth*) I'm there pissing, fucking idiot comes into the loo staring at my dick. I turn round to him, 'What's the matter with you, mate, seen something you like?' 'Fucking battiman!' he says. I goes, 'Fuck off, cunt, me nuh want yuh, me fuck bigga man dan yuh a'ready!'

Karl That was brave.

Donovan I step outside now the pussy pulls a knife. You shoulda seen him as well, skinny little pop-eyed runt, I nearly killed him.

Karl You should be careful who you're trying to pick up.

Donovan I wasn't pickin' nobody up, man, I was havin' a piss.

Karl Those toilets are dangerous.

Donovan Like I said, I wen' in there to have a piss, okay.

Karl How's that?

Donovan Awright.

Karl You might need some stitches.

Donovan It's just a cut.

Karl You should get it seen to anyway. You don't want it to get infected.

Donovan Don't worry about it.

Karl *returns the first-aid kit. Pause.*

Donovan Hey, so what – you guys couldn't stop an' chat the other day when I saw you?

Karl We were in a hurry.

Donovan Oh, yeah?

Karl Didn't think you wanted to.

Donovan   Didn't I say hello to you? I said I was gonna check you, didn't I? Where was you going?

Karl   I was with an American friend. I was taking him out to dinner.

Donovan   What was his name?

Karl   Wendell.

Donovan   Sounds like a girl.

Karl   He definitely ain't that.

Donovan   Yeah – so did he enjoy himself, ole Wendell?

Karl   Yes he did.

Donovan   You showed him a good time?

Karl   We enjoyed ourselves

Donovan   So he's gone now?

Karl   That's right.

Silence.

Donovan   So what you been up to then, Karl, man?

Karl   Not much.

Donovan   You know I ain't working far from here now.

Karl   Where's that?

Donovan   Up in Stockwell Park there. That same garage where you saw me.

Karl   That's a change from the van driving.

Donovan   I'm a good mechanic, man. Thought I'd learn a trade. Well, Susan's idea really.

Karl   Makes sense.

Donovan   I'm glad you only live round the corner here, though. You know sometimes you don't wanna go home. You never know, our friendship could blossom.

Karl *laughs.*

Donovan   What's the matter now?

Karl   Sorry.

Donovan   No, man, what's funny?

Karl   You make me laugh.

Donovan That's what people say. I was always the joker at school . . . the kid who'd make all the other kids laugh an' get everyone in detention.

Karl A disruptive element.

Donovan A born comedian.

Donovan *walks around.* **Karl** *watches him.*

Donovan So, Karl, man, looks like you fixing up the place. Bought some new statues and things. That's nice, man. That's real nice, man. This wood or stone?

Karl Wood.

Donovan I shoulda known, ennit, cos you're into wood. Looks stone to me, though, man. Guy who carved this sure knows his stuff. You never bought these here, though, these musta come straight from outta Africa.

Karl I went home for a while.

Donovan That's perceptive of me, ennit?

Karl *smiles.*

Donovan What you laughing at?

Karl Just smiling.

Donovan It ain't a word you'd expek me to use, is it. Perceptive. I like to surprise people. Like this bloke comes up to me, 'Hey, guy, how you feel?' 'With my hands,' I says, 'how about you?' I tell you he creased up. Ha, ha, ha.

Karl *laughs too.*

Donovan I did too cos I surprised myself.

Karl (*mock Texan*) You shoulda been on the stage, kid.

Donovan Or under it.

Karl Don't put yourself down.

Donovan So what was Africa like, man? What's the people like out there?

Karl Poor and clean.

Donovan Yeah? What part was you in, Guyana?

Karl Ghana.

Donovan That's what I mean, man. Ghana.

Karl Yeah, travelled right through the country this time. From Paga up north to the beautiful Lake Bosomtwe and south down into the dungeons at Cape Coast.

Donovan Dungeons?

Karl Where the ancestors were kept as slaves.

Donovan What, they still have 'em?

Karl Filled with the moans and the crying of ghosts and the scratches they made on the walls with their fingers. The survivors were herded through a dark narrow tunnel to the sea and the waiting ship to another hell.

Donovan Jamaica.

Karl Made me sick to the stomach after all these years. But that's me all over, when I don't know a thing, I always like to put myself in situations that will end my ignorance, and standing in that dungeon on the fossilised shit of my ancestors, suddenly I could feel all your pain, and I understood . . .

Donovan What?

Karl Why you are the way you are. I don't just mean you, Donovan, I mean West Indians. And Africans. The lot of us. Because we Africans lost out too. We lost over forty million of our people.

Donovan You joking?

Karl Half of those bones at the bottom of the sea.

Donovan So what the Jews got to moan about, man?

Karl You tell me. I couldn't see it before looking with eyes only. Now it's made me want to try harder to connect.

Donovan Did you take any pictures?

Karl Too pissed off to get them developed. I just want to get on the plane and go back.

Donovan I'm gonna have to set foot in Africa one day. I just know one day I gotta be there. I was listening to this bredda in Hyde Park one time, chatting about all the things that unite us.

Karl If only we could learn to love each other.

Donovan That's the key, ennit, man. (*Sucks his teeth.*) Chuh! You wouldn't mind, would you, Karl, if I jus' put these clothes in to wash with yours? My jeans got all blood on 'em.

Karl Will they dry in time?

Donovan You got a dryer, ain't you? Do you mind?

Karl Go ahead.

Donovan *undresses.* **Karl** *looks away for fear of revealing his physical attraction, of which* **Donovan** *is aware but plays it cool.*

Donovan Tell you the truth, Karl, man, I been having a bit a trouble at home. Susan, y'nuh, the missus. Don't know what's the matter with her, man. Must be something. Maybe it's me. I dunno. Don't wanna bother you or nothin' with my shit, anyway, y'nuh. Ain't been back there since last Sunday. Jus' need a space to think, man. I mean, seen as though you can't sleep as well. I was wonderin', don't wanna keep you up or nothin' . . .

Karl   You wouldn't be keeping me up.

Donovan   You sure?

Karl   Sometimes, I need to get away myself. The sofa turns into a bed.

Donovan   Cheers, man.

Karl   I'm doing it again.

Donovan   What's that?

Karl   Nothing.

Donovan   Where do you want these?

Karl   Just drop them there.

Donovan   Do you mind if I take a shower?

Karl (*points up*)   You know where it is.

Donovan   You're a mate, you know that.

Donovan *sits next to* **Karl**. **Karl** *gets jumpy, gets up, busies himself with washing and tries to fill the uncomfortable silence.*

Karl   People are funny.

Donovan   I know, I was just thinking that.

Karl   A guy used to come here. I liked him, nothing like that, met him in the street. We got on well. I took him as a brother. He came here about six weeks ago. We sat down one night – drank a few beers, smoked a few joints and chatted. We used up all my weed so he said he'd see me the following day with a draw. But when I woke up the next morning I couldn't find my wallet. I knew I had it when he was here but now it wasn't anywhere. I saw him for the first time yesterday. 'Oh, hello, Karl!' he says. I said, 'Hello!' He says, 'How are you?' I said, 'I'm fine. Couldn't be better!' – even though I'm sick as a dog for being back in this bloody country. And I expect he was waiting for us to chat. I just walked on. I mean, no quarrel, no argument, nothing, to just steal from the hand of friendship like that. How low-down we are. Is it wrong to do good?

Donovan   People ain't used to it.

Karl   But if you don't try how can you ever progress.

Donovan   They don't appreciate it, Karl, man. You should know that by now.

Karl   That's the trouble with the blacks in this country. At least in Ghana we band together. We may still die for the little we want to eat, but at least we have heart. My biggest regret is coming to this country. Because now I might never be able to live in Ghana again, and that scares me.

Donovan Don't worry, man. You'll go back when the time comes. You got any beers?

Karl None at all.

Donovan (*sucks his teeth*)   I was gonna bring a couple as well. Off-licences shut now, ennit.

Karl What's the time?

Donovan Ten past twelve.

Karl I hate this fucking place – can't even sleep and can't get a fucking drink when you want one.

Donovan What's that up there?

Karl Cheap American vodka.

Donovan Vodka?

Karl Try it. The American brought it.

Donovan What, not that Demetri? You wanna kill me? You can drive a car on that stuff. You shoulda told that American to take that shit with him.

Karl I'll have to feed that one to the real winos.

Donovan The wino children would love you. You don't drive, do you?

Karl Love to be driven.

Donovan You got a bike?

Karl Me, no, why?

Donovan I was gonna nip round this Indian offie I know, stays open all hours. You should get you'self a mountain bike, man. A bit a pumping does you good.

Karl Here bicycle-riding is a form of sport. Back home bicycle-riding is a form of poverty.

Donovan It's jus' a different way a seeing things. You miss home, don't you?

Karl Missing home now would be like saying I miss hunger. When I can make something good there, then I'll miss home.

Donovan You've done all right for you'self, though. This place and everything. That's a nice pin you're wearing.

Karl It's a badge.

Donovan Bob Marley, ennit?

Karl Peter Tosh.

Donovan Red, green and gold.

Karl The colours of my heart.

Donovan It's nice, man.

Karl   This guy came up to me in the airport at Accra, 'Oh, my brother, you have returned!', and pinned it on there.

Donovan   Fancy going all the way to Africa and coming back with a Peter Tosh badge.

Karl   We Ghanaians love our reggae.

Donovan   How do you know it's not bad luck or something?

Karl   It's been there ever since and I'm fine.

Donovan   That's nice, though, man. That was a nice thing to do.

Karl   Some round here would kill you for less.

Donovan   Can I have it?

Karl   No.

Donovan   Can I wear it for a while?

Karl   It was given to me.

Donovan   I'll give it back to you.

Karl   I don't give away things that are given to me.

Donovan   I know, it's not good manners, man, but . . . (*Kisses* **Karl**, *takes the badge.*) Thank you.

Karl   Don't lose it.

Donovan   It's all the way from Africa.

Karl   The shower you want is upstairs. I'm going to bed.

Donovan   You gone already?

Karl   Knock me up if anything exciting happens.

They laugh.

Donovan   You know you look familiar.

Karl   You look familiar too.

Donovan   Musta seen you before in one a my other life.

Karl   Good night.

Donovan   See you in the morning. (*Exits.*)

Karl *puts clothes in the washing-machine. Dim lights to darkness.*

Act Three

One month later. We hear the shower running. Maybe a radio plays the news. **Karl** *is writing at the table when the lights come up. More paper balls are scattered at his feet.*

Karl 'I can tell a lie from a mile. After a while you get to know the steely-eyed confidence of a liar. When the person you're going out with, you say to them . . . 'Are you seeing so and so? Are you sleeping with them? Tell me. I won't be upset. I just want to know.' When they look you in the face and say 'No! Never!' And you know the truth. Because when you knocked to call for your best friend to go swimming – she was obviously too busy. So you looked through the letter-box and you saw your lover's coat hanging on the back of your best friend's door. You get to know a liar when you see one.'

Donovan *enters, dressing to go out. He has a shirt in his hand.* **Karl** *screws up the piece of paper and throws it at the bin.*

Karl Where's the broom?

Donovan Leave the cleaning. I'll do it tomorrow.

Karl Tomorrow? What's happening tomorrow?

Donovan I was gonna do . . .

Karl You were going to do what?

Donovan I was gonna do some spring cleaning.

Karl Spring cleaning? What kind of spring cleaning?

Donovan Oh, Gawd!

Karl I never see you touch broom in here before.

Donovan For fuck sake, man!

Karl Don't expect me to do everything round here.

Donovan I can look after myself. (*Goes to the fridge and takes a beer.*)

Karl Those are my beers. Not yours.

Donovan *replaces the beer angrily.*

Donovan What are you playing my music for? Who said you could play my music?

Donovan *turns the music off.* **Karl** *turns it back on.*

Karl This is the one CD of yours I play.

Donovan You locked your music up somewhere.

Karl I locked my music away because my music was going missing.

Donovan Well, it's nothing to do with me or my friends.

Karl I left the ones you like down here so that you could play them.

Donovan Just be careful with my things.

Karl Tell your girlfriends not to keep ringing this number. You brought your woman into this house.

Donovan Who told you that?

Karl You brought your woman into this house, drinking my drinks, eating my food.

Donovan Who told you that?

Karl Nobody needed to tell me that. The whole place stinks of fish every time.

Donovan Ahh, naaaw, man, that's nasty. Where'd you get that from?

Karl You brought your woman into my house, and you have the nerve to watch dirty videos with her in my bed.

Donovan Naw, naw, man. It wasn't nothing like that.

Karl The videos were all over the place.

Donovan Look, I gotta go out now, man. My friends are coming to get me any minute now.

Karl Did you hear what I said?

Donovan What?

Karl I don't want your girlfriends ringing this house.

Donovan Safe! Are you watching telly later?

Karl I'm watching the telly!

Donovan I was wondering if . . .

Karl You don't come and tell me that you want to use the dining-room.

Donovan Did I say that?

Karl You were going to say that.

Donovan Forget it, man. Just forget it!

Karl I'm taking the television up to the bedroom.

Donovan It's your telly, ennit.

Karl You don't come and tell me at ten minutes to ten that you want to use the dining-room.

Donovan For fuck sake, man. Just cos I'm going out.

Karl Ask me if I care.

Donovan I was gonna ask you, as well, if you wanned to come.

Karl *looks at him. Silence.*

Karl We never go anywhere. We never do anything.

Donovan So why bother then, man?

Karl Why did I bother?

Donovan Yeah?

Karl Because . . . because I care.

Donovan   We go out.

Karl   We don't exist, except maybe within these four walls, and that's a bad dream.

Donovan   I'm off now.

Karl   When are you moving out?

Donovan   When?

Karl   Date and time? I'm not about to spend another month in this flat with you. I'm going away for a few days, and when I come back, I'm putting the flat on the market.

Donovan   I been doing my homework on tenants' rights – it ain't as easy as that.

Karl   Speak to my solicitor.

Donovan   I'm speaking to you.

Karl   Well, I don't want to hear it.

Donovan   But Karl, me and you are friends. Just cos I went off with a girl? Sex with a girl is for having babies. She don't mean nothing man. She's just a girl.

Karl   And when you have these kids now – what do you do with them? Fuck them off? Leave them to steal and rot and die shooting each other? What kind of love is that?

Donovan   You and me are friends, man. You can't put me out. You know how things stay already.

Karl   Any sperm bank can father a child, Donovan. It takes a man to show commitment and love. It takes a man to take responsibility for his own. You'll never know.

Donovan   Cos I'm not a man, is that it? (*Holding his crotch.*) This says I'm a man!

Karl   Why – was she a good fuck?

Donovan   That's for me to know and for you to find out, ennit. It can't a been a bad one cos she's pregnant.

Karl   What? (*Pause.*) Donovan, you may turn women on with your boyish charm and straight-teeth smile, but you can't deliver. You could never deliver. Nice body and everything. But you use people.

Donovan   What?

Karl   You lie. You manipulate.

Donovan *chuckles*.

Karl   Stay there and laugh.

Donovan *smiles broadly*.

Karl   You're so stupid!

Donovan   (*pushing* **Karl**)   Don't call me stupid!

Karl   Excuse me!

Donovan   Don't call me stupid!

Karl Excuse me, please.

Donovan Or else what?

Karl Get out of my fucking face!

Donovan Come on then mister big shot big mouth photographer. You think you know it all. What's all this crap?

Karl Put my work down.

Donovan It's crap!

Karl It's my crap. Put it down.

Donovan *very casually throws the photographs to the floor.*

Donovan Sorry about that.

Karl *bends to pick up the photographs and* **Donovan** *pushes him.*

Karl Touch me once more, Donovan.

Donovan What are you gonna do?

Karl Once more.

Donovan *shoves* **Karl**, **Karl** *punches* **Donovan**, *and they begin to fight.* **Donovan** *has strength, but* **Karl***'s agility gives him the upper hand. He has* **Donovan** *in an arm-lock, twisting his hand high behind his back.* **Donovan** *screams.*

Karl You were saying?

Donovan Awright, man, awright! Let me go. You win!

Karl Trying to make me look like a fool.

Donovan I ain't. You win!

Karl Damn right, you ain't! On your knees.

Donovan What?

Karl You heard me.

Donovan No, Karl, my new trousers.

Karl I won't tell you again.

Donovan Okay! Okay!

Karl You wanna play games? Lick my shoes.

Donovan No, man, you mad?

Karl Lick it!

Donovan You joking? You joking?

Karl You think I'm joking?

Karl *yanks* **Donovan***'s arm.* **Donovan** *screams.*

Karl Found something you like, at last – a real man for you. Lick it, I said!

Donovan *licks the shoe.*

Karl   I wanna hear you say, 'I'm a big black battiman and I love big black men.' I wanna hear you say it.

Donovan   No, man, naw . . .

The doorbell rings.

That's my friends them. Come on, Karl, let me up, man.

Karl   I wanna hear you say it.

Karl *yanks* **Donovan**'s *arm again.* **Donovan** *screams.*

Donovan   What's the matter with you, man? You gonna let everybody know what we're doing?

Karl *yanks* **Donovan**'s *arm again.*

Donovan   (*shouts*)   I'm a big black battiman and I love big battimen!

The doorbell rings again.

Karl   Louder!

Donovan   I'm a big black battiman and I love big black men!

Karl *releases* **Donovan**'s *arm.*

Karl   That should teach you.

Donovan   You nearly broke my arm off.

The doorbell rings again for a long time.

Don't answer it!

Karl   It's my door, I'll answer it if I want.

Donovan   I'm not in.

Karl   Oh, fuck off!

Donovan   That's them going now anyway.

Karl   (*picking up photographs*)   Ask me if I care.

Donovan   Yow!

Karl *looks at him.*

Donovan   Undress me. Come on, man. It's a turn-on. I've never been undressed before.

Karl   I forget everything with you is a first. Ain't you going out?

Donovan   No, man, I'll catch 'em up later. What you saying?

Karl Say 'Hello!' to Susan for me. Or whatever it is you call your woman. If you change your mind you know where to find me. I won't be running away.

Exit **Donovan**. *We hear* **Karl**'s *voice-over or he may turn to the audience.*

Karl 'In days two thousand seasons past, our feet roamed freely through golden Ghana soil, our hearts flew up high with birds on a Ghana breeze. You loved me then.

'Of my tortured enslavement from *The Way* you must have heard the stories told. I bear some scars but time has changed me none. I love you now as then. Will we meet and love again? Or is our love for ever tainted by the historic chain of events since then?

'I have never lost hope completely. Don't you despair. This black man still in search of his African Prince.'

Karl *goes upstairs to make the bed. He undresses and gets into bed, turning the lights off. Long pause. Silence. In the dim moonlight,* **Donovan** *appears in the doorway. He sits on the bed with bowed head, then climbs into bed fully dressed.* **Karl** *wakes.*

Karl Donovan? Are you sleeping? I was thinking, you know, about the things we said . . . and just the way the whole relationship is going. And I think we should . . . I'm like . . . I really want things to work out. It's just . . . maybe . . . Donovan, are you asleep? What time is it?

No answer. **Karl** *turns on the light, pulls back the covers.* **Donovan** *is curled up in bed, crying.*

Karl Donovan, what's the matter? Dee, babes, please.

Donovan Don't touch me!

Karl Donovan – what's this? What's going on?

Donovan Just leave me alone.

Pause. **Donovan** *starts to whimper.*

Karl Hey, hey – it's all right. It's all right to cry. Tell me what's wrong.

Donovan It's nothing.

Karl Donovan, please.

Donovan I went to see Susan. She's in hospital.

Karl Susan? Is she okay?

Donovan She ain't having the baby all right!

Karl Oh, Donovan, I'm sorry.

Donovan The doctors just kept going on at me. Talking, talking, talking. Sat me down and did all kindsa tests.

Karl Tests? What tests?

Donovan All these big words they kept coming out with. I didn't know anything.

Karl What, was it a miscarriage?

Donovan I didn't know what the fuck they were going on about. They jus' stuck this needle in me and took out my blood.

Karl What? What for? What's it got to do with the baby?

Donovan She's aborting my kid all right! She's got Aids. Jus' leave me!

Karl Aids?

Donovan *starts to cry.*

Karl You're all right. You're all right.

Donovan When Aids first come out, man, I said, 'Boy, I ain't going swimming again.'

Karl Didn't you and Susan use condoms?

Donovan She look good, man. She look nice. How was I s'pose to know.

Karl We always use a condom.

Donovan I'm dying. I feel I'm dying. I've got Aids, haven't I? It's in my blood. I know I have. Susan gave it to me.

Karl Dee, your nose, is bleeding.

Donovan Oh, my God, my nose, it's coming out my nose!

Karl Donovan, are you HIV positive?

Donovan I'm going, man, I'm going.

Karl What are you talking about?

Donovan I'm dirt, man. I'm filth! You don't want nothing to do with me. I'm no good.

Karl You're a beautiful black man. Come here. I'll have to keep telling you that, because you don't believe me. Do you think I'd let a little thing like this stop us from being together? You don't know me, Dee. I want this relationship.

Donovan I'm no good.

Karl I need you. It's not all gloom, is it? We don't know if you're HIV positive, do we? You've just got to hang on to the goodness and brilliance, yeah? You've got beautiful eyes, do you know that?

Donovan *shakes his head.*

Karl I like big eyes.

Donovan *shakes his head again.*

Karl I'll call you deer eyes.

Donovan You're being soppy again now.

Karl I'll call you Bambi.

Donovan You're being really soppy again now.

Karl I'll be as soppy as I like with you.

Donovan You're being really . . .

Karl Stay there. (*Exits to return with a picture of* **Donovan**.) Look at this picture of you. You look so good when you hold your head up to smile. You should hold your head up to smile more often.

Donovan You remind me of this Rasta bloke.

Karl You've got a thing about Rastas.

Donovan One day I was out with my dad in this pub in Battersea, just after Bob Marley died, and my dad turns round to this Rasta bloke and says, 'Now that your God is dead, who you gonna pray to?' And coolly, you know, this Rasta bloke turns to my dad and says, 'We been worshipping him in the flesh. Now we got to worship him in the spirit.' Nobody said another word. He just come over with it cool like. It was the coolness of it. You remind me of him.

Karl *helps* **Donovan** *up, they hug and hold each other tight.* **Karl** *slowly removes* **Donovan***'s shirt and the belt of his trousers, and then his own clothes. They kiss and hold each other in bed; make love until daybreak;* **Karl** *riding* **Donovan**, **Donovan** *riding* **Karl***; then they fall asleep in each other's arms.*

Next morning, **Donovan** *wakes first and leaves the room, then* **Karl** *wakes.*

Karl Donovan? Donovan? Dee, are you down there? (*Gets out of bed, puts on boxer shorts, and exits. Off.*) Donovan, are you there?

Donovan *enters in dressing-gown and sets the table.* **Karl** *runs in carrying today's newspaper.*

Karl Dee. There you are. I thought you'd left me. I thought you'd decided to call it a day and gone back to Susan.

Donovan No. I'm here.

Karl Hi!

Donovan Hi!

Karl My mouth taste like the bottom of a sewer, so I won't.

Donovan So's mine.

They kiss passionately.

I'm doing us some breakfast.

Karl Good, I'm starving. (*Smiles and looks out the window towards the audience.*) Hello, little birdie-wordie.

Donovan Where? Oh, yeah. His head's all ruffled. Looks like he's growing locks.

Karl (*broad patois*) Wha'appen, star?

They laugh.

Donovan Those birds are really funny. They sit around all day with their mouth wide open waiting for insects to drop in.

Karl That's not gonna get them far. Where's this food – I'm starving.

Donovan It's coming up.

Karl No bacon for me. Did I tell you I stop eating pork? A lotta people never touch pork.

Donovan Unclean meat, man.

Karl There's some burgers in the freezer.

Donovan I'll have to start fattening you up.

Karl I burn up a lot of energy.

Donovan I know you do!

Karl It's about time you did some cooking round here. You can cook!

Donovan I like cooking. Fresh wholesome stuff. I did this course as a chef once. Then I got bored, man. They wouldn't let me cook anything nice where I was working.

Karl I used to hate cauliflower and things like that.

Donovan My mum boils vegetables to mush. Her carrots dissolve on the plate. Serious, man. Her mushy peas turn liquid green, and everything swimming around in grease and Beef Oxo cube.

Karl You shouldn't boil too much of the goodness out.

Donovan Tell her for me, nuh.

Karl Your mum sounds nice.

Donovan She is. We should go up there and see her, you know. She's on her own now. What you smiling at?

Karl You.

Donovan What?

Karl The way you were that night we met.

Donovan Out of order, man. Nothing at all going on up here. I was at that club again the other night.

Karl The Bluenote?

Donovan Yeah.

Karl Haven't been back since. I hear they weren't letting black people in.

Donovan They were letting people in – they close the club three hours early. There was this slave on the door.

Karl Slave?

Donovan That's what we call black guys who check for whites.

Karl Right.

Donovan I don't hate white people, you know.

Karl I prefer my own, myself.

Donovan That's what it is, ennit? We've got white in our blood anyway.

Karl No we haven't!

Donovan I don't mean it like that. I mean, me and my family.

Karl Oh.

Donovan You're funny, you are. You get all worked up sometimes. Sometimes I think your heart's too big for your body.

Karl I let my feelings show.

Donovan You should see yourself sometimes, man. Bang out of order!

Karl I'm sorry.

Donovan Naw, man, it's awright! You know where you are, don't you.

Karl You don't give much away yourself.

Donovan I'm like that, though, you know. You say it's cos I don't give. I used to give to people, you know. I used to give all the time to people. You ask my mum. But the more I give the more people want to take. Take, take, take, that's all people do. And then I don't wanna give, cos I don't wanna feel, and I don't wanna feel cos I don't wanna get hurt. Candy hurt me. Candy my . . . we were gonna get married, man. It's so stupid. D'you know she slept with my brother. My big ole fat ugly brother. If he was the last man in the world I'd rather shag a sheep. She slept with him to hurt me. I s'pose she'd say she wasn't getting enough. Trevor hurt me. Trevor was the first man I met. Trevor is pathetic! That's one of your words, ennit? Do you know he'll swear to God he screwed me. I overheard him on the phone one night showing off to his friend. I said, 'Trevor, you've never screwed me!' He said, 'Yes, I have!' I said, 'When? Where was I?' D'you know what I mean? He's so stupid! I met Nathan right after Trevor. Nathan was quite nice at first. Then he started to want to treat me like a woman. I wasn't having none a that! I met Susan in Safeways. I thought, I ain't having any luck with men. Susan was really good in bed. 'You don't think I'm a slag, do you, Donovan? I'm not a slag, you know. I'm just really really attracted to you!' Susan didn't hurt me. I hurt Susan. She needs love, you know. I didn't mean to hurt her. I wanned to have a son. That's what it was. It was mainly to have a kid. How could I love Susan when all the time I was attracted to men? That'll only breed anger and suspicion, ennit? And anyway, here I am now with you – another man – and feeling good about it for the first time in my life. I ain't making no promises to you, Karl. But just to be with you, you know. Talking to another black man. Someone who can listen without passing judgement. You make me feel so good.

Karl I love you.

Donovan You and me then?

Karl You and me. Where's this food?

Donovan It's coming up, man.

Karl We should get some sleep later.

Donovan I feel like going for a walk, you know, man, but I'm tired too. We didn't get much sleep last night.

Karl We didn't use any condoms last night either.

Donovan I know. How do you feel?

Karl I feel fine. How do you feel? I mean, now?

Donovan You make me feel good, man.

Karl We should go to the clinic and get tested. Every three months, or so they say, we should check again.

Donovan So we can know, if anything.

Karl If anything.

Donovan Yeah.

Karl We'll see how it goes. One day at a time. Shall we go up or eat down here?

Donovan I love you, you know.

Karl *smiles, surprised.*

Donovan I liked you from time, man. It's just me, ennit? Call it progress, if you wanna.

Karl *laughs.* **Donovan** *laughs too.*

Dim the lights to blackness.

Boy with Beer

Boy with Beer is a love story that tells of the relationship between two black men. Though certain of that, however, some theatre-goers have been inclined to assume the obvious: that the theme is the conflicts/contradictions involved in being both black and gay. Confronted by racism in society, and heterosexism in their own communities, black gay men do face formidable challenges, but in fact the theme is much broader than that, and concerns itself with issues of black self-love and the power dynamics at the heart of human relationships.

As a play about power, prejudice and the pressures of machismo, about an odd love affair and an extraordinary 'rite of passage', the struggle of strength in *Boy with Beer* is not just a conflict of men, or of male same-sex relationships, but is a conflict at the centre of any black love. Particularly in the diaspora where black men and women have had to be strong, black love is almost automatically a competitive dance of strength between strong individuals who must find some level on which to communicate and operate as equals. So often what we find in our heterosexual community, for example, is the black man who needs a weaker partner, who is not going to confront him on the level of an equal, going for a spouse of another race, where perhaps the women have been taught to be meeker, more subservient, through their history.

As a story about two black men from different backgrounds, *Boy with Beer* also throws into relief some aspects of the love–hate relationship between Africans and Afro-Caribbeans, and between the working class and the upwardly mobile professional class living in Britain today. It investigates some of the social, emotional, political and historical baggage that black people carry as individuals and collectively. Because Karl is more emotionally and mentally developed than Donovan, we follow his attempts to raise Donovan's consciousness, and how he has to resolve himself in order to share love and understanding with the younger man.

Bar the threat of HIV infection, the ending is ostensibly upbeat – 'and they lived happily ever after' – yet we know in our heart of hearts that there is still more work to be done; for 'Mr Right', our ideal mental construct, does not exist except in our own mind's eye, and we must open our hearts to allow him to emerge in the best approximation that destiny has to offer. In this instance, history has conspired to make black men hate themselves. Yet despite this, black gay men love each other, can protect, comfort and care for each other in a society that despises 'blackness', and a black community that condemns their love. If there is a purity in a love that is as essential as the loving of oneself, then when black men love each other in an environment that negates them, it is not a sign of sickness – it is a sign of health.

Then, on the other hand, and these are crucial questions for the reader and audience, can Donovan really love Karl and put him at risk of HIV infection? Does Karl really love himself when he foregoes the use of condoms? Is this simply a slice of real life? Or is there some deeper spiritual significance, a reunion of souls after 'two thousand seasons past', and a quest for unconditional love that transcends the physical here and now? Is it better for a brother to be prepared to die for a brother or to shoot him in the back with a gun?

Perhaps these musings are purely subjective and find no common ground at all with your own thoughts on the subject. Yet if *Boy with Beer* is nothing more than a simple tale of 'black gay love' and a call for respect, understanding and dialogue, then I believe it benefits every black man or woman who sees or reads it, some of whom I hope may see themselves reflected in the characters.

Very special thanks to Topher Campbell, for seeing potential where others saw none;

Steven Luckie, for commissioning this extended version of *Boy with Beer* and his dedication in bringing it to the public; and to Tunde Oba and Clive Wedderburn, whom I happen to think are two very special actors. My love, respect and gratitude also go out to Patric McCoy, my Chicago buddy, and to Amon James of Washington DC, without whom this afterword would not have been written.

Boy with Beer is dedicated to my friendship with Dave Duncan.

Paul Boakye
New York, 1994

Paul Boakye wrote and produced the original version of *Boy with Beer* through his company HOB Productions (1992). He has also written *Jacob's Ladder* (UK Student Playscript Award winner, 1986), *Hair* (BBC Radio Drama Young Playwrights' Award, 1991), *No Mean Street* for Kuffdem and Red Ladder Theatre Company, Leeds (1993), and *Wicked Games* as writer-in-residence at the Royal National Theatre Studio (1994). He is currently at work on a 'Yardie' play made possible by a Theatre Writing Bursary from the Arts Council of Great Britain (1994), and is putting the finishing touches to *Housecall*, a screenplay for Carlton Television.

Munda Negra

Bonnie Greer

Characters

Anna Eastman, *African-American arts professor on sabbatical in Europe*
Janet Cesaire, *Afro-Caribbean teacher, Anna's old friend*
Emily Braithwaite, *the white wife of a late friend of Anna's and Janet's*
Liam Flannery, *Irish painter and Anna's lover*
David Sinclair, *Afro-Caribbean head-teacher of the school where Janet works*

These main characters, with the exception of Liam, are in their mid- to late forties. Liam is in his mid- to late thirties.

Proprietor, *the white owner of a small bed and breakfast hotel in Brighton*
Little Anna, *Anna's younger self*
The Pope
Mary of Egypt
The Blessed Virgin Mary
A Priest
Neville Braithwaite

These smaller parts can be doubled by the actors.

The play takes place in London in the present . . . and in Anna Eastman's mind.

Act One

Scene One

Anna Eastman *is giving a lecture to a group of teachers at a convention. Behind her are slides of Dürer's 'Portrait Of Katherina' and Degas's 'Miss LaLa Au Cirque Fernando, Paris'.*

Anna . . . that face of Katherina's, open, trusting, vulnerable. It's as if she has looked up and smiled in the face of the artist, smiled in her complete awareness and acceptance of his gaze. As if her innocence was somehow his innocence. This African woman, this black woman, dressed in alien clothing, trapped in a cold, dark climate where winter is eternal. Yet this woman can smile when Dürer looks at her. And he can smile back. He can smile back in his heart, too. He can paint her round face, her full lips, her eyes so unlike the cold, pale eyes of his homeland. He can hold her in his heart, because he has faced the darkness in himself. He has embraced the darkness. His masterpieces are reflections of the darkness that I believe is crucial to confront in these days and times. Degas, on the other hand, paints the circus performer, Miss LaLa, with no face. No features at all. He had seen black women before. He had spent some time in New Orleans, where his relatives dealt in cotton, and he wrote about what he called 'the pretty negresses', but he chose instead to paint his *relatives* at work, and eventually to paint a black woman with no face at all. So, which of these works of art contains the truth, not only about the subject, but about the artist? And are these women 'real', or are they something more? Has there ever really been an accurate depiction of a black person in Western art? And if not, what are we looking at? What are we truly looking at? Can we teach the great masters today without asking that question? I don't think so. Now, I feel, we *must* approach the heart of darkness in Western so-called civilisation. To do so is to approach it in ourselves. It is the last hope for this crazy world. Unless we do, we can no longer teach this work with any credibility. If we teach it anyway, disregarding this darkness, we deny the crisis at the very root of Western society today, its 'munda negra'. My acceptance of this is a key to my . . . well, my sanity. I know this is far out for you English audiences to hear, but I'm sane, free because I can accept what you can't . . . this dark place where *you* function, this secret *you* cannot face. We must all face our hidden selves, because not to do this is to condemn ourselves to a government of fear, a regime of sorrow. Walk into the darkness by looking at these images. Walk into the dark and see yourself.

Scene Two

A hotel room in a Brighton bed and breakfast. **Anna** *is dressed in stockings, suspenders and spike heels. She is putting away a small, ornate box. Suddenly she lets out a loud scream. Enter* **Liam Flannery**. *He is similarly dressed.*

Anna . . . don't look at me like I'm crazy! Get it out of here!

Liam Anna, what the hell are you talking about!!

Anna Just get it out! Get it out, Liam!

Liam   What!!! What!!!

Anna   That goddamn mouse! What in the hell you think I'm talking about!

Liam   Are you out of your tiny mind! A mouse! I don't see anything!

Anna   Look, I know when a mouse's around, trust me! They're all under the floorboards in this goddamn fleabag! Brighton! I was cool the first time I heard them, when we walked in the door. I thought: as long as they're cool. But these ain't! I've *seen* one of them! Don't look at me like I'm crazy, man! Liam, I'm warning you. No tickee no washee, jack! Just do like mommie says and get it out of here!

Liam   Just calm down, will ya? You want the entire British Establishment in here!

Anna   They need to be in here to see this filthy . . .

Liam   . . . this is the last dirty weekend we t–

Anna   Oh yeah? I doubt it. You dig it too much, paddy . . .

Liam   What the fuck did you call me?

Anna   What?

Liam   I'm a what?

Anna   Just find the mouse!

Liam   Answer me, Anna, because if you don't . . .

Anna   No more vodka for you, poopsie.

Liam   What did you call me?

Anna   I'm drunk. So are you. So's the whole world. Nice shape for a couple of schoolteachers to be in.

Liam   What did you call me!!

Anna   Take your paw off my arm, baby. You're too tall to be Al Pacino.

There has been knocking on the door the entire time, which has grown progressively louder.

Proprietor (*outside the door*)   Hello! Hello!

Liam   Bloody hell!

Anna   Shit, it's Basil Fawlty. Fuck it, Liam. Get that goddamn mouse!

Liam   Talk to me, Anna, or I'm walking! What did you call me! And stop screaming, I'm looking, I'm looking!

*The **Proprietor** lets himself in.*

Proprietor   Oh. I beg your pardon.

Anna   Look, man, you've got rats in this joint!

Liam I'm sorry. My wife here's afraid of mice. Everything in creation can assume the shape of a mouse if she allows it to. (*To* **Anna**.) Besides, it's not a rat, it's a mouse that's not even as big as the palm of your hand. (*To* **Proprietor**.) I'm very sorry, but you know women, some of them have this mouse phobia. It's ancient, I think. They believe the creatures'll go climbing into their vagina or something.

Anna Is that what the Christian Brothers taught you!

Liam Honestly, I'm looking and I can't see anything.

Proprietor We've just had the Department of Health come round. Clean bill. We're even in all the guides. I'm assuming that's how you found us. Through the guides . . . I . . . have you looked in the cupboard?

Anna Is it dark in there?

Proprietor Well, yes, I think so . . . the last time I looked, that is . . .

Anna I don't like looking into dark rooms . . . Liam . . .

Liam Calm down, I'll look in the cupboard.

Anna Hurry up, I've got to pee!

Liam Jesus, Mary and Joseph!

Proprietor I'll get a torch. (*Exits.*)

Anna Yeah, this place should be torched . . . for unsanitary conditions. In New York they'd . . .

Liam He's going to get what you call a flashlight, all right! Ow! These bloody suspenders!

Anna You should buy your own stuff, honey. Besides, they ain't got nothin' for them big man's thighs of yours!

Anna *begins kissing* **Liam**'s *thighs, but he pushes her away.*

Liam I haven't forgotten what you called me. Go to the toilet. It's all right. The mouse won't get you!

Anna *leaves. The* **Proprietor** *returns.*

Proprietor Uh, I didn't know the *Rocky Horror Picture Show* was playing in town. My wife and I sometimes . . . That is to say, my wife does . . . the excitement . . . all the young people dressed up and all.

Anna *returns.*

I went once. But I had to leave. It got a bit . . . well, there was a great deal of audience participation if you know what I mean . . .

Anna (*to* **Liam**) Just open the door slow, okay?

Proprietor I didn't know it was playing in town . . .

Liam Nothing. Nothing. Look for yourself, Anna. Come on. Look! Nothing! Nothing at all but the dark insides of your wretched head. *Your* darkness. (*To* **Proprietor**.) We're sorry about this, truly we are.

Proprietor Where is it playing?

Liam Where is what playing?

Proprietor The film. I might be able to sit through it now.

Liam We're not in films. We're teachers. She's a professor. A Ph.D. Doctor of Fine Arts. I'm just an artist. A painter. And lowly primary school art teacher. Most of the time, when I'm not trying my best to keep *her* satisfied.

Proprietor I see.

Anna Any liquor stores around here? We're out. You know, I had this Russian boyfriend once in New York. An appellate judge, bless his heart. Yes indeed. He told me about vodka. He said: (*In mock Russian accent.*) 'Baby, minus forty outside, plus forty inside.' Inside the bottle. Forty proof, he said. Not thirty-nine and a half. Four-oh. Never freeze it. Just keep it cool. Drink it in one quick gulp. Never mix it. Never sip it. Take it right down. Show your gut no mercy. Live your life the way you want to. That's my motto.

Liam She never outgrew Woodstock . . .

Anna Say what you want, but I know one thing: vodka's for its after-effects. That smooth, hot feeling. First take some food. Like this. A quick bite of cold fish and chips will do. Then the chug. Like this. Yeahhh . . . nature's elixir. Baby, we're almost out.

Liam Drink some water for a change.

Proprietor Well, I'm sure that you're satisfied . . . about the mouse, that is . . . that there's no mouse, I mean . . . The theatre? You are in the theatre . . .

Liam Oh. No. I'm painting her. Us, that is. I'm a painter. These are costumes . . . We're posing . . .

Anna Bullshit. This is the way he likes to fuck. Me, too, kimosabee! You know, one of my favourite films is *Brighton Rock*. I love the end when that record is playing over and over: 'I love you, I love you.' Do you like art? You look like a man who doesn't give a fuck about art. Not like me and Sadie over here. We care. I care too much. Why in the hell should I care? These stupid paintings. One of my students at Rutgers University . . . that's in New Jersey . . . big, gorgeous black man, stood up and said, 'What the fuck you teaching us this shit for? We want to study black artists!' And do you know what I said to Mike Tyson? No, that's what I called him . . . I said: 'Know the enemy.' Isn't that a good one? Well, what else could I say? Black people haven't made any art? We have not produced a Velázquez, a Rembrandt. Too busy trying to survive, you know what I mean, Mr . . . Mr . . .

Liam For God sake, Anna. The man's trying to leave with some dignity intact!

Anna So why be a hypocrite? That's what I hate about this country. Janet moaning about Nicola . . . Emily can't handle it . . . Look, Janet knows that . . .

Liam Don't start that again! (*To* **Proprietor**.) I'm very sorry if we've caused trouble.

Anna   And I'm not his wife. Why should I lie? I'm American.

Liam   Oh, I see. And bloody Yanks don't lie. . . !

Proprietor   Well, now that everything's under control. If I can have my torch back, thank you, I'll be going. Breakfast's at seven. Good day. (*Exits.*)

Liam   I don't believe it . . .

Anna   Me either. This placed looked so clean from the outside . . .

Liam *hands her a glass of water.*

Liam   Shut it. Take a big gulp. Now.

Anna   . . . it really did.

Liam   Anna . . .

Anna   Uh, where'd they drag this up from . . . the nude beach? Look, I called you 'paddy' because it's my way of keeping a distance between us. I have to do that.

Liam   So you won't be going to Toulouse with me?

Anna   National Front territory?! *Moi*? Look, baby, I marched in Mississippi twenty-seven years ago and almost got my ass killed. I'm not going to . . .

Liam   I've told you, the locals used to be Communists and after Mitterrand cut the party's balls off they turned to the next group that could get things done. These political parties don't mean a damn thing to them. . . !

Anna   Honey, Europe's much too messed up for me. I've been all over this goddamn continent, up and down, in and out. Pretty soon I'm outta here, baby. Back to Never-Never Land where the President plays the saxophone, and his cat's in therapy. Out of this dark continent, this munda negra . . .

Liam   Mundus negrus . . .

Anna   Yeah, I know, but I like the feminine in all things, honey. Anyway, the Christian Brothers beat your Latin into you. You *had* to get it right. After all, you were a boy. The nuns were much nicer . . . Liam, listen to me. Listen. No, I'm not drunk any more. Listen. Nicola can't stay over here. Not here. No black child, no Asian, no Oriental, no Jew . . .

Liam   Nicola's not your concern! *I'm* your concern! You told me you loved me.

Anna   I was drunk.

Liam   For once . . . for once stop lying! Stop it! Anna, you told me you loved me.

Anna   Okay, I love you.

Liam   Prove it.

Anna   I'll be glad to . . .

Liam   No, not that. Show me what's in the box.

Anna   Off limits, baby.

Liam   Why?

Anna   Nobody looks in there.

Liam   What's in there?

Anna   Don't touch it. Just leave it. Look, I don't love anybody. You're a good lay, all right?

Liam   I'm getting out of here.

Anna   Liam . . .

Liam   You think you can make the world the way you need it to be, don't you? There it is, the world according to you. *You!* Well, not with me. Not any more.

Anna   Liam, Liam . . . I love what you do. I love what we do. I love it. I need it. I didn't know I needed it until I met you. If that's love . . . then I do. I do love you, Liam.

Liam   Open the box.

Anna   Not now.

Liam   Then let me kiss you. Take all this junk off. Take it off. I want to be a man for you now. Your man. I want you to be a woman. My woman. I want you to be soft and yielding to me. I want that, Anna.

Anna   As long as you keep doing what you do, you can have whatever you want.

Liam   Except your heart. I love you. I love your sanity. Anna, don't use me any more. Let me see in the box . . .

Anna   A lovely *double entendre*, baby. I love it.

Liam   Live with me. Marry me.

Anna   I travel light. I came here with nothing, and I'm leaving with nothing.

Liam   You'll leave with my heart. Say it. Tell me that you know that's true.

Anna   Liam . . .

Liam   Tell me. Don't lie there like the great stone woman. Tell me.

Anna   I'm not stone. I'm scared.

Liam   Of me?

Anna   Something's chasing me, baby. Funny, I haven't admitted it before.

Liam   The great doctor Anna Eastman, scourge of Dead White Males?

Anna   Turn over.

Liam   Not until you tell me what it is.

Anna   Do as I say.

Liam   What is it?

Anna   I don't know. Something. I can't sleep . . . that's what you want? Tear myself open for you? That's it. No more opening up, not to anybody.

Liam   Not even now?

Anna   I can't sleep, okay?

Liam   Open, Anna. Don't be afraid.

Anna   Don't talk to me like that.

Liam   Don't, baby. Don't be. I'm here.

Anna   You can't protect me from this. No one can.

Blackout.

Scene Three

A small room off the staff room at Linbrook Primary, West London. **Janet Cesaire** *is eating a sandwich and reading a copy of* Macbeth. **Anna** *enters.*

Anna   What are you doing in here?

Janet   How do I teach this to a group of ten-year-olds? 'I have given suck, and know how tender 'tis to love the babe that milks me: I would, while it was smiling in my face, have plucked my nipples from his boneless gums, and dashed the brains out . . .' Any clues? And if I have to listen to another whinge about the National Curriculum, I'll go crazy. That's why I'm in here, I can't stand how they go on and on and on about it. Why do they hate Shakespeare so much? Back home, that's all I knew. And I loved it. If we didn't learn we were birched, as simple as that. When we came here, my education went right down the tubes, I tell you. Discipline, authority . . .

Anna   All the stuff we rebelled against in the sixties. We changed everything. Now we're reaping the old whirlwind, sister.

Janet   I don't regret that. I don't. Yet Ari and I are having our long-distance calls about whether to send the twins to state school. It's horrible. You fight all your life for something, and when it comes to your turn you're just like everyone else. I don't want them coming out posh little black misfits who don't know whether they're coming or going. But at the same time . . . no one knows Shakespeare!

Anna   I thought every kid in this country knew Shakespeare. This is England! I thought they all went around saying 'To be or not to be' . . .

Janet   . . . and if you do, you have to speak it in RP. With RP attitudes. We rejected all that, and if it meant rejecting Shakespeare . . . it was always a case of throwing out the baby with the dishwater . . .

Anna   But you don't have to.

Janet   I know. I know. We've all gone a bit batty. There've been so many changes. No one's giving teachers any credit at all for anything. If we do too well we've lowered standards, if we don't do well enough we're at fault. And on the salary we're paid. Just about every teacher I know is leaving the profession. It's unbearable. I want to show you something. (*She pulls out a group of holiday snaps.*) The latest pictures from home. Look at that beach.

Anna   Hmmm . . .

Janet   You can't imagine how warm that water is. And so clear! You can see all the way to the bottom! Oh, and the walks! Everything's so green.

Anna   Who's that?

Janet   Oh. My mother's new husband.

Anna   Not bad.

Janet   Forget that one. Look at this. That's the new hotel. I can see myself there right now. Lying on the beach . . .

Anna   You definitely going this time without Ari and the kids?

Janet   Definitely. Want a bite?

Anna   What is it?

Janet   A paté. I made it from the leftovers David brought back. Now he thinks he's the best Caribbean cook in London.

Anna   What is it? Fish?

Janet   Yes, and lots of things. I've mixed it up a bit. I can't stop eating it. Reminds me of home.

Anna   You've been talking about moving back there ever since I met you.

Janet   I know. But Ari, the children. They're British and he's French. French African to be exact. The most precise kind of Frenchman. My husband, Monsieur Aristide Cesaire. He can't bear the Antilles, as he calls it. He thinks we're lazy, backward, illiterate . . . I don't want to talk about it, do you mind?

Anna   He drives you nuts.

Janet   He's been driving me nuts since the day we met, but at least he's in Paris most of the bloody week with his authors and I don't have to hear him bellow for his food every night.

Anna   You think he's got someone there?

Janet   I certainly hope so!

Anna   What would you do if you found out for sure?

Janet   Encourage it! At some point, every married woman should be pleased that her husband has someone else. Then she can get on with her life. If it weren't for the twins he'd qualify for the second worst mistake of my life!

Anna   The second?

Janet   The first was accompanying my mother *here* thirty-three years ago.

Anna Mothers . . . Mine was 'Do this, do that'. Like a fool I tried to please her. But there was one moment when I almost got away . . . one time . . .

Janet Don't start me on that tack. Mine didn't know what love meant. Still doesn't.

Anna She all right?

Janet Like I've said, she's on her fourth husband. The life and the soul . . .

Anna Like Neville was.

Janet Hmmmm . . .

Anna I remember when I first met you two.

Janet We looked hopeless, I know.

Anna Neville was wearing those, what we called 'high-water' pants. Stopped at his ankle.

Janet Just a brilliant Caribbean country boy.

Anna Brilliant. Freaked everybody out.

Janet Brilliant. Knew everything.

Anna Never combed his hair. Loved Otis Redding. And Dr King. Remember that time we took you all into NYC for the first time?

Janet And that hippie chick?

Anna The one who wanted to know if it was true about black men?

Janet She was beautiful though, Anna.

Anna Yeah, well if your daddy's people had come over on the *Mayflower* and you had all those centuries of inbreeding . . . Who'd she say she'd been with?

Janet Jimi Hendrix or something.

Anna At Electric Ladyland.

Janet Yes, and you encouraged him. You told Neville to go for it.

Anna Why not? Check her out. He did. Three days non-stop. I caught them once getting down in the student lounge.

Janet Neville was well and truly liberated.

Anna Think that's when he first got the taste?

Janet You should talk.

Anna Naw. Liam's just my vacation thang. My Wild Irish Rose.

Janet The staff's starting to talk.

Anna So what? I don't live here. Remember when Neville organised that rally after the brothers closed down the school and he asked big, bad Governor Shabazz to speak?

Janet What was his original name?

Anna Milton Dolittle. Used to be an altar boy in church. And when that nigger showed up at the university callin' himself 'Governor Shabazz', I thought I'd die. While he was standing up there with his hands across his chest, all I could see was that white cassock and his sweet little face deep in prayer . . .

Janet He said he did time!

Anna At Morehouse College frat parties.

Janet You're kidding!

Anna I kept his secret. Why not? And there was Neville, so earnest and eager about the black struggle . . .

Anna Yes . . . and he introduces Shabazz, spiritual leader of the Black Students' Union uprising . . .

Janet . . . the applause . . .

Anna . . . Then Shabazz gets up to impart his pearls of wisdom . . .

Janet . . . and this really sweet-faced white girl raises her hand . . .

Anna . . . Neville politely points to her . . .

Janet (*imitating the girl's voice*) 'Governor, Shabazz, what can I do to help the black struggle?'

Anna . . . and Governor Shabazz stares back . . .

Janet . . . The assembled throng holds its breath awaiting his mighty pronouncement . . .

Anna . . . Then Shabazz says in a thundering voice . . .

Both (*imitating Shabazz*) 'Commit suicide, muthafucka! Kill yourself, bitch! That's the best way you can help the black struggle. One less honky!'

Janet He was so rude. And remember that poor girl's face!

Anna Remember ours! We were just two little middle-class girls, we'd never heard anyone speak like that!

Janet And Neville! Poor Neville! I thought he was going to faint!

Anna Didn't he later on?

Janet I think so.

Anna He worked so hard. Bought the whole damn deal hook, line and sinker.

Janet He loved life. Especially when they got Nicola. I'd never seen anyone so happy.

Anna So why'd he kill himself?

Janet I have to go, I've got playground duty.

Anna And Emily's really taking Nicola back to . . . where the fuck is it?

Janet Shropshire's where she's from.

Anna What's that black child going to do in Shropshire?

Janet Be with her mother.

Anna Emily can't raise her properly. That's not what Neville would have . . .

Janet Nev married Emily, don't forget that! They adopted Nicola together. Emily's the only mother Nicola's known, and she's fine, Anna. Besides, you had your chance. Now you're among the great art historians. You write great books, pontificate on the chat shows, cause arguments in academe. Well, you've done it. And I bloody well envy you, too. But you missed your chance with Neville and that's that. Sorry to be so blunt.

Emily (*in other room*) Janet!

Anna Emily can't raise that child, she's unstable! She always followed Nev around like a puppy dog. The man couldn't breathe. You know I know what I'm talking about. I always thought she had a problem.

Janet She's white. That's her problem, isn't it?

Anna Do you know what could happen to Nicola if she stays in England, stays in Europe!

Janet I'm raising my children here. All those children out on that playground are staying here. They have to stay here. This is their home too.

Anna It's not their home. Most of the black children on this continent aren't even citizens of the damn countries they were born in.

Janet You're not in the Black Students' Union any more. This is the real world where people get dirty. Oh, and it's better where you're from? What's it called . . . the 'land of the free and the home of the brave'? The great nation that sticks its bloody nose into the affairs of the entire world whenever it pleases. The great land that overran my cousin's country, the one where she *was* a citizen, because the good old US of A believes in its manifest destiny to determine everything in the Caribbean! The same country that turned my country into a tourist trap. The one that can't keep its own kids off drugs, keep them alive. Is that the one Nicola should go to?

Anna I'm not going to sit here and raise the flag for America. I'm talking about one child. One child. Emily can't take Nicola back to some dead village where she won't even know who she is. And you know I'm right.

Janet It's not your business. You killed the baby Neville gave you. You marched right off to the doctor . . .

Anna I did what I had to do. But let me tell you one thing: I'm not losing this one, Janet, so you can forget it.

Janet What are you talking about? Nicola's Emily's child. She's had enough, Anna.

Janet Whose side are you on?

Enter **Emily**.

Emily Everyone's got their knickers in a twist over this Shakespeare. You can't sit out there and talk about anything else. Even on the playground . . .

Janet I told you about playground duty . . .

Emily No, no, Jan. It's not exhausting. I love it. It gives me something to do. You know, Nicola's quite a bully.

Anna What do you mean?

Emily Well, a boy wanted to talk to her, it was all very innocent, and she punched him.

Janet Like some tea?

Anna Thought you had playground duty.

Janet I've got a bit more time suddenly. Sugar?

Emily Oh yes, please. Punched him!

Anna What did you do?

Emily I didn't know what to do. I'd never seen her like that before. It must be because of Neville. Because of his death, I mean.

Anna Have you talked about it?

Emily Oh, Anna, I've tried. But she won't really open up. We've been so close, and suddenly . . .

Janet Why don't the two of you take a holiday? David'll understand.

Emily No, there'll be enough disruption when we move. Nicola's gone through enough.

Anna You could come to New York.

Emily I hardly consider New York relaxing.

Janet Unless you like carrying mugging money. You have something on you so they don't shoot you.

Anna I'm out on Long Island.

Emily What about school?

Anna She could go to school there. I can pull a few strings.

Emily I'd just be underfoot. Besides, I know this must sound selfish . . .

Janet You have a right to be selfish now. Here's your tea.

Emily Oh, thank you. I know this may sound selfish, but I need to return home. Just for a while. There's a lovely school there.

There's a knock on the door.

Child's voice Mrs Cesaire!

Janet That's me. Playtime's over. Anna . . .

Anna Yes?

Janet Call me.

Anna I'm serious, chief.

Janet *exits.*

Emily This tea is wonderful.

Anna How've you been feeling?

Emily Rotten. If it weren't for Nicola, I'd have gone with him. Because I understand why he did it. I feel the same way. No one, absolutely no one could have told me twenty-five years ago that we would have wound up with the world we have today. It's as if the things we did never happened at all. As if we were in some kind of dream, our own dream. It was just a pause, wasn't it, Anna? Things didn't really change.

Anna Neville was an idealist. I remember when we watched Nixon on TV say his farewell on the lawn of the White House, and then Neville turned to me and said, 'I'm leaving too. I'm going to England. To Europe. It's saner there.'

Emily It was. Then. Anna, sometimes I can't sleep. I turn over and he's not there. I think I must have called his name a lot because I'd wake up and Nicola would be there saying over and over, 'Mummy, mummy.' When someone dies, when someone dies that way . . . you almost hate them. You think to yourself, why couldn't they have lived? Why couldn't they have gone through it with you? Wasn't it good enough with you? I really envy you. So strong, so positive. Black women have such strength . . . My insides feel as if they've been yanked out and trampled. There's nothing left.

Anna Except Nicola.

Emily Our daughter. Anna, I think that, if she could speak to me, tell me what's really on her mind . . .

Anna Maybe she can't.

Emily Yes. She needs time.

Anna She found him?

Emily Yes. Yes.

Anna She needs a change, Emily.

Emily That's why I thought of Shropshire. A village. The city is no place to raise a child.

Anna Are there other . . . you know, black kids there?

Emily No. But Nicola's very strong. Very clear about herself. Neville took care of that.

Anna And what did you do?

Emily Just watched and learned. That's always been my role.

Anna Neville didn't like women to run things.

Emily He tried, poor dear. He did try. In his heart, his great heart . . . he tried.

Anna I think he was scared of women. Scared of what we had.

Emily He didn't scare you. You stood up to him. He always talked about your strength. But he wasn't strong all the time. He wasn't strong at the end.

Anna Emily, Nicola's grown up in London. You know . . . Shropshire . . .

Emily I want some peace and quiet for her. For me. We deserve that. There were always people in the house. It was chaos at times. I . . . we both wanted things to calm down. But Neville became more involved with the militants, people who didn't want peace . . .

Anna Almost time for class. Why don't we meet for a drink?

Emily Yes, let's talk. You knew Neville. There's no one to talk to. His new friends blame . . . they blame me. They say I kept him away from his people, but I didn't. I always supported . . . I'm sorry. I'm very tired.

Anna Tomorrow night?

Emily I don't know. I'd need someone to look after Nicola . . .

Anna I can talk to Janet . . .

Emily Yes, let's meet. Let's meet and talk.

Anna exits. Enter **Janet**.

Janet Forgot my notebook.

Emily I'm sorry I'm so blubbery.

Janet Look, we understand. Under the circumstances . . .

Emily I don't know what my priorities are any more . . .

Janet Giving your child freedom. Loving your child . . .

Emily Are you sure, I . . .

Janet Love her. Proceed from there. There's enough destruction in this world. Enough walking wounded.

Emily I don't know if I'm capable of it. Really capable. I just don't know. I don't know. Jan, I'm afraid.

Janet We all are.

Emily Not Anna. Isn't she wonderful? Still the same. Not Anna. She's not afraid of anything.

Janet No, she's not afraid. But what does that mean in the world we live in now?

Enter **Anna**.

Anna I don't know why people think working with young children is like falling off a log, they wear you out!

Emily I'd better go back out there. (*Exits.*)

Anna See what I mean?

Janet She's human.

Anna She can't cope.

Janet And a forty-something woman who can't even take five minutes on a playground . . .

Anna I can take it. I'm a big girl now, all the confusion of my youth is way past now . . . I like the art work in here. Some of these kids have real talent. (*She picks up a small, ornate box.*)

Janet Nicola. Talented, isn't she?

Anna Don't open it. You don't touch an artist's life unless invited to.

Janet Oh, go on!

Anna No! I'm sorry I'm so freaked out about it. I have a thing about touching an artist's stuff, that's all.

Janet I'd better be going too.

Anna We go back a long way, you and me.

Janet A long way. (*Exits.*)

Anna Don't try it, Janet Cesaire. Don't try it.

Blackout.

Scene Four

Liam's *studio.* **Liam** *is completing an oil-painting of* **Anna**.

Liam Come see this.

Anna (*in next room*) I'm on the phone.

Liam What?

Anna I'm on the phone.

Liam To whom?

Anna New York.

Liam *New York*!!!

Anna I've got my credit card, okay!

Liam Who are you calling in . . .

Enter **Anna**.

Anna What?

Liam Who are you calling in New York?

Anna Mervyn.

Liam Who's that?

Anna (*surveying painting*) Hmmmm . . . getting there.

Liam Woman. . . !

Anna Mervyn's my lawyer. I had to ask him a few things about the New York State adoption laws. You haven't got my left eye right. It should be . . .

Liam Leave it alone.

Anna I'm not going to touch your painting . . .

Liam Leave the *child* alone. Leave Nicola alone. Leave her.

Anna I'm just checking up on things, okay? Don't panic.

Liam Alastair says that it's all right for us to have the house. He's in Japan for six months. He says the neighbours are fine. There's good wine. Beautiful wine. And the light is superb. You could paint a bit, yourself . . .

Anna You're the painter.

Liam You could try.

Anna Not interested. I'd rather write about it. Less bullshit. And wine's not my . . .

Liam . . . He says there's a small American colony in Toulouse. They're teaching the French about computers or something. Alastair says they have these parties, wild parties. Big, crazy things where they play American music, do American things. It's completely incomprehensible to everyone else, these American ways, but to you they'll be . . . well, you'll understand.

Anna What makes you think I understand about America? Because I'm from there?

Liam Just a manner of speaking. Just a way of making conversation with you, darling. No American abroad ever understands anything about America. That's why they left it. Anna . . .

Anna Shut your Galway mouth. You look really beautiful now. In this light. I like it. I like the way it plays on your mouth. You've got the most beautiful mouth. It really turns me on . . .

Liam Then marry me.

Anna Nope.

Liam I won't stop asking you.

Anna Save your breath.

Liam You're not a cold woman.

Anna Neither are you.

Liam Stop it. I'm serious.

Anna I'm going back to New York, baby. I've got a house, plus a jive-ass ex-husband I pay alimony to. He'd come stomping anywhere in the world looking for his money. And there's my work, my refuge.

Liam Let me be your refuge. I can be that, Anna. You know I can be that.

Anna I've got to go call Mervyn back.

Liam   I can. Things are about to happen for me at last. I've got my one-man show in Paris in the autumn. Dublin in the spring. Then London.

Anna   I told you I'd write an article on you . . .

Liam   No, I didn't mean . . .

Anna   No what?

Liam   That's not what I mean.

Anna   Then you don't want the article?

Liam   Yes, yes, of course I do.

Anna   Of course you do, baby. That's why you came on to me in the first place.

Liam   For fuck's sake.

Anna   You can't trick the trickster. I knew what was going on. You checked me out before I even showed up to that party. Then when Lady whatever-her-name-was introduced us, I knew you lined that up too. See, I checked up on you. You've been around. Lots of beds on both sides of the fence. Fine. Everybody has to help their career. No problem. But don't suddenly pull this love thing on me, okay? Don't suddenly do that. Because I know love when I see it. And I don't see it here.

Liam   All right, it was like that in the beginning. But it's all changed.

Anna   Music swells. Clinch. Fade-out. The End.

Liam   It's changed. It shocked me, too. But it's changed.

Anna   Because I found out your little secret?

Liam   I'm not ashamed of what I do in bed. I like lots of things. What about your secret? Are you hiding the hot line in that little case?

Anna   Don't touch it! Sacred fetish, off-limits to white men, especially sexy ones.

Liam   If you don't want me to touch it . . .

Anna   Oops, Mervyn . . . (*Exits.*)

Liam   I want a baby with you.

Anna (*offstage*)   What?

Liam   Come here!

Enter **Anna**.

Anna   Mervyn's . . .

Liam   I want to have a baby with you.

Anna   Excuse me, honey, let me write down what Mervyn just . . .

Liam   I want to have a baby with you!

Anna Whoa! As soon as you have your one-man show somewhere on the planet. That's the thing you really want.

Liam I've worked hard to get where I am.

Anna So have I.

Liam I've worked hard enough. Why not?

Anna He told me to call him right back, but I bet he's still on the phone . . .

Liam I'm painting my way back.

Anna Back to where?

Liam To the time when I first discovered what paint was. The smell of it. The way you could move it around. The way it looked on the canvas and in the light. That moment when nothing else mattered but making that paint work. Shaping it, coaxing it, clearing it out so that only . . .

Anna Let's have a drink . . .

Liam . . . what it was born to do emerged . . .

Anna You mean what *you* were born to do.

Liam Isn't that what I said?

Anna No, you said what the paint was born to do. Anyway, once they take it from you in childhood, you're in a dark tunnel, a dark universe, baby.

Liam I said what the *paint* was born to do? Of course I meant myself. Myself. What *I* was born to do. Don't you see? Somehow, in some miraculous way, you've brought me back to it. Back to that first moment. That moment when I could . . . when it was all in my hands. My heart. My mind. When I could . . .

Telephone rings.

Anna Mervyn's on the case!

Liam . . . when I could truly paint, when I wasn't afraid . . .

Anna I don't know anything about that moment. Too much stuff . . . (*Exits.*)

Liam Do you want to know, Anna?

Enter **Anna**.

Anna Still workin' on it.

Liam You're running too much. What're you running from, Anna?

Anna Got to move fast when you're a black girl in a white man's world.

Liam I'm in a white man's world too. It's the mantle they gave me. Then I was a boy and I knew nothing at all but a very particular world. The house. Fireplace in the kitchen. We all sat round it. The road that seemed to get longer and longer. One day a tinker came along.

Gave me some paints. Something happened when I used them. I could see with those paints. Like a great sigh of relief burning through my whole being. The world became filled with light, a mighty, glistening thing of exquisite beauty and changeability . . . wonder . . . and strange as it may seem to you, no matter how people take me, I've left that white man's world. In my childhood. You never talk about your childhood.

Anna Nothing to talk about. Let's have a drink.

Liam Look at me.

Anna Your eyes are too bright.

Liam You have a secret. I can see the pain. I know. I know. Because I love you. Say yes.

Anna Let me think.

Liam Think.

Anna I don't know what I'm capable of any more. I don't know.

Liam Then be with me.

Anna This is crazy.

Liam So is life.

Anna Give me time, okay?

Liam Not much more.

Anna Don't push me.

Liam *exits.*

Anna Don't push me, Liam. Don't push me. I've got to leave here soon. I don't have much time. I've got to take her back. I've got to.

Blackout.

Scene Five

Anna's *flat.* **Anna** *is on the telephone to Mervyn.*

Anna . . . no, I'm not out of my mind. I want to adopt a kid. She's black, and British, like I told you . . . I know how old I am. I know that. I know it . . . Ten years old . . . So I'll be an old lady in a wheelchair when she's my age, so what . . . maybe I'll be dead and everybody'll be happy. Of course her mother's consented, she's an old friend . . . I told you . . . her husband was an old flame of mine . . . right . . . He's dead and she thinks the child is better off with me . . . What do you mean that's too pat . . . that's the way it is . . . What? . . . Yes, I'm bringing the kid. I just want you to get the ball rolling . . . My research is fine. I'll be back in a few days . . . What do you mean a cooling-off period? What cooling-off period? I don't need a cooling-off period, I know what I'm doing. I'm bringing her with me . . . Why? . . . I'm the better mother, I'm black, remember, Mervyn. If she was a Jewish child . . . I'm making a point, man, and you know it . . . No, I'm not out of my mind . . . The food here is fine . . . What's the food got to do with it . . .

The hall buzzer sounds.

. . . look, I've got to go. I've got to . . . JUST DO IT, MERVYN! Okay? (*She runs to the buzzer.*) Emily?

Enter **Emily**.

Emily Your flat is lovely.

Anna I was lucky. Maida Vale's nice. Reminds me of the West Seventies.

Emily I remember New York. I went there with Nev . . . what . . . ten years ago?

Anna You wouldn't recognise it now. After Koch took over.

Emily There was something in the air, especially in the autumn. It's so sexy in the autumn . . . the scent of the city . . .

Anna Yeah, garbage from the garbage strikes . . .

Emily No, something else. A kind of freedom. Neville loved it. Especially Columbia University and all that.

Anna Ithaca. Upstate New York. The good old days . . .

Emily Oh, Anna, it all just happened so quickly. One day he was here and the next he was gone. Gone.

Anna I know.

Emily No note. Nothing. How could he not leave a note? He was so articulate. He loved to write, loved to express himself. And no note. No note.

Anna I guess he thought he didn't have to leave one.

Emily But he did, Anna. He owed it to all of us, for God's sake, all of us.

Anna Neville always did what he wanted to do. He always did. That was the name of the game for him.

Emily But no note. No word for Nicola.

Anna A drink?

Emily Yes, please.

Anna When I first met him, I thought: this was a brother who did exactly what he wanted. Exactly what he needed to do.

Emily I saw a gentle, sad, lonely man. A man trying to make sense out of the insanity around him. I tried to help him make sense out of it. That was my job. I failed. I don't know. I accused him of having an affair with a young black girl in his office. Oh, Anna, I was so insecure by then. I know he was tired of me, tired of the way we were living. I kept him out of things. Because of what I am.

Anna Neville wasn't a fool. Give him some credit.

Emily There were things he needed me to do, and there I was with my stupid white face . . .

Anna Drink up.

Emily I have to say it. I have to let it out. To you. He respected you so much. So much.

Anna He wasn't a saint.

Emily I know. I know that. Sometimes, he . . . he raised his hand to me.

Anna Did you deal with it?

Emily I called the police around once. They made me feel ashamed . . . the way they looked at me when they saw Neville and Nicola . . .

Anna Why did you feel ashamed?

Emily I didn't mean that, I didn't . . . I meant . . .

Anna My ex tried to hit me upside my head a few times, so I called the law too. A woman's right. Another?

Emily I didn't know you drank so much.

Anna Keeps the demons at bay. Maybe I'm homesick.

Emily I am. I know I am.

Anna What's Shropshire like?

Emily Quiet. Beautiful. Green.

Anna Why'd you leave?

Emily Because it was quiet, beautiful, green.

Anna So you came to the big city looking for adventure.

Emily And did I ever find it. Anti-Vietnam rallies, CND, civil rights . . . did I ever find it.

Anna What happened?

Emily What do you mean?

Anna A rhetorical question. You know, 'what happened?'

Emily We grew up.

Anna Not a good answer.

Emily I suppose not.

Anna Grow up. To what? Me, I wanted to be the biggest, baddest black woman on the face of the earth. No joke. I did. I thought that that was the most important thing in the world. I wasn't going to be tied to my destiny like my mother was and her mother before her. Not me. So I just worked. Worked and worked and worked. Took time off to marry. Big mistake.

Emily   And children?

Anna   Almost.

Emily   Almost?

Anna   Aborted.

Emily   Oh.

Anna   Scraped out and down the whazoo.

Emily   Nev didn't want . . .

Anna   Top up?

Emily   No, thanks. I have to pick up Nicola from her violin lessons . . .

Anna   All around, huh? I saw her box at school. She's good. Now you tell me the violin too?

Emily   She's a genius. All children are. Then they're brought down to earth to take their place amongst the rest of us. Labelled. But you wouldn't know about being labelled, stopped. You've pulled yourself out of all that. It's what Neville . . . loved about you . . . I wake up in the middle of the night and I swear to you I simply don't understand. I just don't. No note.

Anna   Maybe he did leave you a kind of note, but you just couldn't read it.

Emily   What?

Anna   You should know this. He wrote to me, Emily.

Emily   He wrote to you?

Anna   Up until the day he died.

Emily   Neville wrote to you . . .

Anna   He always wrote to me. For years. In fact he never stopped.

Emily   I don't understand.

Anna   Neville and I always had a . . . thing. Right from the start. We couldn't help it. He stopped over to see me in the States when he was last home. I was with him. I think it broke up my marriage, or helped to break it up. It was always the two of us . . . always.

Emily   I . . . I don't . . .

Anna   Neville was trying to escape. He was always trying to escape from whatever he could. That was his way.

Emily   Our life together was an escape?

Anna It wasn't just you. It was me too. I got pregnant by him. At Columbia. I had to get an abortion. That's what he wanted.

Emily Anna, I'm sorry, I can't take this all in . . .

Anna I didn't want you to know all this just like that. But it's true. He told me that he had to leave something other than his speeches, and his books, and his causes. A child. Immortality, Emily. I'll drink to that.

Emily It wasn't real. Our life together. The home we made. Our daughter. Nicola.

Anna He loved her.

Emily He didn't love me. I know that.

Anna He respected you.

Emily Respect.

Anna And he wanted a black world for Nicola. That's what his whole life meant, Emily.

Emily Yes.

Anna Some day it will be different. But not now.

Emily Yes.

Anna He tried to negotiate this as a black man, do you know what that means? In the end it got to him. I know about that, I know what it means. Nicola's got to know what it means.

Emily I couldn't help him. I can't help her. I don't have your clarity. Your sanity. Your strength. I never did. I was wounded in my childhood. Wounded by people who wouldn't let me be what I was deep inside. They had a role for me, a place for me, and I had no choice. But it wounded me inside. Killed me, really. Maybe . . . maybe Nicola was my attempt to redeem my own life.

Anna You can't use a child to do that.

Emily No. But I'm a good mother. I am. I want Nicola to be free. Loved. I'm a good mother, Anna! No matter what Neville thought! Poor you and me. We looked up to him. More than we knew. More than we even guessed. That was his real problem. Because if there was room inside for even one of us, he wouldn't have killed himself. Left us. Women like us appear so self-sufficient, so strong, so capable. But we have a secret even from ourselves, a deep, dark secret that we can't even touch. We loathe ourselves. We do. We give up everything we have, everything we are because we hate ourselves. We give it away to everyone else, our men, our children . . .

Anna *You* might. But not me. He told me about you. The way you clung to him. He thought it would just be a fling with you, a thing, but you wouldn't let it be. He felt sorry for you, you know that? That's what he said.

Emily . . . I didn't know a thing . . .

Anna   Oh, some conspiracy of the dark people, huh? The dark forces ganging up on you. You just weren't his thang, Emily. Period. I've got to tell you the way it is.

Emily   I have to go fetch Nicola.

Anna   Don't freak out. I wasn't his thing, either. He was too busy running. He couldn't take the burden, couldn't take the heat. Yeah, he could have lived a melodrama. That would have been nice for you, and all of those people who looked up to him. But Nev was too far gone for that. And when he saw he couldn't really make a difference with his life, he ended it. Just like that. He didn't have to leave a note. His entire life was a suicide note.

Emily   Nicola . . .

Anna   It's crazy here. Europe made Neville crazy. Nicola has to get out! This European place doesn't give a damn about her. Doesn't give a damn at all. Ask me how I know. I've spent an entire year looking at it. All of your great art, all of it . . . Géricault, Delacroix, Ingres, Manet, Degas, Gauguin, Matisse, Durer, Bosch, Veronese, Rembrandt, Rubens, Velázquez, Watteau, Tiepolo, Reynolds, Blake, Gainsborough, they all painted dark faces. But they didn't see. They couldn't see. Why? Because there's no seeing here, not for me, not for Nicola. Neville didn't want his daughter here. That's why he adopted her. To get her out. And you know that, Emily. You know he wouldn't want her in some goddamn Shropshire. Where the hell is that anyway? *What* in the hell is it? What's it got to do with her?

Emily   She's my daughter! *Our* daughter! She's been with me ever since she was two weeks old. I've been with her, I've seen everything she's done. Who she is. She's my child. What does Nicola mean to you? You're not going to have Nicola. You're not going to take her away from me. You're not going to, Anna! (*Exits.*)

Anna *pours herself another drink.*

Child's voice (*off-stage*)   Anna, Anna, puddin' and pie, kissed the boys and made them cry. Hail Mary full of grace, the Lord is with thee. Blessed art thou amongst women, and blessed is the fruit of thy womb, Jesus.

Anna *follows the voice. She walks into a blaze of light. There are white candles, flowers, an altar decked out for first Holy Communion. A beautiful white child,* **Little Anna**, *dressed for her first Communion, is singing a nursery rhyme.*

Anna   At last. There you are. Out in the open. At least you could've been black.

Little Anna   Oh no, that's not what you wanted when you were ten years old. You wanted to look like Shirley Temple. Remember how you begged for a Shirley Temple doll . . .

Anna   All right, all right.

Little Anna   And mamma said no. She always said no. Except when it was time for Mass. Then she said yes. She thought you were so devote. When all you really liked was the candles and the bells and the Latin, and the priest. Oh, Anna, how could you?

Anna   You're here now. You've been trying to get through for a long time, and you're here now. So get lost. Just leave me alone.

Little Anna   Why didn't you tell Emily?

Anna   Tell her what?

Little Anna She asked you a direct question: 'What does Nicola mean to you?' Why didn't you answer her?

Anna Just leave me alone. Is there a drink around here?

Little Anna Just some holy water. Don't . . .

Anna *takes a gulp.*

Anna Just leave me alone.

Little Anna I want to, but I can't. Because you won't look at me. Look at me, Anna. Look at me.

Anna Don't come near me. I'll kill you . . .

Little Anna You can't kill me. Anyway, I want to go away. But I can't, Anna. Not until you look at me.

Anna I'm not looking at you. I can't stand your skin, your hair . . .

Little Anna Look at me. Love me. Love me. You used to. I can't go until you look at me.

Anna If I look at you I'll go blind.

Little Anna There's nothing wrong with the dark. I know you're afraid . . .

Anna Just go . . . away . . . please . . . please . . . please . . . I thought you'd gone away . . . long ago . . . long ago . . .

Little Anna All the vodka and all the sex and all the power can't make me go away. Look at me . . .

Anna Go away. Let me sleep.

Little Anna Anna . . .

Anna I'm stronger than you. Stronger, better! And you know something, nobody's going to know about you . . .

Little Anna Unless they open the box. Anna, the box. You can't have anything, anything real and true, until you open the box, until you look at me.

Anna Oh yeah? Watch! Watch me. I'm going to have Nicola because she's mine. She's ours, Neville and me. Know something else? The minute I have her, you little white bitch, you'll be dead. And I'll have her, baby, I'll have her.

Little Anna Unless you're betrayed.

Anna I've been betrayed all my life. I thought you knew everything. Damn, the bottle is empty.

Little Anna No it's not, Anna. There's a little left. That's right, turn it up. Drink slowly. Slowly. 'Anna, Anna, puddin' and pie, kissed the boys and made them cry . . .'

Blackout.

Act Two

Scene One

The playground. **Anna** *and* **Janet** *are standing beside a fence watching the children play.*

Janet You look rough. Better lay off the booze. You didn't call me.

Anna I haven't been sleeping, that's all. Look at that kid, the one over there kicking the football. He reminds me of the statue of St Maurice in Magdeburg Cathedral.

Janet Don't change the subject. Why didn't you call me?

Anna I'd love to make those Nazi skinheads go see that. Have you seen my slide of it?

Janet Anna . . .

Anna There was this brief moment in the history of this continent . . . all right, I know it was for political purposes . . . the emperor wanted to shore up his Mediterranean claims, you know how it was in the thirteenth century . . .

Janet . . . Anna . . .

Anna . . . but for a brief moment some white sculptor showed that it was possible for beauty to exist in us . . . that it was possible to depict a black as a black . . . no fantasy . . . no fear . . . *black* and make that blackness just as worthy of salvation . . . of the possibility of life . . . I saw it on a shitty day a lot like this. All the newspapers were full of stuff about immigrant hostels being threatened; the guy who owned the hotel kept turning off CNN . . . it was a lousy day. Then I saw that statue . . . kind of like David your head looks, come to think of it.

Janet Anna, Emily's in a bad way. For Neville's sake . . .

Anna Look at those kids. What's here for them?

Janet The fact they were born at all gives me some kind of hope.

Anna Of what?

Janet I don't know. Sanity.

Anna Wake up and smell the coffee, honey. We're barely here.

Janet You're so . . . black. Wish life was as simple as that.

Anna Do I detect a note of English sarcasm?

Janet I'm not English. And I mean it. You are. Strong. Always sure. Nev and I admired that so much.

Anna I've got to get a move on. Lot to do before I leave.

Janet You're trying to take Nicola from Emily. She told me. You know she's not strong, she'll fight. She won't let you.

Anna I never give up.

Janet I know that.

Anna Anyway, what's happened to you? You used to be the kick-ass-take-no-prisoners-sister.

Janet I'm tired.

Anna Yeah, well if you go to sleep the Man's done got you. I know that. Oh how they hate it when I stand up in their seminars and challenge them on their paternalistic, Christian, Eurocentric point of view. And all this crap about PC. How come they can use funny terms like 'friendly fire', 'economical with the truth', and 'ethnic cleansing' and nobody lifts an eyebrow. But when we want to change words . . . make new meanings . . . That's why I've got all these degrees, why I do what I do. I know their shit. Be the fly in the ointment, baby, the ruffian on the stair, their worst nightmare: a highly educated, loud-mouthed black nigger bitch. I'm tryin' my best. So did you once upon a time, until you took tea with the Queen.

Janet Don't you think I know I've changed? Don't you think I know that I've betrayed my youth? Can't you see that's why I want to go back? I want to go back before I atrophy. Before I become some kind of monster with no history, no home, no life. I have to go back and find that little girl who swam in the sea and didn't care what her hair looked like, how she sounded, whether anyone approved of her. I hate this country. I hate what it's done to me, done to those children out there. They even look at a bloody commercial for bathroom tissues and see themselves.

Anna So you'll help me persuade Emily to give up Nicola? I can give her a better life. A black life.

Janet You live like a bloody maharaja. A black life.

Anna I'm talking about her soul.

Janet Why do you want that child? Why do you really want her?

Anna Boy, they really got to you.

Janet Don't give me that old soap. 'Cause it doesn't wash.

Anna If you'd have stayed home instead of coming here with your mamma, how do you think you'd have been? She brought you and you hate her guts for it. You hate her. That's why you can't go back. Because she's there. And nobody there fought for you, made sure you grew up the way you wanted to, needed to. We both had upwardly mobile mamasitas. They didn't have a plan, just drop us in with the white folks and somehow it will all turn out all right. But I have a plan. I do. Nicola's going to be what I am, only better. And how could you stand in the way of that?

Janet I'm not the one in your way.

owing where everything stands, you know how we Yanks are. By the

ke? He's invited me over to eat. Emily's close to him. Maybe I could

ck solidarity.

avid out of it. He's got enough on his plate.

Anna ot going to hurt him. I just want to fuck him, that's all. Look at those boys. Can you explain this English football to me? And they don't even have any protection. Nothin' like the NFL to show you how to play it right. I better go do my Whoopi Goldberg routine 'cause it looks like a fight's about to start.

Janet Why do you hate white people so much? You think we're stupid, don't you? Too tolerant. The black American way is the only way, the beacon to the world for every black person on earth. It's not.

Little Anna *appears, unseen by* **Janet**.

Little Anna My curls, Anna. Please do my curls.

Anna Oh, oh, the Ugly American rebuked again . . .

Little Anna My curls, Anna. Please do my curls.

Janet Don't you realise how much power we give them by continuously focusing on them as the *'raison d'être'* of our entire existences? When will we stop invoking them?

Anna When they all vanish.

Little Anna I won't disappear.

Janet Are you all right?

Anna I'm writing a thesis on Degas. It's going through my head.

Little Anna Look at me. Look at me.

Anna I don't feel sorry for her. Nicola's not a bargaining chip any more for Neville's love.

Janet Neville's dead.

Anna Then help me. Nicola belongs with me . . .

Little Anna Anna, Anna, puddin' and pie . . .

Anna Let's go. It's freezing out here.

Little Anna Look at me, Anna.

Anna I've got to go. I need a Stoly break. (*Exits.*)

Janet How dare you come back into my life and try to rip it apart?

Blackout.

Scene Two

This scene happens simultaneously in **Janet***'s kitchen and in* **Anna***'s bedroom.*

Janet *and* **Emily** *are seated at* **Janet***'s kitchen table. They have just finished supper.* **Anna** *is sleeping fitfully in her bed.*

Janet (*calling out to her children off-stage*)   No!

Anna (*waking up with a start*)   No!

Little Anna *appears to* **Anna** *dressed in her white First Communion dress. She sits on the edge of* **Anna***'s bed.*

Anna   Look, I told you to go away!

Janet (*to children upstairs*)   No more television, I said! Lights out!

Little Anna   It starts with 'Do you renounce. . . ?'

Enter **Liam** *from the bathroom.*

Liam   You all right?

Emily (*to herself*)   No.

Liam *and* **Janet**   You all right?

Anna   Is there anything left to drink?

Emily   No. No, if I'm honest.

Liam   Why don't you stop?

Anna   An Irishman advising *me* not to drink?

Janet   What is it?

Liam   You know what you are? You're a fucking racist!

Emily   Am I a . . . Am I a racist, Janet?

Anna   So what. What's left in the bottle?

Janet   What kind of question is that?

Anna   Where's the bottle?

Emily   An honest one.

Liam   I poured it down the sink. Right down. So go back to sleep.

Janet   You're tired. You need some rest. Nicola's all right upstairs with the children. Why don't you sleep here? Ari's in Paris.

Liam   Anna, I have to have my answer.

Anna   I don't know the answer to that question.

Liam   You do. And I want it tonight.

Emily   Please answer me. I need to know.

Little Anna 'Anna, Anna, puddin' and pie, kissed the boys and made them cry . . .'

Janet Is that Nicola's voice? I can hear her singing upstairs. Listen.

Anna Listen, baby . . .

Emily Nev taught her to sing. He taught her everything.

Liam I'm listening. Because this time I want a real answer, not one of your fuckin' excuses.

Janet Her voice is so beautiful . . .

Anna (*to* **Little Anna**) I can't hear . . .

Little Anna *stops singing*.

Anna I can't answer you.

Emily Janet, am I? I don't know anything any more.

Anna I can't answer you.

Janet We all are, Emily. We are because that's the way it's been set up. And most of us are cowards.

Emily *and* **Liam** Why?

Anna Baby, it's late. I can't deal with this.

Liam You're flying back to New York in a few days. That's what you're scheduled to do. I'll go back there with you if that's what you want me to do. If that'll prove it to you. Prove what I feel.

Anna Liam, it's too late, baby . . .

Janet Babies, children, adults, it's drummed into us. Even when I was a child and there were no white people around me to speak of, I was aware of them. The difference between me and them. Between me and you.

Anna Me and you? Me and you, Liam? I could go off with you, couldn't I?

Liam We could have our own children. It's not too late.

Emily I remember when I saw a black person for the first time. He was African and walking down the road. I think his car broke down or something, I don't know. I was very young. And I was walking up the road and he came toward me. Like something out of a dream. And I stopped and stared. He was so tall. His skin was so dark. So much darker than mine. There was something in that darkness that I could never forget. I couldn't sleep that night because of it. I just wanted to touch that skin. I just wanted to feel what it was like.

Anna Just like in some dream. Like a fairy tale, huh, Liam? You and me deep in the French countryside with our wine and bread, our tan babies, our dreams.

Emily When I met Neville, I felt that same thing, that yearning. It came back to me. I wanted to touch him. Continuously. Every chance I had. He was like a mirage to me. Never really real. Because he wasn't real. There was no room for his tears, the things that made him afraid. Not with me. I fooled myself into believing there was.

Anna Just like in some dream. Oh Neville, I want to dream.

Liam What?

Janet I can't, Emily.

Emily What?

Janet I can't take it all in. I'm sorry.

Liam You loved him, didn't you? Neville.

Anna No. No. I've never loved anyone in my life.

Little Anna Bingo!

Janet (*calling to children*) Stop that noise! Stop it!

Liam What was it like with him then?

Janet I can't take it on any more. I can't even take on my own children, my husband, myself. I keep seeing myself back there, back home, playing in the waves. Running the sea through my hair. It comes every day now. Once that feeling only came occasionally and now . . . now it's every day. I don't have room for anything else. Nothing.

Little Anna Bingo! You used to like to say that word. Especially when Father Flannery came in the room. The one who'd been in the Congo with the little native children. To the Dark Continent. Remember the stories he used to tell? Walking into the villages and all the little naked children who had no civilisation at all running up to him for salvation. Then he would pour the water on them and ask, 'Do you renounce . . .' Now what's the rest? What's the answer to the question?

Anna (*to* **Little Anna**) What do you want? Why don't you leave me alone!

Liam Leave you alone. Even if I killed you it wouldn't matter.

Anna Oh stop being so corny. We're both big kids. We like to fuck. That's it. You sure that bottle's empty?

Emily Yes . . .

Janet I can't answer your question.

Little Anna (*to* **Anna**) Answer.

Janet I can't.

Little Anna (*to* **Anna**) Try.

Emily Everything's collapsing around us. We can put on a brave face, but . . . this is a kind of . . . Dark Ages. Neville knew it. He knew that it would never change.

Janet Neville was a fool.

Anna (*to* **Liam**) Where do you think you're going?

Liam What difference does it make to you?

Emily Because of what he did?

Janet Why don't you get angry? Why do you sit there like some mewling sheep? He left you with nothing. You're walking around like a corpse. Is that any good for you, any good for Nicola?

Emily I'm not sure I am any good for her.

Anna There are a lot of bad black guys out there this time of night . . .

Liam Fuck off! That's the only way you can possibly see the world, isn't it?

Emily I'm not sure.

Anna I can't afford to see it like you!

Liam And you want Nicola, who was brought up like a human being by two people who tried their damnedest to make her that way, to go to you so you can warp her mind, prove your sick thesis!

Emily Perhaps I shouldn't have her.

Anna Oh, baby, please . . .

Liam You want to know what the real difference between you and me is? Vulnerability. I'm not afraid to show how I hurt. I'm a human being, Anna.

Anna I tried to be a human being. A couple of times. But every time I tried I was reminded of *this*. (*She points to her skin.*) Let me clue you in on something, Liam: the whole world is seen through your eyes, everything through your eyes. And I'm going blind trying to see what you see. I almost cracked up, Liam. But I said no. No, I'm not going to crack. I'm going to learn, and learn, and learn, and be better than you. Better than you could ever be. Do you know what will save you? Becoming like *me*! Being *me*! Then you can see. Then you can hear what I'm saying! Oh yes, I sat in catechism class. A good Catholic girl. Catholic because that was the only school that wasn't segregated. And the priest would come to us, a class full of black children, and bring his snow-white Jesus. And when I was baptised I was asked: 'Do you renounce Satan and all his works?' And something inside me said 'No. No. Because if *you* renounce Satan, then I accept him. I accept the darkness.'

Little Anna That's the answer I've been waiting for. The magic answer! Bingo! (*She disappears.*)

Liam And *you* want to have Nicola. *You* want to have her.

Anna What'll Emily make her into? Another black cripple who doesn't know who she is!

Janet Maybe you shouldn't.

Emily Anna and Neville . . . they . . . you knew about it, didn't you?

Janet It was an open secret. If you'd wanted to see. Anna got pregnant by Neville at university. She wanted the baby. He wanted the Cause. She got an abortion. For a while she didn't see him. But that didn't last long. She came back to him. They were together for a while at graduate school. She wanted to follow him here, but he wouldn't let her. Then suddenly, he married you.

Emily She loved him. And he took her child.

Anna Yes. I want Nicola. And you can think whatever you like.

Liam Oh Anna, Anna, Anna. What's the use. You want to watch satellite TV?

Anna Do you hear what I said?

Liam 'UK Gold'? The Golden Oldies of British TV. Or how about a film. Arnie Schwarzenegger.

Anna Get out!

Liam Watch him beat up people in the worst accent in the world. Come on, Anna.

Anna Let go of me!

Liam Come on. It's what my brothers' wives do. We can be cosy and domestic.

Anna You don't want me to start screaming, do you?

Liam All you like. The London police will show up and prove your thesis. They'll take one look at me, one look at you and assume you're a tart. They'll leave us in peace, *so watch*!

Emily Oh, Janet. It's too much. I think I'll take up your invitation to stay over. I'm really tired.

Janet You love Nicola, don't you?

Emily I don't know any more.

Janet Emily, you have to know. Do you love that child?

Emily Yes. Yes.

Janet I'll get some blankets.

Emily Thanks, Janet. I know my way round.

Anna Liam.

Anna *and* **Liam** *begin to make love.*

Little Anna (*offstage*) *whistles a hymn.*

Liam You don't get it, do you?

Anna I get everything you give me.

Liam Can't you see how it is with us?

Anna I know . . .

Liam How could you give this up. . . ?

Anna I must be out of my mind . . . Don't stop.

Liam I don't want to. I love you.

Anna The girl's supposed to want the babies and the home. I love the way your skin tastes.

Liam Say yes.

Anna Yes! Yes! Yes! Yes! Yes! Yes!

Liam Oh, God . . .

Anna Say yes to me, Liam. Can you do that?

Liam I've always said yes to you. From the moment I laid eyes on you.

Anna Make me say 'yes' again, baby. Make me. Don't leave me.

Emily *exits.* **Anna** *and* **Liam** *stop making love.*

Liam I want you to feel something!!

Janet It's the most important thing. Love.

Little Anna (*offstage*) 'Anna, Anna, puddin' and pie, kissed the boys and made them cry . . .'

Janet . . . my mother on her porch, rocking back and forth in the afternoon. That sound, that creaky sound. Always that sound. Pretending that she couldn't see. She could see everything. Everything. She could see *his* eyes, *him* looking at me. My new father. He wasn't my father. She knew. She knew what was happening. But she just sat there rocking back and forth. Rocking back and forth . . .

Little Anna (*offstage*) Listen, Anna, listen.

Janet . . . pretending that she couldn't see. She didn't defend me. Ever. All I could hear were the waves, the way the water came in and out. In and out. And what it must be like to just go down, down deep inside the water, let it cover me up for ever, take me away. Take me where he couldn't touch me. Away. Where there was love.

Little Anna (*offstage*) WHERE ARE YOU? Can't you hear me?

Janet Her love.

Liam I'm sorry, baby, I'm sorry. Jesus . . .

Anna I . . . wish . . . I . . . could . . . for . . . you . . . I . . . wish . . .

Liam Come to bed, darling. Come to bed with me.

Anna In a minute. In a minute. You go on.

Liam Anna, I'm sorry.

Anna It's not you. It's just tonight. I usually go off like a twenty megaton neutron bomb. Go to bed, honey. I'll be there in a minute.

Liam I love you. (*Exits.*)

Anna Do I love that man? Do I love anyone?

Little Anna *appears.*

Little Anna Maybe yes. Maybe no.

Anna (*to* **Little Anna**) I didn't mean to tell you to go away. I didn't mean it. I was drunk. I'm always drunk.

Little Anna Whose fault is that?

Anna What am I going to do with Liam? I wouldn't be any good. My God, my God. Little Anna, Little Anna.

Little Anna Feel it?

Anna I can still feel Neville's baby inside me. I can feel them scraping it out. Scraping. Everything inside me is screaming 'No!'

Little Anna I don't know anything about that. I'm just a little kid.

Anna When Liam and I make love, sometimes I can feel that stirring in me. Then I know. He's making love to make babies. And I can feel myself, just for a second, feel myself go under. Say yes. Again. I want to feel that life inside me again. Life that Liam and I make. Then I think it's possible. I do. But it was all scraped out. Scraped out when I saw that white Jesus, when they put that white wafer on my tongue. It frightened me. Liam frightens me. I turn over and look at his skin. It's so . . . white. And my skin . . . I can't see anything else. It's made me a little bit crazy.

Little Anna Janet's not crazy, David's not crazy.

Anna They don't want as much as I do.

Little Anna If only mamma'd loved me a little bit more . . .

Anna Shut up! That's over! It's all over! Neville owes me. He owes me a child. He owes me a girl child because that's what they dug out . . .

Little Anna Bingo!

Anna Come here so that I can talk to you face to face.

Little Anna You're looking at me! You're looking at me!

Anna I'm owed. I'm owed. Even by you, you little bitch. If you can't give me what you owe me, stay away! STAY AWAY! Everybody, stay away!

Little Anna *disappears.*

Anna There's no real love in this world. There's nothing but darkness. Darkness.

Blackout.

Scene Three

David Sinclair's *flat.* **David** *is setting the table for a meal he has just prepared for* **Anna**.

David . . . then to Cambridge. Trinity. I didn't last. I couldn't stand it. I came down and went to what we call here a 'red-brick university'. Yes, there were times I regretted not staying on. But it worked out for the best.

Enter **Anna**.

Anna   Excuse me for being so nosy. I love the things you have here.

David   Nev's taste, to tell the truth. He thought I needed some culture.

Anna   This statue is gorgeous.

David   There's a story about that. Nev knew this frightfully English former memsahib who had a garage full of loot she'd brought back from her life 'in the colonies'. Nev met her at some embassy do. He was always winding up in the strangest places, and the old girl'd had a bit too much and started telling him about her garage. Nev thought that this loot should be returned to its rightful owners, or at least their descendants, so to speak . . . (and this is the most dishonest thing I have ever done) . . . We posed as community leaders, appealed to what social conscience she had, and she gave us the stuff. I was stunned. But then Nev pointed out to me that she owed this to us. She'd gotten it by trickery, so we got it back by the same means. *We* didn't use mirrors and beads to do it. Nev kept some, I kept a bit, and the rest's in the school. I think it's considered too ugly for the kids to steal.

Anna   That's pretty wild. Hmmm . . . sorry for sticking my finger in that, but it smelled so good.

David   If you allow me, I shall take you on a gourmet tour of the Caribbean, the southern states of America, and Africa.

Anna   All in one meal.

David   If you'll allow me. Please sit down. Now, what you stuck your finger in is called 'ital'. What you tasted is called 'rundown', a method of slowly cooking coconut milk. It makes a thick, creamy sauce that can be used with fish, meat. 'Ital' belongs to the Rastafari. Mostly vegetarian. The sauce: coconut milk, onion, garlic, thyme, parsley, cloves, cinnamon, fresh ginger, hot peppers. Add vegetables: carrots, white cabbage, sweetcorn, etc.

Anna   Great. Anything to drink?

David   Are you through the one I gave you already?

Anna   Just thirsty. Might be the reason I haven't been sleeping well.

David   You might be a little keyed-up about going back to New York. Sit down, I'll massage your shoulders.

Anna   That's all right . . .

David   Sit down. Good. Drop your shoulders. What's a beautiful woman like you carrying on your shoulders? They're so tight. You shouldn't be carrying anything at all.

Anna   Why'd you leave Cambridge? Racism?

David   Oh no. In the sixties everyone was tripping over themselves trying to be nice to you. No. It was just that I discovered a frightening trait about Englishmen.

Anna   And that is?

David   When Englishmen don't get their way, they throw tantrums.

Anna   Excuse me?

David Yes. Full-blown, livin' tantrums. The Latins duel, the Americans shoot you, and the English throw tantrums. I didn't know what was going on at first. But I had a friend there by the name of The Honourable Hugo Fitzmaurice, who was the best steel drummer I have ever seen. And he was with me when this tantrum happened after a cricket match. I can remember him smiling and then saying: (*Imitating Fitzmaurices's voice.*) 'It's tear-off-the-sailor-suit, bang-the-head-against-the-nursery-wall time. One of our national characteristics.' And he was right. I couldn't take it. So I left. There, your shoulders feel better.

Anna I could go to sleep right now, but I can't. I can't close my eyes.

David Not until I feed you . . . Miss or Mrs Eastman?

Anna Mrs Eastman, I'm sorry to say. It sounds better than Rufus.

David Anna Rufus. It's got something. Here's your drink.

Anna Why do you talk like that?

David Talk like what?

Anna Like you're a refugee from *The Importance of Being Earnest*?

David I'm nervous.

Anna Why?

David I've never been this close to you.

Anna Oh. Confessions of a Head-teacher.

David May as well take the plunge.

Anna May as well, as you'd say.

David I know you've met Liam, my art teacher . . . are you with. . . ?

Anna No.

David Somehow that didn't sound too convincing. I just thought . . . you looked so . . .

Anna I said no. What else you got to eat?

David Yassa. A Senegalese dish. You traditionally use lots of lemon and oil with this, but I've toned it down. Lemon juice, malt vinegar, groundnut oil, onions, thyme again, hot peppers, bay leaves, stock . . .

Anna Toned it down? I like dark meat.

David It's very hot.

Anna I like hot things.

David That's the American Way, isn't it? Upfront.

Anna Only way to fly.

David Like to switch to palm wine?

Anna Whatever you got. And it looks like a lot.

David Neville used to talk like that. You know, that accent.

Anna   Picked it up in America.

David   He loved it there.

Anna   No he didn't. That's what he told you. Hmm . . . this is strong . . .

David   I suppose we should sit down.

Anna   This looks wonderful.

David   Hope it tastes that way.

Anna   I'm sure it will.

David   *Bon appetit.*

Anna   Cheers, David.

David   Speaking of names, I was named after the Duke of Windsor. My mother thought he was wonderful. She loved the way he dressed. She saw the photos after he'd become Governor of the Bahamas. Loved him. Didn't care for Wallis, though. Like it?

Anna   I certainly do.

David   The food.

Anna   Oh. Absolutely. You're hired.

David   Thanks. Would you like to go to the theatre with me next week?

Anna   I won't be here next week.

David   Oh, I forgot.

Anna   I'm not supposed to be. It's up to Emily.

David   Emily?

Anna   I'm trying to persuade her to allow me to take Nicola back with me.

David   I don't understand.

Anna   Well, why not? What's Nicola got here? Shropshire?

David   Let me see if I understand this: you intend to take Nicola back to the States?

Anna   Yep.

David   I don't . . .

Anna   You don't understand? How long have you been head-teacher of Linbrook Primary, the school they dump all the problems in? Don't look at me like I'm crazy. Linbrook, England, Europe's no place for Nicola.

David   Anna, she's a British child . . .

Anna   *British!* What does that mean?

David It means that this is where she was born and raised. What in the hell would it be like if we all left? It would be like we had never been here. Certain people would cover over what we've done, what we've achieved, as if we never existed. They'd win. And I won't let them win. The children belong here. England is all Nicola knows.

Anna She's ten years old. She'll adapt.

David Besides, Emily wouldn't know how to even deal with this right now.

Anna That's why I need your help.

David Anna, I've just told you . . .

Anna Okay, everything you say may be right, I don't know. I do know that this is the safest place for black people to live on this whole damn continent. But what does that mean? Give one kid a chance, David.

David I don't believe I'm hearing this after I've said . . .

Little Anna *appears and begins eating the food.*

Little Anna Ugh! I hate spicy food!

Anna (*to* **Little Anna**) I'll wipe you out after I have Nicola . . .

David Anna, what are you saying?

Anna What I'm saying is that she can come back here and live when she grows up. I'm not going to take her citizenship away. I just want to give her a chance, that's all.

David Is that why you came here tonight? To enlist me by any means necessary?

Anna Have to give it my best shot.

David Guess I'd better call you a cab. (*Exits.*)

Anna You know I'm right. You know the way it is. What future do those kids in your school have?

Little Anna My hair needs a ribbon. I'm losing a curl!

Anna Hmm . . . this palm wine is wonderful . . .

Little Anna Palm wine won't get rid of me!

Enter **David**.

David Five hundred years of running stops here! My stand is here and the children I teach, their stand is here! Right here!

Anna Easy for you to say. Easy for me. How long do you think it'll take before they're accepted, really accepted in the 'fabric of society'? A generation? Two? What about *now*, David!

David Now is what I'm talking about. Besides, you're not motivated by Nicola's welfare. It's something else.

Little Anna My hair! My hair!

Anna Shall I lie on your couch while you diagnose me?

Little Anna My hair! My hair!

David No, it's not Nicola. It's about you. You need her. For yourself.

Anna What's that supposed to mean?

David I've worked with children and adults half my life . . . You don't love that child. You don't even know her. She's some kind of prop that you need.

Little Anna Bingo!

Anna You call that cab?

David Yes, I understand now. When you first came to Linbrook I can't tell you how privileged I felt. A big American art expert coming to work in my little, poor, inner-city school. My little school fighting to survive. I thought you were an angel come down from heaven. But you came to take Neville and Emily's child away.

Anna What were you doing in the sixties in that little red-brick university. . . ?

Little Anna In the sixties, I tried to help you. I wanted you to look at me. But you ran away, far away. But it didn't make me vanish. It didn't make me go away.

Anna (*to* **Little Anna**) Just shut up!

David You won't stop me from saying what I have to say to you. You may not like this, but I'll tell you a little story. Neville was a womaniser. Couldn't keep his hands off the ladies. Didn't care where he was. Especially toward the end. Humiliated the hell out of Emily. But she put up with it. She loved him. Nicola was her link, her bond. She brought that child up as well as she could. She knows more about black history than any of those children out there with two living black parents! Oh, Nicola knows who she is! More than I do, more than you do.

Little Anna But she doesn't have beautiful blonde hair like I do.

David Emily listens to me. Watch this. (*He picks up the telephone.*)

Anna Okay! You win.

David *replaces telephone.*

Little Anna Good. My ribbon, please.

Anna I've got a terrible headache.

David It's not a matter of winning or losing. England is Nicola's home.

Anna No more palm wine. What about vodka?

David Look at me. Stop running.

Anna Empty.

David We're from the same generation. I had to grapple with what was expected of me. Neville carried on, I didn't. I became a schoolteacher. No wife. No children. It's been a kind of waste. I'm in there all day and half the evening. It's like carrying a boulder uphill. You get to the top and then you fall back down. I've lost everything, not just my accent.

Little Anna Anna, Anna, he loves you! Love, Anna, love! You and David could have a little Nicola of your own.

Anna (*to* **Little Anna**) Please, I can't breathe.

Little Anna *disappears.*

David Anna, sit down.

Anna You're wrong, David. You haven't lost anything.

David You got a cigarette?

Anna Smoking's the only thing I don't do.

David I keep a few hidden. I'm trying to give them up. Guess supper's finished.

Anna Maybe what you lost had something to do with being . . .

David Black?

Anna . . . in a white man's country . . .

David 'Save Nicola from a fate worse than death.'

Anna Save Nicola from what happened to us. To Neville.

David In America? That doesn't make any sense.

Anna Africa eventually. The Caribbean. Any place but here.

David Nicola's all Emily's got.

Anna Emily, Emily, Emily. What about the kid?

David Truce? The food's cold.

Anna Life's a bitch and then you die.

David I'm sorry.

Anna You said what you had to say. I'd better go. Where's that cab number?

David I can drive you.

Anna I'm all right.

David I'm sorry you're leaving.

Anna Are you?

David Yes.

Anna You're out on a limb, aren't you, brother?

David Aren't you out there from time to time?

Anna Can't afford to be.

David Try it.

Anna No I'll step off a cliff.

David Try.

Anna Gotta go back to America, the 'Evil Empire' awaits.

David You'll miss the dessert.

Anna I have a mighty fierce sweet tooth. Always have.

Blackout.

Scene Four

Anna *is dictating to her tape recorder while finishing a bottle of vodka. Behind her, projected on the wall, is a slide of the painting 'Portrait d'une negresse'.*

Anna (I've got to get some sleep) . . . '*moi égal à toi*' . . . the black *citoyenne* . . . that golden moment in French history between 1794 and 1802 when slavery was outlawed . . . Perhaps this is the meaning behind the dignity of Benoist's portrait, one of the most beautiful paintings of a black woman ever created. No servitude, no fear, she radiates confidence, serenity, security in herself . . .' (*To the painting.*) You cow! Look at you. Bet you didn't have parents who wanted you to be the first black woman President of the United States, bet they didn't have garden parties for the NACP – the National Association for Certain People – bet they gave you room to breathe . . . yeah, you breathed all right. You got away. Went to France. Well, I'm not going to France. Listen to this: (*Reads letter.*) 'Dear Liam, I've thought a lot about going away with you. But it won't work and we both know it. Too much time has passed, baby, too much water under the bridge for you and me to . . .'

Little Anna *appears.*

Little Anna 'Anna, Anna, puddin' and pie, kissed the boys and made them cry.'

Anna Don't you have some homework to do?

Little Anna What ya drinkin'?

Anna Get out of there!

The Pope *appears.*

Pope I beg your pardon. What did I hear you say?

Little Anna Like a drink?

Pope I've had enough, thank you. I've just said Mass. Now, I think this calls for a confession.

Anna You want one? Okay, here it is. I think everything you forced down my throat stinks.

Pope The catechism: 'Who made you?'

Little Anna 'God made me.'

Anna I made myself!

Pope Impossible. 'Why did God make you?'

Little Anna 'God made me to show forth his goodness, and to make me happy with him in heaven.'

Anna I need some sleep.

Little Anna Listen.

Anna No, you listen. I made myself. No thanks to you. No thanks to your little petty rules, your lies, Holy Father.

Pope You can't blame it all on me. I'm just the scapegoat.

Little Anna He's just . . .

Anna Shut up! I know who he is. Know what I really want?

Pope Get thee behind me, Satan!

Anna I want you and everything you represent to own up. God! *He's* even a white man! He's even a fucking he!

Pope Blasphemy! I won't stand for it!

Little Anna You'd better be quiet. He's got the power.

Pope Will you repent?

Anna And live with Liam in some little cottage in France, baking bread and stroking his brow, or be with David and carry the angst of his life on my shoulders? You gotta be kidding!

Little Anna You did it once.

Anna I was a fool, okay? Not again.

Pope Tell me something. What would bring you back to the fold?

Anna Down on my knees again?

Pope I would have put it more delicately.

Anna Your head on a pike, paraded through the Vatican in the front of a column of free black women, naked and dancing!

Little Anna Liar!

Anna Why don't you . . .

Little Anna Liar! That's the 'correct' answer. That's your trouble. That's what you always give . . . the 'correct' answer. Except to one person . . .

Anna Who's that?

Pope *and* **Little Anna** NEVILLE!

Neville *appears*.

Neville Anna . . .

Anna Just go away.

Neville I have to talk to you.

Anna   About what? About what you did?

Neville   I knew you'd understand. I didn't have to explain everything to you.

Anna   And why not? Because I'm some kind of goddess who sits on top of things and sees all?

Neville   No. Because you're on the verge of it every day.

Anna   The verge of what?

Neville   The darkness that finally swallowed me up. Nicola. When I saw her that day in the hospital . . . I wrote you about that . . . I wanted her. I wanted her . . . with Emily.

Anna   How could you do that to me!!! You made me kill our baby!!! You didn't . . .

Neville   It wasn't me. You know that. It was you. You did it. Because you love me.

Anna   I loved you. What did you expect me to do? What was I going to *be* if I had a baby? *Nothing, man*!! I loved you. I wanted to be with you.

Little Anna   Bingo!

Anna   You didn't want our kid! I could have loved that child! I need another chance.

A Priest *enters.*

Priest   Thought I'd join the party. Is this yours? (*He holds up the ornate little box.*)

Anna   Don't touch that!

Priest   I need to bless it.

Anna   Don't touch it!

Heavenly music fills the room. **The Blessed Virgin Mary** (*the White Virgin*) and **Mary of Egypt** (*the Black Virgin*) *stand on opposite sides of the room. The* **Priest** *throws them the box. They pass it back and forth like a football while* **Little Anna** *tries in vain to catch it.*

Anna   Stop it! Stop it!

Pope   Father?

Priest   Oh yes. (*He makes the sign of the cross.*) '*In el nomine patre, et fili, et spiritu santi, amen.*'

Mary of Egypt *returns the box to* **Anna**. *The* **Priest** *tries to bless her, but she rejects him. Instead,* **Mary of Egypt** *tries to bless him.*

Priest   Heresy! Anti-Christ!

Mary of Egypt   That's my middle name.

Blessed Virgin Mary   I can't bear this!

Mary of Egypt   Who asked you anyway!

Pope   Silence!

Mary of Egypt If anybody's God's mother, it's me. This little lightweight dolly-bird couldn't be anybody's mother. Who's ever heard of a virgin having a baby? Does that make sense to you?

Blessed Virgin Mary I'm a miracle.

Mary of Egypt I'll say.

Little Anna *hands the* **Priest** *a bowl of water. He washes his hands.* **The Pope** *extends his ring, the* **Priest** *kneels and kisses it. The* **Priest** *sprinkles holy water on* **The Blessed Virgin Mary** *and* **Mary of Egypt**. **Mary of Egypt** *wipes it off. Suddenly, a sixties Stevie Wonder tape, 'I Was Born to Love Her', rings through the room.* **Neville** *begins to dance.*

Anna Neville, don't let them take my box! Please!

Neville I love this song.

Anna They want to take it!

Neville . . . it was my first night in America. Things looked so fresh and free. We were on the verge of something great then, yes we were. Something great we black people were going to do. I worked for that all my life and then one day I couldn't work for it any more . . . I sat in my car, the car Emily bought me for a birthday present, and I played this song, our song, Anna. Then I went to sleep . . .

Anna I don't care how you died. Just don't let them have this box. No!

Neville Hide it. You always have. Even from me . . . the 'love of your life'. I didn't betray you. *You* betrayed you.

Little Anna Bingo!

Anna I'm going to have Nicola no matter what you say! No matter what any of you say! I'm going to save my life, I'm not going to end up in the foetal position suckin' gas like you did, Neville!

Neville I knew one thing about Emily. She would love Nicola.

Anna What's love got to do with it, baby? Answer me, all of you, you bunch of self-righteous hypocrite-losers! I'm not walking around blind!

Neville Blindness is not always a bad thing. You can develop a second sight.

Anna So you say, the man who could deal with it all. Well, I'm not Janet. Or David. Let them run you to the ground, the blacks and the whites. Just like it does some good, like it means something. It means nothing because in the end you die. You die whether you've been good, or whether you've been bad. That's what I found out. So you might as well have what you need. I need Nicola.

The **Priest** *is now swinging incense all over the room. He is chanting.* **The Blessed Virgin Mary** *and* **Mary of Egypt** *now face one another as if they are about to duel.*

Little Anna Love me! Love me!!

Mary of Egypt What is this about the candles? I'm black because of the candles?

Blessed Virgin Mary   You know the mother of God is white. If you find black statues of the mother of God in Europe it's because of the candles. She's been burnt!

Mary of Egypt   Those Black Virgins are black because they were made black! Ask Anna!

Pope   Ladies, ladies. I mean, Blessed Ladies. All of this is nonsense. Only one of you could be the true mother of God, despite Anna's thesis to the contrary.

Anna   Those statues were black. I can prove it . . .

Pope   But what a waste of time to do so. You spent an entire year travelling, trying to prove that the colour black is some sort of beautiful thing. Something with meaning. And where has it got you?

Neville   Where had it got *me*?

Priest   Neville, my son, at least you can look forward to some fifteen-year-old filmmaker in the south Bronx negotiating the rights to your story.

Mary of Egypt   It doesn't matter that no one read Anna's book on the Black Virgins. She did the talk shows. All the major ones. Signings.

Little Anna   But nothing changed. Everything's still the same.

Blessed Virgin Mary   Because I am the truth. But don't despair. Trust in . . .

Mary of Egypt   Trust? We live in the real world, right, Anna? We know the way it really is. Look at me. I've been ignored for almost a thousand years. There I am. Statues of me all over Europe and they say I'm burnt! Let's go for it! Winner gets the box!

Anna   No! I tried so hard. I tried so hard to be what everyone wanted me to be. I used to pray that I could be what everyone wanted me to be. Then one day I couldn't do it any more . . . one day it all came tumbling down on me . . . I couldn't be another day in this world unless I stopped it, all the humiliation, the pain . . . Can't you hear me? How can I stop it? How can I stop it?

Mary of Egypt *and* **The Blessed Virgin Mary** *wrestle.*

Pope   Now, now. Father, please . . .

The **Priest** *tries to pull them apart. He's dragged into it.* **The Pope** *raises his crosier and they all stop.*

Pope   My children. Peace on earth. Goodwill towards men.

The Pope *leads them all off except* **Neville**, **Anna** *and* **Little Anna**.

Neville   Two of a kind. Except you must go inside that darkness I could no longer confront . . .

Anna   I don't want to die. I don't want to die.

Neville   We survived the Middle Passage . . .

Anna   Did we, Neville?

Neville   You have.

Anna   Just be quiet!

Neville You never wanted to hear my pain. Your own is too intense. That's why it couldn't be the way it should have been between us.

Anna Then Emily came along.

Neville I loved you. Then Emily came along. She was good. There was something calm about her. She made a home for me, a refuge. When things got bad at the end, she was still there.

Anna She didn't stop you from dying!

Neville No, she didn't.

Anna Now you expect me to go on living!

Neville Say it, Anna. Say 'I want to live'. (*He vanishes.*)

Anna I need a drink.

Little Anna Me too! Me too!

Anna No! No!

Little Anna I know what's in that box. The letter. You wanted to be the May Queen, but they picked Lisa O'Brien because she had blue eyes and blonde hair. Beautiful hair, like a fairy's hair. All tumbling down to her waist. Everyone thought she was so beautiful. So did you. You wrote her a letter. To tell her about her beautiful hair. When you had to draw a picture of yourself for art class, you drew a picture of beautiful Lisa instead. Because that's who you wanted to be. Beautiful Lisa. You drew picture after picture of her.

Anna Then one day the nun caught me. She hung the picture up on the board and everyone laughed. She said, 'Who is this, Miss Anna Rufus? You don't look like that. You're black.'

Little Anna And then when you told mamma and daddy about it, all they could talk about was how strong Negroes had to be, how Negroes had to be better than white people.

Anna But they didn't see that picture pinned to the board for a whole week. They didn't see the way Lisa looked at me after that. She felt sorry for me.

Little Anna (*sings*) 'Anna, Anna, puddin' and pie, kissed the boys and made them cry.'

Anna Everyone laughed. I just want to sleep now. I just want to sleep.

Little Anna Go to sleep, little black girl. Sleep, sleep. Tomorrow is a busy day. You have to take that picture down from the blackboard. You have to take it back. Go to sleep now. Sleep.

Anna I can't. I can't.

Blackout.

Act Three

Scene One

Anna *and* **Emily** *are having a drink in a bar.*

Emily Then it's agreed?

Anna You sure?

Emily Yes. I've thought about it. It's the hardest thing I've ever done, but it's what Neville would have wanted. You're right. I know you're right. The way things are today, I want her to grow up properly. With the proper mother for her.

Anna You won't regret it. And I won't turn her American, I promise. I'll send her to one of those Manhattan girls' schools. In Harlem. Another drink?

Enter **Little Anna**.

Anna Too late.

Emily Anna, did you say something?

Anna Boy, I always say you Brits make some strong drinks. I don't see how you stand up half the time. I remember the first time I came over here, I went to some pub somewhere and asked for a beer. First of all, it wasn't even cold, and . . .

Little Anna *sits at the table.*

Anna (*to* **Little Anna**) Thanks a heap.

Emily *starts to cry.*

Emily I'm sorry.

Little Anna *playfully flips the hem of her dress up and down.*

Anna (*to* **Little Anna**) Beat it.

Little Anna I was in confession. I told all my sins. And yours too. And do you know what my penance was? I had to keep on living!

Emily I don't think I'll go to the airport with you. It'll seem strange to Nicola, but I think it's for the best.

Little Anna New game.

Emily You know, I've come to realise something. . . . Anna? . . .

Anna I've got to go. Where's the waiter?

Emily Anna, are you all right?

Anna Guess that's why he loved you. I'm taking your child away, and you ask about me. (I hate saints! . . .)

Little Anna 'Anna, Anna, puddin' and pie, kissed the boys and made them cry . . .'

Anna Where's the waiter?

Emily There are things we have to sort out.

Anna What's her favourite food?

Emily What?

Anna Her favourite food.

Emily I'm sorry. It's just that . . . I could see her when we first got her . . . bangers and mash. She likes chocolate milk. She never eats everything on her plate. She pushes her food around. I can't break that habit. She cooks her own tea. For both of us. Sometimes if she's good I let her take the shopping trolley and then she gets what she wants. I'm always worried when she has that trolley. She has this glint in her eye. The same kind she had when she was a baby. Just when I'd say 'Nicola, no!', off she'd go with that look on her face.

Little Anna 'Anna, Anna, puddin' and pie, kissed . . .'

Anna Did you make her stop playing with her food?

Emily Not completely. I can't get her out of my mind . . .

Anna What did you do?

Emily What?

Anna About the food.

Emily Oh, I used a combination of tactics, most of them around authority. Nicky hates authority, just like . . . Neville did. I often accused Neville of actually being Nicky's father, she was so like him. She's allergic to chocolate. She breaks out in spots, swells a bit too. And she snores like a man, you wouldn't believe it . . . She hates blue because she has to wear it all the time . . . The doctor said there's a good possibility that she may start her period earlier than most . . . I don't quite know how to broach that with her, yet . . . Oh, she grows very quickly, so you have to buy . . .

Anna I'd better get going.

Emily I know you're right. Let me take care of the bill. I insist.

Anna *and* **Emily** *exit.*

Little Anna 'Anna, Anna, puddin' and pie.'

Scene Two

Anna's place. **Liam** *is pacing with* **Anna**'s *note in his hand.*

Liam You're trying to build a life with that child that can't possibly exist.

Anna I can't hear you!

Liam Piss off!

Anna We'll stay in touch.

Liam No we won't. It's over. You know, I feel like that line in 'Old Man River', 'tired of livin' and scared of dyin' '. You feel that way too. But that would be the last thing you'd let me see.

Anna And what would you do with it if you saw it?

Liam Stay with you. Love you. Always love you. Goodbye, Anna. May the wind be always at your back.

The telephone rings.

Anna Honey, I've got to go . . . (*Exits.*)

Liam *stares at the flat for a moment, then leaves.*

Enter **Anna**.

Anna Liam, please, let's talk. I . . .

She has stepped into the domain of **Little Anna**: *white flowers, white altar, etc.*

Little Anna Bingo! I'm going to be the May Queen! The first coloured girl to crown the Blessed Virgin. Whee! (*Sings.*) 'Oh Mary we crown thee with blossoms today; Queen of the Angels, Queen of the May. Oh Mary, we crown thee with blossoms today! Queen of the Angels. Queen of the May!

The scene segues into **David Sinclair**'s *office at Linbrook Primary, although we still retain a sense of* **Little Anna**'s *world.*

David . . . of course we'll forward whatever you need. Whatever it takes to make Nicola happy in America.

Anna You're a good guy . . . I think I left my bracelet behind . . .

David I know. Is this it?

Anna Thanks. David, I . . .

David I want to thank you, Mrs Eastman, for the work you've done for us at Linbrook Primary. I won't ask you again to allow Nicola to stay with us.

Anna Don't. I'm doing what's best.

David Yes. I understand that. I've spent the past twelve years or so dealing with people in the education establishment who knew what was best.

There is the loud ringing of a trolley bell. **Anna** *leaves* **David**'s *office, which segues back into* **Little Anna**'s *world.* **Anna** *and* **Little Anna** *are standing on a sidewalk in* **Anna**'s *old neighbourhood, the neighbourhood she grew up in.*

Little Anna Here he comes! Here he comes!

Anna I don't see him.

Little Anna He's coming! I can see him!

Anna   He won't look at me.

Little Anna   Yes he will, if you smile nicely.

Anna   I'm scared.

Little Anna   What did you say?

Anna   I'm scared.

Little Anna   Repeat after me: 'Anna, Anna, puddin' and pie . . .'

Anna   He won't remember he taught that to me. He still won't see me.

Little Anna   Do as I say!

Anna   'Anna, Anna, puddin' and pie, kissed the boys and made them cry.'

Little Anna   Stop sobbing. Here he comes. Oh, look! Look! He is looking at you. He is! Call him!

Anna   Daddy! Daddy!

Little Anna   That's him. Not that other guy mamma married. Not the one she told you was your father. She told you that because your real father wasn't good enough. So she got herself a new man.

Anna   I hate her.

Little Anna   Naw. Don't blame it on her. What could she do? She had to get ahead for you.

There is a loud banging, which continues through the scene.

Don't blame her. You grew up exactly the way she wanted. You even surpassed her wildest expectations. She tried to reign you in, and you told her where she could go. Poor woman. Can't blame her. But daddy. Dear, old, invisible daddy. If you can't have him, *be* him. Only better. Daddy. He always knew who you were. He always acknowledged your existence. From the streetcar. Ring that bell, daddy! One day he brought you some jonquils. They were so pretty they made you cry. Then you painted a picture of the jonquils for him. And when you gave it to him he said:

Anna   'You have talent. You must paint, little Anna.'

Little Anna   And he even bought you some paints. Must have been hard to do that. You didn't get much on a trolley conductor's salary. He said 'paint'. You did for a while.

Anna   I was no good.

Little Anna   Liar! You were brilliant. I want to see the paints! I want to see the paints!

Anna *finally opens the small, ornate box.*

Little Anna   There they are, the little letter you wrote to the little blonde girl, and the paints. They've been barely touched.

Janet (*off-stage*)   Anna?

Little Anna   Touch them.

Anna   I can't. I can't touch anything in here.

Little Anna   Try.

Anna   I can't.

Little Anna   Do you have to be the best all the time?

Anna   Can't you leave me in peace? Why can't you?

Little Anna   Because you're afraid of the dark.

Janet (*off-stage*)   Anna!

Anna   Yes?

Little Anna   Hold the paints. Hold the letter.

Anna   No! No!

Enter **Janet**.

Janet   Your door was open.

Anna   Was it? I act like I haven't lived in New York for the past twenty years.

Janet   Those paints are beautiful. They look like they belong to a child. I love to look at children's things. There's something powerful and delicate about them. Whose are they?

Anna   It doesn't matter. What do you want?

Janet   They're gone.

Anna   Who's gone?

Janet   Emily and Nicola. They've gone to Shropshire.

Anna   What are you talking about?

Janet   I persuaded her to go.

Anna   You persuaded her?

Janet   Yes.

Anna   She can't just go. She promised me. I'll call her . . .

Janet   How?

Anna   I'll . . . I'll get the number from David. I'm sure he's got some solidarity left.

Janet   He won't help you. Go home, Anna. Go back to America.

Anna Not without Nicola. Well, I never thought I'd see the day. A 'brother' and a 'sister' giving up a black child to a white woman.

Janet Save that for your lecture podium. This is real. You'd make her like you, and that's one too many Anna Eastmans in this world. This childhood business, it's all a gamble, isn't it? We were born to who we were born and have to make the best of it. But Nicola can be different. She has someone who has chosen her, chosen to bring her up, to love her. She has a chance with Emily to be whole and sane so that, when she has to step out into it, she'll have a better base than we had.

Anna Are you crazy? Emily'll ruin that child!

Janet Those are yours.

Anna What?

Janet Anna, you've opened the box . . .

Anna No, don't touch it. Janet, Emily's not stable. She said so herself.

Janet I'm not as strong as you, Anna, you know that. I'm weak. But I'm not running away any more. I'm staying. Nicola's staying.

Anna I can get a court order . . .

Janet That's a long process. Let her go.

Anna So she can stay over here! With Emily! With *you*! *You* the loser, the little island girl loser. Dreaming about your emerald green sea, your lazy times under the sun? You'll never give up dreaming about that. 'Cause you haven't got it. You never did. Neither you, nor David, nor Neville. The next generation's going to sweep you away, right into the garbage can. And I'll be there to see it. 'Cause you betrayed them. You betrayed everything you fought for.

Janet You may be right there. But you won't be in charge. The young will disown you, too. The young always do. I have to get the twins' tea. There's a parent–governors' meeting tomorrow and Ari's coming home tonight. He'll talk my head off. He always does. (*Exits.*)

Anna Nicola!

The trolley bell rings again.

Little Anna Oooh, Anna. He's going.

Anna No!

Little Anna Let's play a game.

Anna Nicola!

Little Anna Let me blindfold you.

Anna Please, please help me.

Little Anna Stand still. There. The blindfold tight? You can't see, can you?

Anna I can't see.

Little Anna Don't worry.

Anna   So many faces whirling around my head . . .

Little Anna   People who loved you.

Anna   I can't stop them from whirling around faster and faster . . . Nicola!

Little Anna   I can take you to her.

Anna   Can you? Can you help me? Can you?

Little Anna   Now you have to walk straight ahead. Don't pull back. It's a trust game. Just walk straight into this world where you have to invent everything with your own hands.

Anna   I . . . I don't understand . . .

Little Anna   Trust me?

Anna   I . . . I . . .

Little Anna   Trust me, Anna. Trust me.

Anna   It's too dark.

Little Anna   Take my hand.

Anna   Yes.

Little Anna   Off we go to our great adventure. Are you scared, Anna?

Anna   Yes . . .

Munda Negra

I think I was about nine years old when I wrote my first play. I can't tell you how I came to write that play (it was about Mary and Joseph and Jesus and a problem Mary was having in coming to accept her fate, and eventually how she came to do it), but I wish I hadn't thrown it away because I don't think I'll ever top it. All that I can recall about it was hearing it read in class and then getting back to writing another one as soon as possible.

Besides, writing was the best thing you could do in Arctic-cold Chicago in the dead of winter. I managed to write all the school plays, plus conduct a story-time session after school, when all the neighbourhood kids came and listened to me weave a serial about life on the moon. I guess it beat dodging the gang warfare raging in the ghetto at that time.

I didn't see my first real professional production until I was almost twenty-one. It was the late Joe Papp's musical version of *Two Gentlemen of Verona*. This turned out to be quite an auspicious thing because I ended up in New York working for Joe Papp and one of the things I did was teach Shakespeare to black and Hispanic kids.

I studied in Chicago for a while with David Mamet before *American Buffalo*, and what I recall most of all was his great ability to tell theatrical anecdotes. I thought that this was what playwrights did, so I set out to learn a few myself.

Then, in 1976, I read something about Bertolucci's film *1900*, which traced the history of Italy right up to the end of World War II. I loved history as much as I loved drama (and still do), so I decided that I wanted to do the same thing for black Chicagoans. I wrote a play called *1919*, which centred around the 'Red Summer' of 1919 with its horrific race riot.

This play was the beginning of what I call my self-delusion. That self-delusion was based on the fact that I thought I was writing 'black' plays to tell black people about their history etc. Now, a historical thing may have sparked me off, but that's not what got me writing. What got me started was boredom. I was bored with all the 'perfect' black mothers who managed to carry the world on their backs and stay strong. Of course, there are women like these – my own mother is like this in some ways – but I honestly can't think of a less challenging character to ask people to come out of the comfort and safety of their homes to see.

As a little kid, all my plays were about life on the edge, the farthest extreme of things, and I wanted to write about a black mother who was not a paragon of light, but an extremely incorrect and imperfect human being. And so Louvenia in *1919* became a cross between Lillian Hellman's 'Regina' from *The Little Foxes* and Tennessee Williams's 'Blanche'. Her daughter had to decide between life in the big house on the hill or down in a ghetto on the verge of a race riot. She chooses the ghetto.

After the play got favourable notices I moved to New York, because that's where you had to go to see if you were any good. I studied with Steve Carter at the Negro Ensemble Company, then I was invited to join the Actors' Studio Playwright and Directors Unit, to which I still belong. At the same time I began to work with Lee Breuer, the grand old man of what is now called 'live art' but was then called 'performance art'. So I was running from the Actors' Studio, where I might find myself sitting next to Paul Newman, to downtown, where I was writing plays with no words and working with six-foot-seven Australian drag queens; then uptown to a black theatre company where we wondered when we would ever be noticed by the artistic director. In between I read plays for Joe Papp, taught playwriting, and saw and read everything I could.

By the way, reading plays, seeing plays and reviewing plays are some of the best things a playwright can do. It develops your style through the Buddhist negation technique of 'not-this', plus it helps your plays become more and more director- and actor-proof. Directors and actors wax and wane; texts abideth for ever.

This New York madness went on for eight years. All the while, as I've said, I thought I was writing plays for black people; this gradually extended to women, then to black women. They were very correct plays with some interesting bits. I had lost track of that little girl who wrote because she loved stories, and enjoyed writing about people *in extremis* and the life-or-death choices they had to make. Yet all the while this character, the main character of my first adult play, a black woman on the edge and not very nice with it, refused to go away. And because I had no defence against her, Anna Eastman was born, a brilliant and very angry woman.

Munda Negra is about a woman whose childhood was shattered, full stop. She was a black girl who drew a self-portrait of herself as a white girl with blonde hair and was ridiculed for it, and somewhere in her young heart she decided to take revenge: she got smarter than everyone else. It is very difficult in life to observe such an angry character, but Anna is my Macbeth – no, not Lady Macbeth, but Macbeth. She makes a wrong turn and then can't stop herself. She is potentially full of poetry, but she can only spew bile. Anna is offered love by two men, but she cannot accept it; she can only stay on her vengeful path. This makes her a hero to me. She is a hero because she keeps going in spite of the fact that she cannot win, a bit like Don Giovanni – or Bessie Smith. She defies God, although in the end 'God' triumphs. I like to think that, in giving in at the end of the play, Anna is really only biding her time.

When I work with young black playwrights, I always tell them that there is nothing you can say on the stage that the audience has not thought about or seen or felt. As Sam Goldwyn said: 'If you want to send a message, call Western Union.' Or in other words, as Robert McKee, in his brilliant story-structure class, says, 'The audience is smart.' To me it's outrageous for someone to stand up and tell me how to live in the guise of a dramatic production, no matter how well-meaning they may be. This happens too much in black theatre. Too many black playwrights, on both sides of the Atlantic, in seeking to push their world-view, take advantage of an audience hungry to see itself reflected on-stage. I think black audiences are starting to get hip to this.

I believe in giving the audience a good story, as well told as I can. I think a writer has failed if the audience talk about nothing but the performances, or the directing, or the design, or the price of the programmes. The root word of audience, after all, is the verb *to hear*. And if the writing is as true as possible, and the play as well structured as possible, then the audience will take the relevant bits to their heart and create meaning for themselves. Now that's 'entertainment'.

Bonnie Greer
London, 1994

Bonnie Greer was born in Chicago but now lives in London. Her play *In the Country of the Young* won the 1992 Verity Bargate Award. *Munda Negra* was short-listed for the 1993 John Whiting Award. Her latest play, *Dancing on Black Water* for BTC, opened at the Warehouse

Theatre, Croydon in September 1994. Her film *White Men are Cracking Up* was broadcast on BBC2 in December 1994 and her first novel, *Hanging by her Teeth*, was published by Serpent's Tail in 1994. She is also a theatre critic for *Time Out*.

Scrape off the Black

Tunde Ikoli

To my Mum, Rose, Dad, Tunde and Brother Ade

Characters

Rose Ikoyi
Trevor Ikoyi, *her elder son*
Andy Ikoyi, *her younger son*
Mary, *her neighbour and best friend*

Scrape off the Black was first produced at the Riverside Studios, London in 1981. The cast was as follows:

Rose	Mary McCloud
Trevor	Brian Bovell
Andy	Okon Jones
Mary	Sue Porret

Directed by Peter Gill

The play was revived at the Theatre Royal Stratford East in 1987. The cast was as follows:

Rose	Jill Gasgoine
Trevor	Gary McDonald
Andy	Chris Tummings
Mary	Kate Williams

Directed by Philip Hedley

Act One

Scene One

Rose's *flat. The living-room. Early morning. It is dark. The curtains are drawn, but a single shaft of sunlight from a gap in the closed curtains lights the room. We can just make out the figure of* **Rose** *sitting on the sofa, feet up, a telephone resting on a small table by her side.* **Rose** *smokes a cigarette. Smoke from the cigarette swirls and climbs in the beam of sunlight.* **Rose** *is looking at a small framed photograph.*

Rose *sighs and coughs. The telephone rings.* **Rose** *stubs out the cigarette she has been smoking, takes another from the box, lights it, then picks up the phone. To do so she has to bend forward into the shaft of sunlight. We see her face for the first time: expectant, soon to be disappointed.*

Rose Hello and . . . (*The pips go.*) Trev . . . the silly bastard!

She slams the phone down, takes another puff on her cigarette. She leans back out of the sunlight. A pause. She quickly takes the photograph and hides it behind a cushion. She coughs.

I'll kill 'im!

A knock at the front door.

I'll fuckin' kill him!!

The front door is knocked again. **Rose** *struggles to get up from the settee; all the while her leg is giving her pain. She yells.*

Wait a bloody minute!!! Ouchh . . . Fuckin' leg . . . ouchh . . . (*To herself.*) I'll kill 'im.

She has finally managed to get herself up from the settee. She steadies herself. The front door is knocked again.

Just you wait, you hardened bugger!

She slowly limps off towards the front door.

Trevor (*off, cheery*) Good morning, Mother.

Rose (*off*) Don't you good morning me!

Trevor (*off*) Well, may I take this oppor –

Rose (*off*) Shut up.

Trevor (*off*) Right.

The living-room door opens and in comes **Rose** *followed by her son. In the darkness we cannot tell what he looks like.* **Rose** *sits on the sofa.*

Trevor Did I wake you?

Rose Yes!

Trevor Sorry. (*Pause.*) I was passing by and thought I'd call in . . .

Rose   Next time you're passin' by, do me a favour and just keep on walking. You got no business comin' round here at this time in the mornin'.

Trevor   It's not that early . . . 'alf eight.

Rose   I don't need you comin' round here tellin' me the time . . . disturbin' me, I get precious little sleep as it is.

Trevor   Your leg playin' you up, is it?

Rose   Never you mind about my leg. It was you that phoned!

Trevor (*pause*)   Yeah.

Rose   Why the fuck didn't you speak?

Trevor   Didn't want to waste any money. Just makin' sure you was in.

Rose   'Course I'm bloody in. Where am I gonna go at this time of the mornin'?

Trevor   The post office, change your SS cheque.

Rose   I hope that's not the reason you've come round here. I've got no money to lend you. All my money's got to be paid out in debts . . .

Trevor   All right, calm down, don't give me your life story. I don't want any money.

Trevor *is about to draw the curtains.*

Rose   Leave 'em . . .

Trevor   Why?

Rose   The loan man's due today.

Trevor   So?

Rose   So, I don't want 'im looking through the bastard windows and seein' that I'm in. So leave them closed!

Trevor   But it's dark.

Rose   It's not dark . . .

Trevor   I can't see . . .

Rose   What, are you blind?

Trevor   No. It's dark.

Rose   It's not. You need glasses.

Trevor   I don't need glasses.

Rose   Didn't anybody tell you that you should have eat carrots as a kid.

Trevor   Didn't anyone ever tell you, that's an old wives' tale.

Rose   No it's bloody not.

Trevor   Shall I switch the light on?

Rose   Switch the bloody light on, what do I care!

Trevor *walks over to the light switch.*

Rose What d'you want?

Trevor *switches the light on, and the contents of the living-room are revealed: best mail-order tradition, colour television, three-piece suite, fitted carpet, record-player.* **Rose** *is dressed in nightdress and gown, hair greying, dishevelled and done up in a bun on top of her head.*

Rose Well?

Trevor Do I have to have a reason to visit you?

Rose You, you're always after somethin'. Why ain't you at work?

Trevor I gave it up.

Rose You'd only been there a week.

Trevor Packin' boxes all day. I've had enough of it.

Rose An' what's 'She' got to say about it?

Trevor 'She' – the woman that I am living with, the mother of my child, the lady I love – Marcia. She won't say anything.

Rose Have you told her?

Trevor No . . . not yet . . . I need somethin' a bit more fulfillin', you know, somethin' to tax my brain . . .

Rose What brain?

Trevor Has he been?

Rose What?

Trevor Come on, Mum, you know what I'm talkin' about.

Rose No . . . he hasn't.

Trevor Aren't you looking forward to seeing him?

Rose All I can see is the same old trouble . . .

Trevor It's been over a year. He'll of changed . . .

Rose Do me a favour. Borstal didn't do him any good, if anythin' it made him a better thief than when he went in. What's prison going to do for him?

Trevor He's older . . .

Rose That boy's set in his ways. Nothing or no one is going to change him.

Trevor We should really try and make things different for him this time.

Rose I've done all I can.

Trevor Yeah, sure . . .

Rose Don't you start your cheek with me.

Trevor I'm not, I'm agreeing with you.

Rose   He never gave me anythin' . . . What did he ever give me?

Trevor (*pause, quietly*)   What did you ever give him?

Rose   You trying to be funny?

Trevor   No, Mum.

Rose   I'm his mother, I gave him life, what more am I supposed to do for him?

Trevor   Shall I make some tea?

Rose   If you want . . .

Trevor   And toast?

Rose   Haven't you got any food at home?

Trevor   'Course. I'm peckish, that's all . . .

Rose   She's not feeding you properly.

Trevor   All I want is some toast, Mum . . .

Rose   Go on, have some then . . .

Trevor   Thank you.

Rose   Just two slices mind, and when you make the tea use one tea bag between the two of us . . .

Trevor   After I've done that, I'll hang it out on the line to dry with the other tea bags.

Rose   I've warned you about your bloody cheek, if you want to take the piss, you can forget about the tea and toast and get out.

Trevor   Okay, okay, it was a joke. I'm sorry. What is it about me that gets you so excited?

Rose   You're a bloody fool.

Trevor   Thank you . . . I'll make the toast. (*He goes off.*)

Rose   As you're eating my bread, you can do a slice for me . . .

Trevor (*off*)   I've put one on already . . .

Rose   Don't let it burn . . .

Rose *quickly and furtively takes the majority of cigarettes from the packet and hides them in her handbag.*

Trevor (*off*)   In all the years that I've been making toast for you, have you ever known me to burn a single slice?

Rose   There's always a first time . . .

Trevor (*coming back on*)   You've no confidence in me, have yer?

Rose (*having managed to hide her cigarettes*)   How's little Trevor?

Trevor   All right. He's at home with his mother, lookin' forward to seein' 'is uncle . . .

Rose   He's never met Andy yet.

Trevor   No.

Rose Andy wrote and told me how pleased he was to be an uncle, you should've taken little Trevor up on a visit . . .

Trevor Well . . . Marcia and me didn't think that one of Her Majesty's Prisons was the right environment for a one-year-old child.

Rose Don't be so bloody daft. I took you up to see your father when you were that age.

Trevor And look how we turned out . . .

Rose You turned out all right. (*Pause.*) It's hard to believe it's over a year since I last saw him . . .

Trevor I offered to take you on a number of visits.

Rose It was me bad leg, playin' me up somethin' awful . . . it was. Couldn't move . . .

Trevor Didn't stop you goin' to bingo.

Rose That's my business! None of you have been any help to me. Bingo's the only place I can go to get a bit of extra money . . .

Trevor You can't really believe that . . .

Rose It's a fact.

Trevor When's the last time you had a win and paid off any of your debts?

Rose None of your business!

Trevor When, eh. . . ? You can't tell me, can you?

Rose The toast!

Trevor The toast?

Rose Don't you dare let it burn . . .

Trevor *runs towards the kitchen.*

Rose If it's burnt you'll just have to scrape off the black, don't you dare throw it away. If you weren't so busy stickin' your nose into other people's business you'd know what you were doing . . .

Trevor (*coming back on*) It's all right, I've turned it over.

Rose You'd better stay in the kitchen with it.

Trevor It'll be all right.

Rose I'm warnin' you, if it burns that's the last slice of toast you'll get off me.

Trevor The toast is not going to burn. How many times d'you want me to tell you. You want me to pay for the bread or what?

Rose I'm not sayin' that. I don't like to see things wasted, that's all.

Trevor It's on a low light, the toast will not burn.

Rose It better not.

Trevor So tell me, how's the leg today?

Rose A bit painful, it's the cold . . .

Trevor It's not cold in here . . .

Rose I know that, you daft sod, but that doesn't stop the cold from outside gettin' to it, does it? I can feel it, my leg turns funny whenever the cold weather is comin' on . . .

Trevor Like a barometer, you mean, you can predict the weather. You ever thought about applyin' for a job as a weather forecaster?

Rose You tryin' to be funny?

Trevor Who, me? Wouldn't dream of it . . .

Rose Because I don't think that's very nice – laughing at my affliction.

Trevor Yeah, you're right. I'm sorry. You know what you should do; put yourself to bed for a couple of days, give the leg a rest.

Rose Who's goin' to do the housework?

Trevor I'll do it for you . . .

Rose I like to do it myself, then I know it's been done properly. No offence.

Trevor Mum, come on, you can be honest with me. It's bingo isn't it, afraid you might miss a few games.

Rose Can't afford to . . .

Trevor You talk as though bingo is a guaranteed income. I can't understand it. You never win anythin'.

Rose You tell me where else I'm goin' to get the sort of money I need to pay off me debts?

Trevor Not at bing –

Rose The toast!!!

Trevor Oh yeah. (*Once again he runs off into the kitchen.*)

Rose Is it burnt?

Trevor (*off*) No.

Rose You sure?

Trevor (*off*) 'Course I'm bloody sure. I've got it right in front of my eyes . . .

Rose Don't you start swearin' at me.

Trevor Bloody ain't swearin'.

Rose Yes it fuckin' is, as far as I'm concerned.

Trevor (*enters with tea and toast on a tray*) Your toast, madam. Completely unburnt.

Rose (*examining her slice of toast*) I hope you haven't put too much butter on it . . .

Trevor Haven't you got anythin' to say to me?

Rose (*eating her toast*) Do what?

Trevor Two little words . . .

Rose Piss off.

Trevor I was thinking more along the lines of 'thank you'.

Rose Gettaway, it was my bread, my tea, my milk . . .

Trevor But I made it . . .

Rose So you should. I'm your mother.

Trevor Where would you be without me?

Rose A lot better off.

Trevor What, down in Cornwall. The wife of a farm labourer, up at the crack of dawn, milking cows and picking potatoes! Your leg'd never 'ave lasted out.

Rose My leg would've been just fine. I'd've been happy.

Trevor But Mum, you would never of had us . . .

Rose Bloody good job.

Trevor That's a matter of opinion . . .

Rose Yeah, mine, and that's all that matters.

Trevor (*pause*) You got any fags?

Rose You come round here to scrounge?

Trevor No . . .

Rose Smoke your own.

Trevor I haven't got any . . .

Rose (*showing* **Trevor** *the contents of her box*) I've only got a few. You can only have one.

Trevor Clever as I am, I can only smoke one at a time. (*He snatches a fag.*)

Rose You'll get no more.

Trevor That's what I love about you, so generous, so willing to give . . .

Rose I suppose you'll want a light now . . .

Trevor It would help . . .

Rose You'll have to light it off mine. I'm not wasting a match . . .

Trevor (*taking* **Rose**'s *fag*) Wouldn't expect you to.

Rose And don't puff mine.

Trevor (*handing back fag*) I'll buy you some later . . .

Rose That'll be the day.

Trevor I promise.

Rose I've heard your promises before . . .

Trevor Twenty fags is what we're talkin' about, Mum, not a house by the sea.

Rose Cigarettes are expensive, and on the money I'm gettin' from the social I can hardly afford to smoke.

Trevor Give it up.

Rose Why should I? It's one of the few pleasures I have left. Why don't you bloody give it up, then you wouldn't need to smoke mine.

Trevor It's a right liberty, ain't it, nearly a pound for a packet of fags . . .

Rose I don't know what the world is coming to.

Trevor Not like the old days, eh?

Rose No . . . it's not. (*Pause.*) I can remember my dad buying ten Woodbine and still havin' change out of two shillings. Use to cough 'is little heart out on them Woodbine he did. (*She laughs to herself.*)

Trevor I remember . . . Those days are gone. Not to return.

Rose Worse luck.

Trevor I don't know why you ever left Cornwall.

Rose I know why I did. It's now that I wish I hadn't. D'you know when I wrote and told my parents I'd had a kid to a black man, I got a letter by return post, with the train fare, begging me to come back with you. As if they thought, they could save me . . .

Trevor Why didn't you go?

Rose Spent the money on a lovely siren suit for you.

Trevor You should've gone, taken me with you, while you had the chance.

Rose I suppose I should have. But your dad – I really did love your father in those days, I couldn't imagine life without him. Took me everywhere he did – parties, dances, clubs and pubs. Me and him hardly ever went to bed before four o'clock in the mornin'. Cornwall seemed so far away, quiet and boring. Fuckin' idiot I was.

Trevor If you'd taken me back, I might've been the only black yokel in the whole of the West Country.

Rose You're not black!

Trevor I'm not white!

Rose You're half-caste.

Trevor Can you imagine me walking about on a farm, with a straw in me mouth.

Rose You wouldn't be like you are today, bleedin' hopeless. You'd of helped your mother.

Trevor I will . . . I'll buy you a house.

Rose When?

Trevor When I'm rich.

Rose Don't talk daft. You've never managed to hold down a job for more than a week.

Trevor That's because there's going to be more to my life than being a labourer.

Rose Like what?

Trevor I don't know, do I . . . I haven't found it yet. Wouldn't mind bein' a chat show host, like that Michael Parkinson, but the last time I went to the labour they didn't have any vacancies for chat show hosts.

Rose You're soft . . . soft in the head. You'll never be rich.

Trevor Yeah, I know. I don't really want to be.

Rose Then how you goin' to buy me a house?

Trevor I'll squat in one for you . . .

Rose Don't bother . . .

Trevor You're a real snob . . .

Rose You watch your tongue . . .

Trevor I was only jokin'. You are a wonderful mother really.

Rose Oh yeah, and what are you after?

Trevor After. . . ? Me. . . ?

Rose Yeah, You?

Trevor Nothin' . . .

Rose Don't act the innocent with me. You want somethin'. You've bin actin' strange all mornin', not arguin', no backchat, making me talk about me past. You want somethin' or you're up to no good.

Trevor It's a sad day when a son can't be nice to his mother without her gettin' suspicious.

Rose I've told you, I've got no money . . .

Trevor I've got me own . . .

Rose On a Monday morning? Don't make me laugh.

Trevor I've bin savin' up . . .

Rose You save up . . . You, who lets money slip through his fingers like water off a duck's back. What are you savin' up for?

Trevor Today . . .

Rose What's so special about . . . So you've got money?

Trevor Yeah.

Rose Why didn't you buy any fags?

Trevor Didn't have the time. I came straight here from home.

Rose How much you got?

Trevor Enough.

Rose For what?

Trevor What I need.

Rose So where d'you get it?

Trevor That's my business.

Rose You haven't been up to anything silly, have you son?

Trevor Who me, na.

Rose How much you got?

Trevor Enough. I told yer.

Rose Let me see it.

Trevor It's in me pocket.

Rose Well show us.

Trevor No, it's mine.

Rose You ain't got nothin'.

Trevor Haven't I? (*He rustles paper in his pocket.*)

Rose Don't you start playin' your stupid games with me. What the fuck do you want?

Trevor I just thought I'd stick around today. Keep you company.

Rose What's the matter? Your wife kicked you out again?

Trevor No, nothin' like that.

Rose Well I don't want you round here all day, drivin' me mad.

Trevor I thought we'd have a party . . .

Rose A party? Why?

Trevor Celebrate. Andy's release.

Rose Where?

Trevor Here . . .

Rose You've got to be fuckin' jokin'!

Trevor Not a big party.

Rose There'll be no party here.

Trevor A small party.

Rose Oh no.

Trevor In fact a very small party . . . just family.

Rose What family?

Trevor Our family.

Rose Like who?

Trevor You, me, Andy and . . .

Rose What?

Trevor Andy. You, me and Andy! You know, all of us together, a family. Go on, Mum, just for Andy.

Rose I've done enough for him. Who was it who put up bail for him last time, even though I didn't have the money . . . I could have gone to jail . . . I don't know, I've got enough troubles on me mind without having the two of you in the same room as me . . .

Trevor I'll give you money to go bingo this afternoon.

Rose It's four pound.

Trevor Don't worry, you don't have to pay me back.

Rose I wasn't going to. You said give.

Trevor Did I . . . ?

Rose If you're goin' to start, there'll be no party.

Trevor I was havin' you on.

Rose I'm not in the mood.

Trevor Sorry.

Rose So how much money you got?

Trevor *makes a big show and takes a lot of time pulling three fivers out of his pocket.* **Rose** *is unimpressed.*

Rose Is that it?

Trevor Fifteen quid.

Rose You call that money?

Trevor Yeah, what would you call it?

Rose Fuck all, the way you was goin' on, I thought you had a couple of hundred.

Trevor Where am I going to get two hundred quid?

Rose Don't ask me.

There is a knock at the door. **Trevor** *and* **Rose** *freeze. They look at each other. Pause.*

Trevor Who's that?

Rose How the fuck do I know? I'm not outside am I.

Trevor D'you think it's Andy?

Rose Na, it's not his knock.

Trevor How can you be sure? It's over a year since the last time he knocked on this door.

Rose I know his knock!

Trevor Shall I get it . . .

Rose No . . . yeah . . . wait. If it's Andy, he'll call.

They wait in silence. The door is knocked again.

Trevor Well?

Rose That's definitely not Andy's knock.

Trevor I'll get it then . . .

Rose No, no wait.

Trevor Mum, we're never goin' to find out who it is if we don't open the door.

Rose (*almost a whisper*) If it's the loan man, tali-man or tele-man, tell 'em I'm not in . . . and I'll see them next week.

Trevor Not payin' again?

Rose I haven't got it.

Trevor If you didn't go to bingo . . .

The door is knocked again.

Rose (*yells*) Shut your mouth and open the door!

Trevor Okay, okay, I'm only tryin' to offer some advice . . .

Rose Day I need your advice is the day they'll take me out of here feet first in a coffin. Now get the poxy door.

Trevor Yes sir. (*He salutes and runs off.*)

Rose Bugger (*She looks in her cigarette box: no fags. In frustration she screws the box up. Then she remembers, takes a single fag from her handbag.*)

Trevor *comes back on, after 'rhubarb' is heard off.*

Trevor The loan man says that he can't wait till next week, he wants payin' now. So I let him in . . .

Rose (*angrily attempting to get up from the sofa*) You little fucker. I'll kill . . .

In walks **Mary**, *mid-forties but looks older. Once a very smart and striking woman, she has fallen on hard times. Her coat and dress are perhaps the remnants of her glorious and well-dressed youth. She makes an effort: her clothes, although old and slightly worn, are spotless. Her hair is coiffured into a beehive. She tries very hard to hold on to her dignity, although some would say it's her sanity she should worry about.*

Mary Hello love.

Rose Oh, it's you.

Mary Who were you expecting, your fancy man?

Rose Do me a favour, I need a fancy man like I need a cold sore.

Mary Well . . . er . . . yes . . . I suppose that's . . . well . . .

Rose Sit down, Mare, take the wait off your brain.

Mary Thanks love. When I had to knock three times, thought you were out, gone to the post office.

Rose It's this bastard. (*Pointing at* **Trevor**.) Pissin' about.

Trevor Mum and Dad weren't married, did you know?

Mary Not everyone feels the need to these days . . .

Trevor I'm talking about the old days . . .

Rose Will you shut up. Take no notice of 'im Mare, he'll drive you mad . . .

Mary He's getting much bigger . . .

Trevor Six weeks.

Mary Pardon?

Trevor Since the last time you saw me . . .

Mary Is it really . . . that long . . . time doesn't fly.

Trevor I grow very quickly . . .

Rose Only your head.

Trevor Take after me mother.

Rose You'll take the back of my hand. (*To* **Mary**.) Want a cup of tea?

Mary If it's no trouble . . .

Rose No trouble at all. Make Mary a cup of tea, love.

Trevor Love, now, is it. Now you want somethin' done.

Rose Go on, piss off.

Trevor You want to be careful, you might give people the impression that you don't love me. (*He goes off.*)

Mary Spittin' image of his father.

Rose Too much for my likin'.

Mary Come now, Rose, your Trev was a lovely lookin' man.

Rose He was. But that one takes after him too much. Mad just like him.

Mary I always thought Trevor was an intelligent boy.

Rose He's a bloody fool, gets on my nerves. Kids are all right as babies and at school but after that you can't tell 'em a thing.

Mary   It's livin' round here. Can't expect to bring up kids right. Rubbish over all the streets and courtyards, shit and piss in the lifts. It's a disgrace.

Rose   True enough.

Mary   Have you seen the number of Pakistanis that have moved into this estate?

Rose   We'll soon be havin' sewing-machines goin' day and night. I don't know where they find the time to have so many kids. All they seem to do is work. And the Council don't care. If you happen to live there that's your hard luck. They let the place get turned into a dump.

Mary   Still, you've managed to bring your two up all right.

Rose   I've tried, Mary, God knows I have tried.

Mary   I'm sure they appreciate your efforts.

Rose   They couldn't give two fucks.

Mary   They do, Rose, don't say that.

Rose   You don't know them like I do. (*Pause.*) So what happened to you last night? I missed you at the late session.

Mary   (*blushes*)   Well . . .

Rose   So you let him go home with you?

Mary   Well, it had been a long time, Rose.

Rose   What was he like, then?

Mary   Nothing special. A bit like all the rest. Left this morning without a word . . . telly went too.

Rose   You're a silly cow!

Mary   I know.

Rose   Haven't you learnt your lesson by now? None of 'em are any good.

Mary   Oh no, Rose, he wasn't black! This was an English bloke.

Rose   You think I don't know that? I saw him, didn't I? I'm talking about men. None of 'em are any good. After what you've been through I would've thought you'd know better. Mare, you had it all.

Mary   Oh don't go on, Rose.

Rose   A beautiful house, money in the bank. You were a bloody fool.

Mary   You know what they say, easy come, easy go.

Rose   It's criminal what you did.

Trevor   (*coming in*)   What was that?

Rose   None of your business.

Trevor   I see. Here you are, Aunty Mary.

Mary   Thanks, pet. (*She takes a syringe out of her handbag and prepares to stick it into her arm.*)

Trevor I didn't know you were a junkie . . .

Mary Oh no . . . I'm a diabetic . . .

Trevor I know. It was a joke . . .

Rose Well it's not very funny . . .

Trevor Accept my apologies . . .

Mary That's all right . . .

Trevor Do you have to do that every day?

Rose 'Course she does . . .

Trevor Don't it get on your nerves?

Mary You get used to it . . .

Trevor Fancy that, a needle every day . . . Ukkk, I hate needles . . .

Mary It's not bad. I live.

Trevor What'd happen if you didn't take it?

Rose Mind your own.

Trevor I'm interested . . .

Rose It's none of your business . . .

Mary Really, I don't mind . . .

Trevor See, I told you.

Rose Go on, piss off out of it! Where's my tea, then?

Trevor Your tea? You've drunk it, Mum.

Rose So?

Trevor *goes into the kitchen with* **Rose**'s *mug.*

Mary He's a good boy . . .

Rose He's a sod . . .

Mary I thought he was working.

Rose Mare, he's had more jobs than you and I have had hot dinners. And he hasn't managed to stay in one of them for longer than a week. He'll never amount to anythin' . . .

Mary Shame . . . Still, your Andy's due out soon . . .

Rose Today, God forbid . . .

Mary I thought you'd be pleased . . .

Rose   Too much bloody trouble. At least while he was in there I'd know where he was and that he couldn't get into any trouble. I didn't have to worry about phone calls telling me that he'd been kicked or stabbed.

Mary   That's true . . .

Rose   The fights that boy got into. Bottles, knives, axes. Anything he could lay his hands on. But I warned him the day he lifts his hand to me that'd be it . . .

Mary   He hasn't, has he?

Rose   'Course not!

Mary   Perhaps being inside will do him some good.

Rose   Don't be daft. The last time he came out, it wasn't more than a week before he was up to his old tricks.

Mary   Shame . . .

Rose   A bloody shame.

Mary   He was such a nice boy.

Trevor (*coming in with tea*)   Talking about me again?

Rose   Shut up . . .

Mary   So your brother's free today?

Trevor   Thank God.

Mary   Always been close haven't they . . . then they usually are, aren't they, brothers . . . and sisters . . . sisters and brothers as well, of course . . . families . . . It must be wonderful having your family around you . . .

Trevor   That's what I say . . .

Rose   Nobody's interested in what you've got to say . . .

Trevor   That's where you're wrong . . .

Mary   I had a sister . . . Allison.

Pause.

Trevor   Well? What happened to her?

Mary (*shrugs her shoulders*)   I don't know . . .

Trevor   You don't know what happened to your sister?

Rose   Will you leave Mary alone . . .

Mary   Last time I saw her, she was eleven, I was fifteen. Leaving home I was, for the bright lights of London. 'Bye,' I said, 'when I'm rich, I'll send for you . . .' 'Course I never did.

Trevor   Where was home?

Rose *kisses her teeth, irritated.*

Mary   Scotland.

Trevor   You ever been back?

Mary   Oh no . . . never . . . I can't.

Trevor   Why?

Mary   It's a long story . . .

Rose   And we haven't got time to go into it now. Do we Mare?

Mary   Don't we?

Rose   No we don't. (*An awkward silence.*) We're havin' a party!

Mary   Oooooh that's nice, can I come?

Rose   'Course.

Trevor   Not a party, more of a family reunion, you know, Mum, me and Andy . . .

Mary   Oh . . . well, I wouldn't want to intrude . . .

Rose   You won't be.

Trevor   It was meant to be just for family.

Rose   It's my house. I say who's coming and who's not.

Mary   But I'm not family.

Rose   It doesn't matter.

Mary   There'll be things you want to talk about . . .

Rose   What bloody things?

Trevor   Family things . . .

Mary   And I've got to wash the cats.

Rose   Mary, you're coming and that's that!

Mary   Okay love, thanks. I can always wash the cats next week.

Trevor *sighs, walks over to the window, looks out.*

Trevor   These windows are filthy . . .

Rose   Then you can wash 'em, can't you.

Trevor   Anythin' you say, Mother dear.

Mary   He's a good boy . . .

Rose   He's a daft swine.

Trevor You don't mean it.

Rose Don't I?

Mary No, you don't.

Trevor They should've let him out of the gates by now.

Mary On his way to see his mum . . .

Rose He always come to see me first . . . Last time half past nine he was straight here from Borstal.

Mary You must've been so proud.

Rose I don't know about proud. After all, he had only just come out from Borstal. More pleased I'd say.

Mary It's only natural. You being his mother.

Rose When we were alone here, just me and Andy, he was as good as gold, no cheek, backchat or swearing . . . do anythin' for me he would, but fuck me the minute someone came through that front door he'd change . . . get nasty, cheeky, step on the dog's paw.

Mary Jealous maybe . . .

Rose Could be . . .

Trevor When he was good, he was very, very good and when he was bad he was horrid . . .

Rose You tryin' to be funny?

Trevor Who, me?

Mary Andy was always your favourite though . . .

Rose A long time ago.

Trevor What about me?

Rose You didn't need it. Your father gave you more than enough attention . . .

Mary Would be, wouldn't it, with Africans. First born and all that . . .

Rose I don't know what his father would have done to me if he'd been a girl. He used to dote on him. So I had to give Andy some attention . . .

Mary He had to stay in hospital once when he was a baby, didn't he?

Rose Yeah! Some sort of lump in his stomach . . . He was always cryin'. Had to have an operation in the end . . .

Mary Shame . . .

Rose His father weren't too keen at first. Didn't trust doctors or hospitals . . .

Mary Well they don't do they, Africans?

Rose Had to in the end. There was nothing else they could do.

Mary Thank God he's better now . . .

Trevor I should think so. It was over twenty years.

Mary That long, oh Rose, he must be getting old.

Rose Yes, love, what a waste . . .

Mary Just imagine if their father hadn't gone to prison that time, you and him might still be together . . .

Rose That was the biggest piece of luck I've had in my whole life. I would've had twenty-one kids instead of two by now.

Trevor But twenty-one kids! Just think of the family allowance.

Rose Never gave me a rest. I was lucky when he went to prison. I wouldn't've had the nerve to leave him while he was out . . .

Mary They could be bastards . . .

Rose You're tellin' me. Couldn't do anythin' I wanted. Had to breast-feed both of them. Didn't dare say I didn't want to. Had no say whatever in their names . . .

Mary But when they first arrived in this country they were lovely men. Always willing to take you out to pubs or a party, no matter what day of the week it was, even if you lived with the man . . .

Rose When I first met their father, gentle as a lamb he was. I'd just come up from Cornwall and was as green as the grass. He gave me some money for housekeeping, I went out and spent it all on chocolates . . .

Mary Oh Rose, you didn't . . .

Rose I did . . . I didn't know any better . . . He said get some food . . . and I liked sweets . . . Anyway, I was just a kid.

Mary What did he do?

Rose Nothing, just laughed . . . Didn't laugh the next time, though, just gave me a clout . . .

Mary Cruel . . .

Rose At times, but it's in their nature . . .

Trevor If he was so cruel why didn't you leave him before he went into prison, and find yourself a nice friendly English man?

Rose Me go with an Englishman?! . . . Don't be silly . . .

Mary *laughs.*

Trevor Why?

Rose I just couldn't bring myself to.

Mary Once you've tasted the sweet, you don't want the bitter.

Rose   And what Englishman would have looked at me with you two darkie children . . . trailing behind me?

Mary   Once you've been with a black man, Englishmen think all you're good for is one thing!

Rose   You kids'll be a scar on me for the rest of my life . . .

Trevor   How . . .

Rose   You know how . . .

Trevor   You tell me . . .

Rose   You're not that stupid . . .

Trevor   Damn right I'm not . . .

Rose   Don't start swearin' . . .

Trevor   Damn ain't fucki – oops, sorry, I let that slip out.

Rose   You watch your mouth.

Trevor   Come to think of it, you haven't been the best example of what we should and shouldn't say . . .

Rose   I'm your mother, I can say what I like . . .

Trevor   It would've been better if you had set up some sort of example . . .

Rose   Shut your bloody mouth. It's not up to me to set an example for anyone . . .

Trevor   Doesn't Mary's hair look nice. Had it done, have yer?

Mary   Yesterday.

Trevor   Yours is beginning to look like a mess, Mum. Why don't you have yours done?

Rose   I will when you give me the money . . .

Trevor   I'll buy you your own shop one day . . .

Rose   Leave off, will you . . .

Trevor   Oh yeah, I forgot, a bingo hall is what you want . . .

Rose   You want a clip round the ear . . .

Trevor   You and who's army. (*Sucks teeth.*)

Rose   You're not too old for me to hit . . .

Trevor   I need a fag . . .

Rose   Not off me . . .

Trevor   Mary'll give me one. Won't you, Aunty Mary. . . ?

Mary   I've only got these, they're non-tipped.

Trevor   I'm not fussy. (*Taking a fag.*) Yeah, you're really looking smart. Goin' somewhere?

Rose   She's goin' bingo with me . . .

Trevor   Bit early for bingo isn't it?

Mary   The morning session . . .

Trevor   Bloody hell, it's like that shilling machine thing where you have to win five thousand games to get a token and then you'd be lucky to cash it in for a second-hand teddy bear? . . .

Rose   It's better than sittin' here listening to you rattlin' on . . .

Mary   Somebody won a kettle once . . .

Trevor   Did they now, wow.

Mary   You get to meet people . . .

Trevor   It's all just an excuse . . .

Rose   What for?

Trevor   So that you don't pay your debts . . .

Rose   Debts, debts, debts. Is that all you can think about? I am gettin' fed up with it. D'you ever think about why I've got 'em? . . . it's you bloody lot. Buildin' a home for you! I don't have no man, your father gave me nothing. How the fuck did you expect me to do anythin' with the money I got from the social? . . . None of you thought to help.

Trevor   We didn't ask to be brought into the world . . .

Rose   Piss off . . .

Trevor   Don't you ever get tired of the life you lead? . . .

Rose   Don't you ever get tired of the sound of your voice? . . .

Trevor   I don't know why I bother . . .

Rose   Nor do I . . .

Trevor   I won't in the future . . .

Rose   Thank God . . .

Trevor *sits down in the chair.*

Rose   Not goin' to sulk, are you? Peace at last . . .

Trevor   You'll never have any peace the way you carry on . . .

Rose   Don't be upset . . .

Trevor   I'm not . . .

Rose   Then you'll still clean the windows for your mummy?

Trevor (*sighs, turns away from the window to face his mother*)   Yeah . . .

Rose   . . . go to the post office . . . and do the housework?

Trevor   Of course. (*He moves slowly towards* **Rose**.) As always, your wish is my command.

Trevor *has reached* **Rose**. *He bends down and is about to kiss her when the door knocks.*

Mary   Ooohh. D'you think that's Andy?

Rose   It's not his knock . . .

Mary   Isn't that wonderful, a mother knowing her son's knock? Not many mothers can say that without fear of retribution . . .

Rose   What are you talking about Mary?

Mary   I don't know, Rose.

Rose (*to* **Trevor**)   Go and get the door. Remember what I told yer.

Trevor   What's that?

Rose   Next week, whoever it is, I'll pay 'em next week.

Trevor *goes off.* **Rose** *signals for* **Mary** *to listen by the living-room door.*

Rose   Who is it, what's he sayin'?

Mary   I can't hear properly . . .

Rose   He's takin' his time. All he has to tell the bloke is . . .

Mary   It's Blundel! . . . I think . . .

Rose   Him, no trouble.

Mary   Nice wee Jewish man . . . So many folk owe the poor man money . . .

Rose   If he's fool enough to offer it, I'm clever enough to take it.

Mary *quickly moves away from the door.* **Trevor** *enters.*

Rose   What took you so long? Tell 'im your life story?

Trevor   I really feel sorry for that bloke . . .

Rose   Whatever for? He's got more money than you'll ever have . . .

Trevor   I made up some story about you bein' in hospital, because of your leg, and he told me how sorry he was, started enquirin' about your health . . .

Rose   Wants to know if he can come and collect his money at the hospital . . .

Trevor   No, I don't think so, he seemed to care . . .

Rose   Don't be so bloody daft, all he cares about is his money.

Trevor   The bloke was almost in tears . . .

Rose   Ahhh, what a shame . . .

Trevor   He asked if there was anything he could do . . .

Rose   You should've asked him for another loan.

Trevor   Asked me if you'd left any money, started at two pounds, went down to twenty-five p, that's when I gave him . . . three pound!

Mary   You did what?

Rose (*struggling up from sofa*) You, you're daft as bloody arseholes, Blundel see you comin' a mile off . . .

Trevor What?

Rose You're too bloody soft. (*She limps towards her bedroom door.*) It better not've been my bingo money . . .

Trevor It wasn't . . .

Rose There'll be no party if it was.

Trevor It wasn't. (*Takes fiver from his pocket.*) Here's your money . . .

Rose *snatches the money and goes into the bedroom, slamming the door in* **Trevor**'s *face.*

Trevor You said you only needed four pound . . .

Rose (*off*) The other pound's for all the trouble you've caused me this morning! Mare, I'm gettin' changed, be ready in a minute.

Mary Okay, love. (*She takes a half-bottle of vodka from her bag, unscrews cap.*) Me and your mother are going to bingo . . .

Trevor I bloody know.

Pause.

Mary So what time are you expecting Andy?

Trevor Anytime . . . He's usually here by now . . .

Mary You don't think he's been and gone. . . ?

Trevor No . . . Don't be silly . . .

Mary I had to knock three times . . . Not everyone is endowed with my sort of patience . . .

Trevor Na . . . he would've . . . (*He quickly goes over to* **Rose***'s bedroom door and knocks.*)

Rose (*off*) What the bloody hell d'you want? I'm trying to get changed . . .

Trevor I was wondering . . .

Rose (*off*) Oh my God, what about now?

Trevor D'you think I should phone the prison . . . make sure Andy's been released. . . ?

Rose (*off*) Don't be so bloody daft: this time of the morning, long distance, can't afford it. He'll be here, don't you worry . . .

Mary (*taking a sip of her drink*) You could set your watch by him, couldn't you Rose . . .

Trevor *sighs, opens the curtains. Early morning sunshine pours in.*

Scene Two

The lights come up. The heavy curtains are drawn, the net curtains have been taken down. The windows are covered with Windolene, so you cannot see out of them. We hear **Trevor** *whistling and the front-door opening. The sitting-room door opens.* **Trevor** *comes in with a shopping-bag in either hand. He rests them on the table. He takes milk, bread and tea bags from one of the bags and goes off to the kitchen. He returns with a hoover. He finds a place to hide the other carrier bag. He puts a record on the player: 'Patches'. He then starts hoovering, quickly and efficiently. He sings along with and dances to the record.*

During this scene there should be a very gradual and subtle light change from morning to afternoon.

Trevor *finishes hoovering. He takes Mr Sheen furniture spray polish from carrier bag and a cloth, picks up the phone, dials, polishes tabletops and television while speaking on the phone.*

Trevor   All right . . . Yeah, just phoned you up to find out how you are . . . Little Trev all right. . . ? (*Indignant.*) 'Course I'm at work! Where else would I be. . . ? I think that's really bad, accusin' me of not bein' at work . . . What's the matter with you. . . ? I am at work! The music. . . ? That's a bloody radio ain't it. (*Shouts at imaginary workmate.*) Oy, turn it down. I'm tryin' to have a conversation here with me wife. (**Trevor** *turns music down. Then back into phone.*) Yeah . . . so you're all right. . . ? Yeah, listen, I'll be a bit late home tonight . . . No, don't be silly . . . I'm passin' by Mum's . . . To see Andy . . . I told yer . . . Yes I did . . . No I won't be . . . Yeah . . . see you later . . . Bye.

He puts the phone down, sighs. Pause. Surveys the room. He's content. Takes another cloth from the carrier bag. Exits living-room. He starts wiping and polishing the windows from the outside.

Rose (*off*)   Has he been?

Trevor   No. You seen him?

Rose (*off*)   Don't be daft. What's he goin' to be doin' at a bingo hall!

Trevor   Any luck?

Rose (*off*)   Luck? What's that? Every other fucker in the world has a bit of luck not me . . .

Mary (*off*)   Your mother was so unlucky . . .

Trevor   Story of her life . . .

The sound of the front door opening and closing. **Rose** *and* **Mary** *enter the room in their coats.* **Rose***'s limp is more pronounced. She is in a foul mood.*

Rose (*to* **Trevor**)   No, you're the story of my life, it's yous that have given me all this bad luck . . .

Mary   Well Rose, you nearly won . . .

Rose   Nearly's not going to pay the bleedin' bills, is it?

Mary   No, I suppose not . . .

Rose .It's that poxy Vera, she's the one with all the luck, and it's not as if she really needs the money. When she called out 'here-are' on the last house, I could've stubbed me cigarette out, right on her nose. She has too much luck if you know what I mean. . . ?

Mary (*puzzled*) Er . . . yeah . . .

Trevor *pushes a window open to clean inside.*

Rose Somethin' dodgy goin' on if you ask me!

Trevor Not a fix???

Rose Nobody should have that much luck . . .

Mary That Vera wins practically every night . . .

Trevor You're such bad losers. You should learn to take defeat with dignity like I do . . .

Rose We've got nothing to learn from you. Now hurry up with those bloody windows, it's gettin' freezin' in here!

Trevor *moves away from the window, towards the front door.* **Rose** *takes a fag from her handbag. She notices her bingo books, takes them out and rips them to pieces, leaving the pile of torn bingo books on the coffee-table.*

Rose It's like they're takin' the piss – one number – the difference between winnin' and losin' . . .

Mary (*to herself*) So near and yet so far away.

Rose What?

Mary He was too fast, don't you think?

Rose Do what, Mare?

Mary I said, he called those numbers too fast. I was frightened to even light a fag in case I missed a number.

Rose I don't miss numbers. No matter what I'm doin'. I've never missed a number.

Mary He wasn't bad looking though . . .

Rose Do me a favour, I've seen better faces on the dead.

Mary He wasn't that bad . . .

Rose Leave off . . .

Trevor *enters, tut-tuts as he scoops the pile of torn bingo books off the coffee-table.*

Mary Perhaps I was sitting too far away. I'm not very good without me glasses.

Trevor I didn't know you wore glasses, what happened to them?

Mary Sold 'em years back, only use 'em for reading. Don't read much now, in fact I don't read at all, can't, you see, without my glasses.

Trevor   Don't you think it'd be a good idea to give bingo a miss and buy a new pair of glasses . . .

Mary   Don't be silly, what would I do for fun . . .

Trevor   All right, National Health?

Mary   I wouldn't be seen dead in a pair of National Health glasses. I've got my reputation to think of . . .

Rose   What d'you think you are, a bloody social worker? We don't need your bloody advice, what we need is money . . .

Trevor   Money's not all there is to life, Mum . . .

Rose   Gettaway you daft sod. Without money you can't live.

Trevor   But . . .

Rose   But nothing. Have you been to the post office yet?

Trevor   No . . . I was just on me way . . .

Rose   Get a move on then, instead of standin' about natterin' like some old woman!

Trevor   I was just going to let you know that I've done the housework, windows and shoppin' . . .

Rose   I want me money . . . now . . .

Trevor   I thought I'd have a cup of tea . . .

Rose   Now . . .

Trevor   It's just down the road, won't take five minutes . . .

Rose   Now!

Trevor   You want me to go now?

Rose   You little bastard . . .

Trevor   I'll go now then . . . See you later. (*He goes.*)

Rose   Bloody kids!

Mary   Where?

Rose   Where? What?

Mary   The bloody kids?

Rose   I was talking about Trevor . . .

Mary   Oh . . . I would've thought he was older than that . . .

Rose   Forget it, Mare, just forget it . . .

Pause.

Mary   He's made a good job of it, don't you think . . .

Rose   Who? What?

Mary The sitting-room. The windows. Your Trevor.

Rose It's all right. Though I don't wanna tell him that, he might get a big head. Anyway, I like to do these things myself. You know it's done properly then.

Mary He's a good boy.

Rose Only when he wants something.

Pause.

Mary So Andy's not been . . . then?

Rose Doesn't look like it . . .

Mary You don't think anything could have happened to him?

Rose He can look after himself.

Mary Missed him, have yer?

Rose A little, but I wouldn't tell him that . . . though.

Mary Why's that, Rose?

Rose He'd think I was soft . . .

Mary Oh . . .

Rose They take liberties if you're soft. You have to be hard.

Mary I know, Rose. I'm soft. I used to be hard when I was younger, but I'm soft now . . .

Rose I'm hard enough for the both of us.

Mary Yes, Rose, you probably are. (*She takes a half-bottle of vodka from her bag.*)

Rose What d'you think you're doin'?

Mary Oh . . . I thought I'd have a wee drink . . .

Rose It's that, that's what's made you soft . . .

Mary I know . . .

Rose It'll do you no fuckin' good!

Mary Just the one, I thought I'd have just the one . . .

Rose That's what you said at bingo . . .

Mary That was such a long time ago . . .

Rose Not more than half-hour . . .

Mary Just the one, Rose?

Rose Just the one, mind. Go on, get a glass.

Mary Thanks, Rose. Thanks . . . (*She gets herself a glass from the cupboard.*)

Rose You've got to give it up . . .

Mary (*pouring her drink with as much speed and dignity as she can muster*)   Yes . . . I know . . . I will . . .

Rose   It's ruined your life . . . Ouchh . . .

Mary   What's the matter?

Rose   It's me leg, Mare, it ain't half givin' me some pain.

Mary   Can I get you anything?

Rose   No . . . I'll stand on it . . . I'm goin' to lay down in a minute . . .

Mary   You all right, love?

Rose   Yeah . . .

Mary   Sure?

Rose   Yes. I'm sure!

Mary   Perhaps it means we're going to have a bit of luck . . .

Rose   Don't be so bloody daft, it's been painin' me all day, didn't bring us any luck in the last session, did it . . . We didn't win anythin' did we . . .

Mary (*pause*)   No.

Rose   We never win anythin' . . . I'm gonna give it up.

Mary   What's that, Rose?

Rose   Bingo.

Mary   How many times have I heard you say that?

Rose   I mean it this time, my luck's out, I'm gettin' fed up with it. No wins, no money . . . up to me ears in debts. What's the point?

Mary   Rose, you've got to have your bit of enjoyment and if bingo's your only hope . . . play.

Rose   I never win . . .

Mary   You've had wins. I've bin with you . . .

Rose   Not what you'd call real wins, big money. All I seem to get is ten or twenty, that's nothin', that sort of money goes nowhere these days. I've never had that big win, you know somethin' that would put my head above water, where I could see some bleedin' hope for the future . . . Sometimes I feel like endin' it all . . .

Mary   Not you, Rose . . .

Rose   That's the way I feel . . .

Mary (*pause*)   If I hadn't heard it out of your own mouth . . . I'd never have believed it . . .

Rose I get so depressed what with me leg an' all . . . but it's the worry, Mare . . . in my mind . . . the worry . . . My mind, it never rests . . . if it's not one thing . . . it's the damp . . . the debts . . . Andy . . . this fuckin' flat, the windows . . . I wrote to the Council but did they . . .

Mary Wha's the matter with the windows, they look nice and clean to me, Rose?

Rose The ground floor, Mare . . .

Mary I thought you wanted ground floor, 'cause of your leg . . .

Rose Mary, I know that, but it's the windows, there's no wire mesh on the outside . . .

Mary Wire mesh?

Rose You live on the ground floor, you're a sittin' duck for any thief that comes along. All they have to do is tap a hole in the window, undo the lock and they're in . . . My Andy told me and he should know . . . I wrote to the Council, every week . . . but do they do anythin' . . . Do they fuck. No, Mare, it's all gettin' too much for me . . .

Mary Well your Andy's coming out today and there's the party . . .

Rose Oh Mare, don't, you're making it worse, if anythin' it's the boys who'll give me the final push . . .

Mary Don't say that. I'm sure they love you . . .

Rose Doesn't really make much difference . . .

Mary Take some black and greens. They'll make you feel better.

Rose They're in the kitchen, there on the window-ledge.

Mary Take a couple . . . I'll join you.

Rose Not that they do much good, I think. After all these years I've grown immune to them.

Mary These the right ones? Ooh, you've so many.

Rose nods, **Mary** hands her two pills and then the water.

Mary You have so many . . . Have a sip of water . . . that's it, dear . . . There you are . . .

Rose Ta . . .

Mary And two for me. (*She takes hers with a swig of vodka.*) Rose, all those pills you have in the kitchen . . . you won't do anythin' silly . . .

Rose Not before bingo tonight.

Mary (*handing bottle of pills to* **Rose**) You'll feel better soon.

Rose Some hope . . .

Mary Talking of bingo – at the lunch-time session when you shouted at the caller 'Shake your balls up mate!', were you talking about the bingo balls or were you talking about his?

Rose (*laughs*) Both, Mare, both.

Mary See, I told you, you feel better. I knew it. 'Cause I feel better already and there was nothing wrong with me. I like to have a good stock of pills about me . . .

Rose D'you need some?

Mary What's that, Rose?

Rose Black and greens?

Mary I could do with a few. My doctor won't give them to me, says I might be addicted to them.

Rose What do doctors know. (*She throws the bottle of pills to* **Mary**.) Take them home with you.

Mary You sure you got enough?

Rose I've got plenty and I can always get Trevor to run up to the doctor's for some more . . .

Mary I'll pay, of course . . .

Rose Don't be silly . . .

Mary No, I insist . . .

Rose It doesn't matter . . .

Mary How much d'you want?

Rose I don't know . . . what can you afford?

Mary Say ten p a tablet . . .

Rose There were about fifteen in the bottle . . .

Mary That's one pound fifty . . .

Rose Don't you want to count them . . .

Mary Don't be silly, I trust you. (*Offers money to* **Rose**.)

Rose There's no need . . .

Mary Go on, take it. I'd only pay more elsewhere.

Rose *needs no more encouragement. She takes the money.*

Rose I've got some sleeping-tablets if you need them.

Mary I've got all I need. (*Goes into her bag and pulls out another bottle of pills.*) Look, I've got these . . .

Rose Let me see. (*Taking the bottle and examining the contents.*) These are no bloody good . . .

Mary Aren't they?

Rose 'Course not. How many d'you take?

Mary Two or three a night . . .

Rose What did I tell you – rubbish. My doctor used to give me those. Hopeless. I told him straight: 'I don't want this shit' . . . The ones he gives me now are so strong I guarantee you take one and as soon as your head touches the pillow you're asleep.

Mary Really?

Rose Take a couple of mine home with you. Try one before you go to bed tonight. One, mind – take two and you won't wake up tomorrow morning.

Mary I couldn't . . .

Rose 'Course you can . . .

Mary You're too kind . . .

Rose If you like them, I'll sell you some tomorrow. And you better find a decent doctor.

Mary My doctor's no good, keeps tellin' me how ill I am but he won't give me anything except advice on what to eat, what to drink and to make sure I rest enough.

Rose Paki?

Mary I –

Rose I thought so . . . Then you definitely want to change him. They won't give you anything. Frightened of being called up in front of the Medical Council. Them being foreigners, they won't take chances.

Mary All the good doctors are dead . . .

Rose Mine's not. Gives me anything I ask for . . .

Mary Wasn't there something about him in the papers a couple of months back? . . .

Rose All lies. I won't hear a word said against the man. He's a bloody good doctor . . .

Mary I suppose he's better than a Pakistani . . .

Rose I'd trust him with my life. Been with him ever since I came to London. I'll have a word with him, get him to put you on his books. Then you won't be short of anything.

Mary That'd be a relief . . .

The sitting-room door slowly opens.

Trevor Hello ladies . . .

Rose Ahhhh . . . oh fuck, you bastard . . .

Trevor That's a nice welcome for someone who's just run to the post office and back for you.

Rose How d'you get in?

Trevor The door was open . . .

Rose Anybody could've walked in . . .

Trevor I thought I'd leave it open for Andy . . .

Rose He can knock like anybody else . . .

Trevor I've been standing outside that door listening to you two. You're just a pair of junkies . . .

Rose You shut your mouth. And where's my money? . . .

Trevor (*hands over her money*) D'you think I was going to leave the country?

Rose I wouldn't put it past you . . .

Trevor Here's the fags I promised you . . .

Rose I hope you didn't buy them out of my money . . .

Trevor Check it and you'll see. And don't say I never give you anythin' . . .

Rose About time . . .

Trevor And twenty for you, Aunty Mary . . .

Mary That's nice of you . . .

Trevor Why do I call her aunty, she's not your sister . . .

Rose She's an old friend . . .

Mary You don't have to if you don't want to . . .

Trevor If it's good enough for my mother it's good enough for me . . . You have been invited to the family reunion.

Mary Well, Rose, I must be on my way, I've got to feed the cats . . . I'll see you outside the bingo tonight . . .

Rose Okay, love . . .

Trevor You're going to bingo again! . . .

Rose Mind your own . . .

Mary Got to try your luck . . .

Rose Don't forget the sleeping-tablets by the window . . .

Mary Right . . . Bye. (*She leaves. Door slams.*)

Trevor So you're a drug dealer now?

Rose Don't be so bloody daft. I just lent Mary a couple of sleeping-tablets! (*She lies on the settee.*)

Trevor You goin' to sleep . . .

Rose What does it look like. . . ?

Trevor You goin' bingo again?

Rose Yes . . .

Trevor But Andy should be comin'. You don't wanna miss him, do yer . . .

Rose He'll still be here when I get back . . .

Trevor Not the same, is it . . .

Rose I'm not rearranging the whole of my life to suit him . . .

Trevor Nobody's askin' you to. Just one evening. You could give bingo a miss tonight. You've already been twice today.

Rose No, now shuddup. I wanna sleep . . .

Trevor Where you gettin' the money? . . .

Rose Mary . . .

Trevor She's beginning to get on my bleedin' nerves.

Rose She's all right . . .

Trevor Or she will be till she stops lendin' you money . . . same with all your friends.

Rose What d'you mean? I always pay back . . .

Trevor I know, and as soon as you do, you ask again . . .

Rose That's my business.

Trevor Oh come on, Mum. Just for Andy. It won't hurt once. It would be nice. You might be overcome with a swell of motherly affection, and you want to give all that up for one night at bingo? You listenin'? . . . you asleep? . . .

Rose How can I be with you babblin' on . . .

Trevor Do you want me to rub your leg?

Rose If you want . . .

Trevor Time was, you'd pay me to rub your leg. Sixpence. When I was a kid I used to pick the dead skin off your heel, d'you remember. . . ?

Rose Hmmmmmmmmmm.

Trevor You goin' to pay this time . . .

Rose Get off . . .

Trevor 'Course it'll be a lot more than sixpence now. Inflation an' all that . . .

Rose In Cornwall, when I was little, my father would go for a sleep. Head on his arms at the kitchen table. Forty winks, he'd say. He would ask me to look in his hair for fleas. I was promised a penny for every flea . . .

Trevor D'you ever find any?

Rose No. Used to search for hours. Threw my heart and soul into that search for fleas, but I always used to get a penny when he woke up . . .

Trevor In one of his letters Andy said that he might move to Cornwall, get away from the East End . . .

Rose   It's a pity your grandfather's dead. He would have sorted Andy out. He wouldn't stand for no nonsense. He used to wear his belt with the buckle at the back. When you were goin' to get hit with it, he'd slowly turn it round. 'Ere . . . you're supposed to be rubbing, not scratchin' . . .

Trevor   I'm sorry, out of practice . . . I think I'll go to Cornwall soon.

No answer. **Trevor** *gets up from the settee, takes one of* **Rose***'s fags* . . .

Rose   Put it back . . .

Trevor   I thought you was asleep . . .

Rose   Well I'm not . . .

Trevor   Just this one. I forgot to buy some for myself . . .

Rose   I don't know what you do with your money . . .

Trevor   Spend it . . .

Rose   On what?

Trevor   I do have a wife and kid to support . . .

Rose   I warned you, didn't I?

Trevor   It would be the same with any girl . . .

Rose   No it wouldn't . . .

Trevor   You're talkin' rubbish . . .

Rose   Am I? After what I've been through with your father, I always expected you to have more sense.

Trevor   Mum, I'm not white . . .

Rose   You're half . . .

Trevor   Which half, top or bottom? . . .

Rose   Don't be silly. You know what I mean. Black girls are free and easy, I mean it's not their fault it's just what they're like . . .

Trevor   You don't know what you're talkin' about . . .

Rose   Yes I do, you ask your father, he's the one who told me . . .

Trevor   I don't believe that. He never said anythin' to me . . .

Rose   You ask him next time you see him . . .

Trevor He's glad I'm with a black girl. He's proud of me. The only sensible thing to do in this country, he says . . .

Rose Your father's a two-faced cunt. He's never been with a black woman in his life . . .

Trevor Yes, and look where he is today – in a shitty one-roomed flat.

Rose That's not my fault . . .

Trevor You helped put him there . . .

Rose You're fuckin' mad . . .

Trevor I know what I'm talking about.

Rose Now you shut up, I wanna go to sleep . . .

Trevor He told me he was waiting for the right one to come along . . .

Rose Right what?

Trevor Black woman . . .

Rose He's full of shit . . .

Trevor I do believe you're jealous . . .

Rose Who me? Jealous of your father! You must be joking.

Trevor Light still burnin', eh?

Rose That light went out a long time ago.

Trevor I bet if he did get together with a black woman that'd really crease you, wouldn't it?

Rose Don't make me laugh.

Trevor It would.

Rose I couldn't care less about your father . . .

Trevor It would really upset you. You'd have lost your hold . . .

Rose I've got no hold on your father . . .

Trevor Why d'you think he never married again . . .

Rose I don't know. We was never married in the first place . . .

Trevor Oh I see, I'm a bastard now . . .

Rose For want of a better word, yes . . .

Trevor You really know how to make me feel secure . . .

Rose It didn't worry me . . .

Trevor It doesn't worry me, but it is nice to know these things . . .

Rose Nobody cares these days . . .

Trevor I've just had a thought: I must be what they call these days, a love child.

Rose There was no love . . .

Trevor It's all clear now, the root of all my problems. Parents who never married or loved each other.

Rose (*sits up*) Here . . . I just figured you out . . .

Trevor You what?

Rose You invited your father!

Trevor Pardon?

Rose You bloody heard. You told your father to come round here . . .

Trevor No I didn't . . .

Rose That's what all this has been about. I should've known . . .

Trevor I don't know what you're talkin' about . . .

Rose (*kicking her feet, which* **Trevor** *is still holding*) You fuckin' little bastard. I don't want him round here, I've told you that, I don't know how many times. I had enough of him when I was livin' with him, I don't want to see his ugly mug now. If he comes round here I'll push him over the fuckin' balcony . . .

Trevor You haven't got a balcony any more, Mum, you live on the ground floor . . .

Rose Don't you tell me where I live, you fucking little bastard . . . let go of my leg . . . You can go and tell him I don't want his black, African, bastard backside in my house!

Trevor (*still holding on to her leg*) Sssssssh, Mum . . .

Rose Don't you ssssh Mum me . . . You think he's an angel, he's no fuckin' angel, left all the aggravation to me . . . go and have the fuckin' party . . . reunion up his poxy bedsit . . .

Trevor Calm down, Mum. (*Furiously rubbing her foot.*) Don't be silly . . . would I invite him knowing how you feel? Come on now, I'm not that stupid . . .

Rose (*calming down*) You better fuckin' not have . . .

Trevor I haven't . . . My life . . .

Rose Got enough on me plate without seein' that bloody old African . . . don't want him drivin' me mad . . .

Trevor I know you don't . . . Sssssshhh now, Mum . . . you wanna sleep . . . you've had a long day . . . your legs been achin' . . . You wanna get some sleep before you go bingo tonight . . .

Lights fade to blackout.

Act Two

Scene One

It is dark except for an orange glow from the street lights. The curtains are open. Most of the furniture has been pushed neatly to the edges of the room. The table and four chairs have been set, rather formally, in the centre of the room. On the table a bowl of fruit, four candles, a bottle of Bacardi, a bottle of Coca-Cola and four glasses. **Trevor** *lays asleep on the sofa, facing the audience.*

A knock at the front door. Pause. **Trevor** *stirs, then turns and faces the back of the sofa, still asleep. A figure stands at the window, looks in, taps on the window.* **Trevor** *still asleep. The figure moves away from the window.*

The sound of a window opening. Pause. Then the sitting-room door opens. The figure enters, walks coolly around, notices **Trevor** *asleep on the sofa. The figure tiptoes around, looking for something. He does this quickly, quietly and efficiently. He can't find what he is looking for. He goes into* **Rose**'s *bedroom, off. Pause. He comes out smiling, walks over to the settee and kisses* **Trevor** *on the forehead.* **Trevor** *wakes with a start.*

Trevor Hmmmm . . . Eh . . . Do what . . . Andy!!!! It's you! Fuckin' e'll! You an' half give me a fright . . . What time is it? Where've you been? How are you?

Andy Which question d'you want me to answer first?

Trevor Sorry, just woke up . . .

Andy I'd've never have known . . .

Trevor How you doin'?

Andy Can't complain. Yourself?

Trevor Knackered. Mum's had me runnin' about all day . . .

Andy Didn't expect to find you here . . .

Trevor . . . waitin' for you?

Andy How long?

Trevor All day. I mean, you usually come and see Mum first. What happened?

Andy Change of plans . . .

Trevor You all right?

Andy 'Course.

Trevor *moves towards the light switch. He switches the light on.*

Andy Close the curtains!

Trevor What?

Andy The curtains – draw them.

Trevor Why?

Andy It's the ground floor. Don't want people to see what we're up to, do we.

Trevor The ol' bill aren't after you already, are they?

Andy Don't be silly. Just close the curtains, will yer.

Trevor Right. No problem. (*He draws the curtains.*) It's really great to see you.

Andy It's good to see you.

They stand facing each other. Pause. They hug.

Trevor Yeah. You used my name. It was a bit of a shock to come home from work and have Marcia tell me I'd been arrested for burglary . . .

Andy Had to do it. I was up on other charges and yours was the first name that came into my head. Sorry about that.

Trevor It's all right. I was glad to be of some help . . .

Andy Your wife didn't like the idea . . .

Trevor No . . . She was all for it.

Andy She wasn't.

Trevor She was . . .

Andy Why are you lying?

Trevor I'm not, she is the one who suggested it.

Andy Marcia wrote to me while I was inside . . .

Trevor Oh . . .

Andy Telling me how unfair it was that I should give you a criminal record, when you had not done nothing wrong . . .

Trevor It's none of her business. You're my brother.

Andy She's your wife . . . So how is she?

Trevor Who? Marcia?

Andy No. Mum.

Trevor Oh she's all right.

Andy Her leg?

Trevor Plays her up now and then, but not enough to stop her going to bingo . . .

Andy You couldn't stop her goin' to bingo if she was a double amputee . . .

Trevor A what?

Andy Never mind . . . Where's the dog, didn't bark as I climbed in the window . . .

Trevor She sold it. Needed the money for bingo, although she'll tell you she sold it to pay off her debts. Then for weeks after she tried to win the money to buy back the dog. It never happened. Shame, really, Mary and Patch were the only company she has . . .

Andy Good fuckin' job. She showed that dog more affection than she ever showed us . . . (*He moves around the flat, examining the contents.*) New settee . . .

Trevor She got it from the catalogue . . .

Andy Colour television?

Trevor Visionhire . . .

Andy Record-player?

Trevor Rumbelows . . .

Andy Carpet. . . ?

Trevor Blundells . . .

Andy You think there's anythin' in this flat that's not on h.p.?

Trevor Hmmm . . . the net curtains . . .

Andy Na, she gets them off the tali-man . . . The coffee-table?

Trevor Na, that came with the record-player from Rumbelows, she owes money on them all . . .

Andy Tell me somethin' new.

Trevor She wants them to take her to court, she gives her sob story and ends up payin' twenty-five p a week for the lot of it.

Andy You'd of thought they would've caught up with her by now . . .

Trevor She uses so many names, she sometimes forgets who she is when she opens the door.

Andy *runs his hands over the table and chairs.*

Andy (*pointing to candles, bowl of fruit, etc.*) What's all this? Mum holding a dinner party?

Trevor For you . . .

Andy For who?

Trevor You.

Andy Me. . . ? Mum bought all this for me?

Trevor I did.

Andy What?

Trevor Bought the stuff . . . you know . . . it was my idea . . .

Andy Idea . . . what idea?

Trevor A party . . .

Andy This is a party?

Trevor To celebrate your release and freedom . . .

Andy I see, a party.

Trevor More of a family reunion . . .

Andy   Four chairs . . . I take it the Cornish and Nigerian branches of the family haven't been invited?

Trevor   Not all of them.

Andy *points to each chair individually. As he does so, each time he asks a question, and each time* **Trevor** *nods his head.*

Andy (*points chair one*)   You? (*Chair two.*) Me? (*Chair three.*) Mum. . . ? (*Chair four.*) Well. . . ?

Trevor (*mumbles*)   Dad . . .

Andy   You invited Dad here?

Trevor (*quickly*)   Mum with think the fourth chair's for Aunty Mary . . .

Andy   She's not our fuckin' aunty . . .

Trevor   Well, Mary then . . .

Andy   Who invited her?

Trevor   Don't look at me . . . it was Mum . . . we'll soon get rid of her . . .

Andy   Will we?

Trevor   I'll have a quiet word in her ear . . . say her cats have been electrocuted or somethin'. What d'you think?

Andy   I was just wonderin' who has hit you over the head with a sledgehammer . . . inviting Dad here! (*Ruefully shakes his head.*)

Trevor   I thought it'd be nice . . .

Andy   Nice . . . For who?

Trevor   You, me, Mum, Dad . . . all of us . . . the family, together in the same room . . . I thought . . .

Andy   I think you're fuckin' crazy . . . Mum and Dad hate each other.

Trevor   No they don't . . .

Andy   Yes they do!

Trevor   Not really . . .

Andy   Not really. The last thing I heard them say to each other was: 'Get back to Africa, you black bastard' and 'May you burn in hell, you pink-faced cow!'

Trevor   Sticks and stones. . . ?

Andy   Mum and Dad don't fight with sticks and stones, they fight with bombs and mortar, on clearly defined lines, black against white, men against women. It's total.

Trevor (*laughing*)   I thought you coming out of prison might make it different . . .

Andy   Different. Some optimist you are. It certainly will be a family reunion, with a difference . . . More like an Armageddon. A white person who doesn't like black people, a black man who doesn't like white people, a hopeless dreamer, an ex-convict and, to round it all off, a Scottish diabetic alcoholic. Thanks, brother of mine.

Trevor (*still laughing*)   Well I tried, And . . . God knows I've tried . . .

Andy   Bacardi . . . that makes it complete . . .

Trevor   And Coke . . . Rod Stewart's drink . . . So I thought, what's good enough for Rod Stewart is good enough for the Ikoyi family.

Andy (*unscrews the cap of the Bacardi*)   Let's drink to that disparate band of desperadoes: the Ikoyi's!

Trevor   Shouldn't we wait?

Andy   For what?

Trevor   The rest of the family . . .

Andy   You and me are family enough.

Trevor   Yeah, right.

Andy *pours each of them a drink.*

Trevor   Wait . . . one minute . . .

Trevor *rushes off towards the kitchen. While he's off,* **Andy** *lights two of the candles with a gold lighter he has taken from* **Rose***'s room.* **Trevor** *comes back on with lemon, a knife and a small ball of ice, which he hands to* **Andy***.* **Trevor** *slices the lemon.*

Trevor   Can't drink Bacardi and Coke without ice and lemon. (*Pops a lemon into* **Andy***'s glass.*) It's not the done thing.

Andy (*holding up his glass*)   To my brother!

Trevor (*holding up his glass*)   Likewise!

They clink classes.

Andy   Cheers!

Trevor   Cheers!

A pause.

Andy   So what's happenin'?

Trevor   What, with me?

Andy   Yeah, with you . . .

Trevor   Nothin' much. I'm out of work and Marcia's pregnant. Don't tell Mum.

Andy   Again? She's pregnant again?

Trevor   We've only had the one little Trev . . .

Andy   He's only a little over one . . .

Trevor Eighteen months . . .

Andy Haven't you two ever heard of contraceptives?

Trevor 'Course . . .

Andy Do you use them, though?

Trevor Marcia's on the pill, when she remembers . . .

Andy What about you?

Trevor No, I don't take the pill . . .

Andy Ha, ha. Don't you use anythin' like Durex?

Trevor Na, don't be silly, I can't be bothered with all that. Anyway this baby's wanted. It was planned, it wasn't no accident.

Andy Yeah, sure. So what are you going to do with your life? You got a family. You need a job.

Trevor So everyone keeps tellin' me . . . But packin' boxes, lumpin' crates, sweatshops, that's all that's out there. I want more . . . (*He pours himself another drink.*) I was educated for more, better. You remember Miss Scott, our foster mum, well she had me playin' the violin and speaking fluent French at the age of nine, remember that little primary school in the village.

Andy But you failed your eleven-plus and left secondary school without a qualification to your name . . . You've got to face up to reality. You've got a son, another kid on the way, you need money for a decent place to live, clothes on your back, food in yer mouth. You don't get money by dreaming. Grab whatever job's going. Things aren't going to get much better for you unless you do somethin'.

Trevor What can I do. . . ?

Andy Night school . . .

Trevor Night school?

Andy Yeah, you know, a school that gives classes at night.

Trevor Funny.

Andy You've got to make an effort . . .

Trevor 'Old it, 'old it, 'old it. We've got it all arse backwards. I'm the elder brother. I'm the responsible one, I'm the one who hasn't just been released from prison. (*Pause.*) Why is it I feel you are my older brother now?

Andy I've had a bit more experience than you, read a few more books, had more time to think, plenty of time . . .

Trevor But I used to look after you, I was your bodyguard, from when you was four up until you was thirteen. All the while we was in care I never let anyone take liberties with you . . . Don't you forget that . . .

Andy I won't. I appreciate it.

Trevor You remember the rubber tomahawk . . .

Andy Yeah, in the cottage home . . .

Trevor Your tenth birthday . . .

Andy Donald Meakle . . .

Trevor He was a big fucker . . . (*Acting himself as an eleven-year-old.*) 'If my brother wants to buy a rubber tomahawk, he should have a rubber tomahawk, it's a nice red tomahawk. And if you think that's so funny . . . I'll stuff it right down your gob!' Now Donald Meakle was big for an eleven-year-old, but his two pals were even bigger . . . all three of them jumped on me and beat eighteen different kinds of shit out of me, and where was my little brother, whose honour I was trying to avenge?

Andy Hiding in the broom cupboard. My older brother was taking care of things . . .

Trevor I was seeing stars . . .

Andy I was scared . . .

Trevor You don't scare now.

Andy Yes I do, but I don't show it.

Trevor *pours himself another drink, starts searching his pockets.*

Trevor D'you wanna fag. . . ? I've got some here . . . somewhere . . . (*Starts looking around the flat.*) Mum's been havin' goes at me all day for smokin' hers, so I bought a packet. I'll give you one when I find them, they're around here somewhere . . .

Andy (*taking out his own*) Have one of these . . .

Trevor I definitely had a packet.

Andy Take one!

Trevor Ta . . . I'm always losin' things . . .

Andy You haven't changed. (*Offering* **Trevor** *a light with the gold cigarette-lighter.*) Have a light.

Trevor Nice lighter. Hey, isn't this the one you gave to Mum before you went inside?

Andy What if it is?

Trevor I was just wonderin', that's all . . .

Andy I took it back.

Trevor When?

Andy Just now, out of her bedroom while you were asleep. I wouldn't apply for a job as security guard if I were you . . .

Trevor She treasured that lighter . . .

Andy Too bad . . .

Trevor She hardly ever used it.

Andy She wasn't supposed to . . .

Trevor She'll be upset.

Andy She's got no right to be. I stole it in the first place. Poetic justice . . .

Trevor (*handing back the lighter*) Who are you livin' with?

Andy Karen . . .

Trevor She's a nice girl.

Andy A nice 'lookin' ' girl.

Trevor You stayin' there?

Andy Only till I find somewhere else. I'm fed up with her . . .

Trevor Give her a chance. You've only been out a few hours.

Andy It's convenient, that's all. I've got no feelings for the girl. I'm a different person from the one she met.

Trevor Mum likes her . . .

Andy What does Mum know or care . . .

Trevor Geoffrey and Stephen.

Andy Fair hair . . .

Trevor Blue eyes . . .

Andy White skin . . .

Trevor Brown freckles . . .

Andy Wonderful, caring mother . . .

Trevor Strong but fair father . . .

Andy Big house . . .

Trevor Big garden . . .

Andy With trees . . . A tree house . . .

Trevor Our own rooms . . .

Andy Our own bicycles . . .

Trevor Tailor-made school blazers . . .

Andy Light grey shorts pressed so sharp you could cut your fingers . . .

Trevor Knee socks that stayed at your knee . . .

Andy   Car to school . . .

Trevor   Satchels with our initials. G and S.

Andy   Geoffrey and Stephen.

Trevor   You be Stephen and I'll be Geoffrey . . .

Andy   No . . . you're always Geoffrey, I want to be Geoffrey and you be Stephen.

Trevor   And run like this.

They both ape Geoffrey and Stephen running. High knee and arm action. They both laugh. Then stop, out of breath.

Andy   We wanted to be G and S when we were how old . . . six and seven?

Trevor   About that . . . Hastings . . .

Andy   Lowestoft was the best place we were ever in. Our Miss Scott. She made you learn French and play the violin . . . Her plans for me were less ambitious. She just wanted to stop me being a thief . . . She tried so hard, not once did she ever shout at me or hit me . . . I really liked that woman . . .

Trevor   I nearly drowned down there . . . I couldn't lift my arms and legs above the water . . . my head was poppin' up and down, one second blue skies, next dirty green sea water burning my eyes and filling my throat . . . I was apologising to everyone . . . promising God I'd never be a naughty boy again. Then by some miracle I was lifted from the water . . .

Andy   The bloke said he saw this black, squiggly thing. At first he thought it might have been seaweed, then a cat or a dog, and it was you. Saved by your long, black, curly hair . . .

Trevor   I used to hate those fuckin' curls. Every night, I use to comb my hair. Comb? Tug at it, pull at it, trying to make it straight. I used to watch them white guys when they used to come up out of the sea and flick their heads back and this giant spray of hair and water, like that red fur on a Roman's helmet. When I flicked my head, all that would happen is that water would fall out and my hair would do a little quiver from side to side and up and down like it was on springs . . .

Andy   There wasn't many of our sort in Lowestoft in those days.

Trevor   God how I wished I was white in those days . . . I must've been sick.

Andy   We had no other role models . . .

Trevor   You taken some sort of course while you was inside?

Andy   Not really, I've just been thinking about it a lot . . .

Trevor   I'm glad I know what I am now . . .

Andy   And what's that?

Trevor   Black, of course . . .

Andy   Why of course?

Trevor   Because that is what we are . . .

Andy   We?

Trevor We're not white. Our father's black. We're black.

Andy You're what people say you are. I'm what I say I am, and that is brown.

Trevor Brown?

Andy Not white.

Trevor But being black is . . .

Andy I know what being black is . . . I suppose that's why you married a black woman . . .

Trevor That's right. I see what happened to Mum and Dad, I didn't want anyone calling me a black bastard because we weren't getting on . . .

Andy You usually marry someone because you love them or something, not because you're afraid they might call you a black bastard.

Trevor I do love her . . .

Andy That's all right then . . .

Trevor You used to be all for it, the salute, the haircut . . .

Andy I've changed . . . I know, you see . . . It's all about money, economics . . . That's how it all started . . . Money, that's the way to end it . . . Get as much as you can, then you won't owe anythin' to anybody . . .

Trevor You can't turn your back on what you are . . .

Andy Don't be stupid. I'm just lookin' after myself . . . that's all.

Pause.

Trevor Yeah, right . . . D'you wanna another drink?

Andy No. And I think you've had enough.

Trevor It's supposed to be a party . . .

Andy Some party. A Scottish prostitute, a Nigerian pusher . . .

Trevor Prostitute . . . Mary?

Andy Uhh . . . huh . . .

Trevor Mary is a prostitute?

Andy She was a very successful one. You didn't know?

Trevor No . . . no, I didn't . . .

Andy All those jewels, flash clothes . . . She had houses all over London. How d'you think she came by that?

Trevor I thought some African sailor had left her his life insurance policy . . .

Andy Jesus, you can be so naïve. I used to see her myself in the West End when I was much younger . . .

Trevor But Mary's a diabetic . . .

Andy Yeah, a diabetic prostitute. According to Mum, she was very beautiful. Yeah, Mum's known Mary since she came up from Cornwall, Mary showed her the ropes . . .

Trevor Mum never told me . . .

Andy Yeah, she told me . . . They use to hang round together when Dad first went to prison and we were put into homes . . .

Trevor And Mum . . . did she . . .

Andy Sell herself?

Trevor *nods.*

Andy No, after a couple of years with Dad, all Mum wanted was a good time.

Trevor Mum told you all this?

Andy Oh yeah . . .

Trevor Wow . . .

Andy I sometimes wish Mum had done that . . .

Trevor What? Been a. . . ???

Andy Yeah, instead of puttin' us in homes.

Trevor You're jokin'?

Andy I'm not. I would've been really proud of her. It would've been heroic, don't you think, to make that sort of sacrifice for her children?

Trevor No I don't . . .

Andy Why?

Trevor It wouldn't've bin right.

Andy You're too sentimental . . .

Trevor Because I love Mum . . .

Andy What d'you expect in return?

Trevor That's what all this is about . . . Me, you, Mum and Dad together . . . Have a drink . . . go over old times . . .

Andy You've got to be jokin'! We don't have any old times, leastwise any worth reminiscing about . . .

Trevor Mum's goin' to need us . . . All she has now is bingo and a mountain of debts . . .

Andy   What am I supposed to do? Turn round and say none of it matters any more, let's pretend to be a family.

Trevor   It would help . . .

Andy   Who? Mum? Dad? Certainly not me. We never existed as a family. You've got your own, take care of that. The one you are trying to create never got off the ground!

Trevor   It's not too late . . .

Andy   You know your trouble, you attach too much importance to belonging to or being part of something – a family, a race – when in reality you're better off on your own, answering to no one but yourself . . .

Trevor   I can't rely on myself . . . I need more . . .

Andy   You've picked the wrong person in Mum, she doesn't know us well enough to love us. Fuck her!

A pause as **Andy** *gets up from the table, goes over to the curtains, looks out, then turns to look at* **Trevor**.

Andy   Not once did she come and visit me, while I was inside!

Trevor   It's her leg . . .

Andy   If it's so fuckin' bad, why doesn't she have the damn thing amputated . . .

Trevor   It has been pretty bad . . .

Andy   How bad's 'pretty bad'?

Trevor   Painful . . .

Andy   Feel her pain for her, do you?

Trevor   No . . . she told me . . . She acts as though she is in pain . . .

Andy   Acts is the right word. She is a fucking great actress. She never visited me because she didn't care. I don't know why I'm surprised she's never wanted to know, the only time she showed us any affection is when we came home for weekends and she was drunk. Why are you making excuses for her?

Trevor   I'm not . . .

Andy   Yes you are. And she wouldn't thank you . . .

Trevor   For God's sake, And, she is our mother . . .

Andy   When has she ever been a mother to us? We were in children's homes from the time we were three up until we were ready to leave school and go to work. You think that was all by chance . . .

Trevor   She had it hard after Dad left . . . on her own in London with two black kids . . .

Andy   What was she doin' with a black man if she didn't want black kids?

Trevor She was young, green up from Cornwall, what the fuck would she know about the East End, black men and children . . .

Andy So what am I supposed to do, sympathise with her for messing up my life?

Trevor Andy, she needs us now . . .

Andy Too bad, ain't it. I don't need her or anyone. (*He gets up from the table.*)

Trevor So why d'you come round?

Andy To get my lighter. . . ?

Trevor Your lighter?

Andy That's right. Why d'you think I came at this time? I knew she'd be at bingo . . .

Trevor All you care about is a poxy lighter . . .

Andy It's worth a lot of money . . .

Trevor That's all you and Mum ever talk about is money. As if nothing else matters . . .

Andy That's because we're both realists . . .

Trevor I'm glad you have at least one thing in common . . .

Andy This lighter is worth nearly three grand . . .

Trevor Do what?

Andy Solid twenty-four-carat gold. The little glass beads, as Mum called them, are tiny little diamonds. The little beauty is so old, it probably is the first of its kind . . .

Trevor Mum never knew . . .

Andy She wasn't supposed to. Say the police raided the place, she thought she had a couple of thousand under her roof, she'd of shit herself . . .

Trevor All that time, she's been going to bed, sleeping on three grand.

Andy I was gonna let her have it, to pay off her debts, when I was first inside, but a couple of weeks before I was due to be released I thought, why the fuck should I, what's she ever done for me?

Trevor I don't know. And . . . I don't know.

Andy You got money?

Trevor A bit . . .

Andy (*pulls out a wad of fivers*) Here's twenty for my nephew . . . and twenty for Mum . . .

Trevor Andy, you haven't . . . not already . . .

Andy   Relax, brother, an advance on the lighter. I've told you . . . Listen, Trev . . . I want things . . . beautiful things. Clothes, cars, stereos, music, food, travel: all the things you see on the telly or in glossy magazines . . . Real high class . . . I want to look at it . . . feel it . . . I want to be comfortable . . . It costs money . . . I'm never going to be able to afford all that workin' on some stall down a market or in some factory . . . So I have to take a risk . . . I'm no different than the so-called big shots in the city – stockbrokers, bankers – except the collateral I'm using is my freedom . . . what else is there?

Trevor   Night school?

Andy   Very funny . . . See you . . .

Trevor   You're not stayin'?

Andy   No!

Trevor   How are you goin' to get out? The door's locked.

Andy   Easy . . . (*He draws one of the curtains, and is about to open a window.*)

Trevor   Stay, And, please . . . If not for the family, then for me . . . Help me handle them two . . .

Andy   Bollocks!

Trevor   What am I goin' to say?

Andy   Don't say anythin' . . .

Trevor   Remain silent while the battle rages?

Andy   Don't be here . . . be gone, leave before it starts . . .

Trevor   When?

Andy   Now.

Trevor   With you?

Andy   If you want.

Trevor   Up and out of the window . . . Na, I couldn't, Mum'll go spare . . .

Andy   So . . . why should you worry?

Trevor   Yeah, why should I worry? If they hate each other it's their problem. Not mine . . .

There is a knock at the door. **Trevor** *stands frozen.* **Andy** *stands by the curtain, ready to make an exit.*

Trevor   What should I do?

Andy   Answer the door . . .

Trevor Say it's Dad . . . he's not goin' to be very pleased. I invite him here but I can't let him in . . .

The door is knocked again.

Andy That's not Dad's knock, it's too feeble.

Trevor Who can it be?

Andy I don't know . . .

Trevor I know . . . You answer the door . . .

Andy I can't.

Trevor Why?

Andy Say it's the police . . .

Trevor The police! . . . Shit, the ol' bill . . . Oh my God . . . what are we goin' to do?

Andy Don't panic. I've got the stuff on me . . .

Trevor Stuff. . . ? What stuff? Never mind . . . I don't wanna know.

The door is knocked again.

Trevor Why don't they go away? . . . Why don't we just climb out of the window?

Andy If it is the police, they are going to assume, if we're breakin' out, we must've broken in.

Trevor Yeah, right. Breakin' and enterin'.

Andy Go to the door. Ask who it is. If it's someone for Mum, tell them to come back later, if it's Dad we'll climb out of the window and escape, and if it's the police, I'm fucked. Right?

Trevor Right . . .

Trevor *slowly makes his way to the front door, leaving the sitting-room door open.* **Andy** *stands by the curtains, ready for any eventuality.*

Trevor (*off*) Who is it. . . ?

Andy, *noticing the living-room door is wide open, tiptoes across the room to close it, when . . .*

Mary (*off*) It's me, love . . . Aunty Mary . . .

Andy *breathes a sigh of relief, tiptoes back to the curtains and hides behind them.*

Trevor (*off*) Bloody hell . . .

Mary (*off*) Are you all right?

Trevor (*off*) 'Course I'm all right.

Mary (*off*) I'm relieved . . .

Trevor (*off*) Mary, Mum's at bingo!

Mary (*off*) I know . . .

Trevor (*off*) I can't open the door . . . I don't have a key.

Mary (*off*) I've got a key.

Trevor (*off*) Your key?

Mary (*off*) Your Mum's key . . .

Trevor (*off*) Mary . . .

Mary (*off*) Yes, love . . .

Trevor (*off*) Why don't you open the door?

Mary (*off*) All right.

The door is unlocked. **Trevor** *rushes in, surprised not to see* **Andy**. **Mary** *follows.*

Trevor Why did you knock?

Mary I was just makin' sure there weren't any burglars in . . .

Trevor Burglars!!!

Mary You can't be too careful . . . (*She looks around.*)

Trevor Mary, what are you doin'?

Mary Checking . . . just checking, love . . .

Trevor Where's Mum?

Mary At bingo. I left her there . . .

Trevor Is she coming home?

Mary Of course, love, she lives here.

Trevor Now?

Mary Pardon?

Trevor Mum – is she coming now?

Mary No . . . She's at the bingo.

Trevor Mary . . . (*Very, very slowly.*) You know this isn't your flat, don't you?

Mary Of course, love. You feeling all right, love, the excitement not getting to you . . .

Trevor No, it is not.

Mary And I always took you for such an intelligent boy. (*She sits.*) Would you get me a glass, I've got to take a couple of black and greens, for my nerves you know.

Trevor, *irritated, sighs, goes off to the kitchen.* **Mary** *sits, her back to the curtain.* **Andy** *steps out from behind the curtain.*

Andy Hello.

Mary, *frightened, grabs the Bacardi bottle swivels round and brandishes the bottle all in one move.*

Mary Don't yer come near, you'll get this in the flat of your face!

Andy Aunty Mary . . .

Mary (*frozen*) Oh . . .

Andy How's tricks?

Mary   Oh no, I don't do that any more . . .

Andy   I know. I mean, how are you?

Mary (*confused, looks towards kitchen*)   Trevor. . . ?

Andy   Andy . . .

Mary   Andy. . . ?

Trevor *enters with glass.*

Trevor   Aunty Mary . . .

Mary   Andy. . . ?

Trevor   No, he's Andy . . . I am Trevor.

Mary *turns her back to* **Andy**, *totally confused. She quickly takes the glass, unscrews the cap off the bottle, pours herself a glass, takes two black and greens, washes it down with the Bacardi, recovers her composure.*

Mary   I've never been able to tell you two apart. It's my glasses, you see, I've never been very good without my glasses.

Andy   You still haven't told us what you're doing here?

Mary   Andy . . . it's wonderful to see you. You're looking so well. Now you've got to be a good boy, you don't want to go back to prison again and give your mother all that worry . . . I know we all like to have a bit of fun when we're younger, think we know best, but we don't, it's not worth it and I should know. So you be a good boy, all right?

Trevor   Mary, why are you here?

Mary   Your mum sent me . . . It was her leg, you see, she didn't want to expose it to the cold . . . It's the break between sessions and she told me I could get here and back to the bingo much quicker than she can, she didn't want to miss the second session, you know . . .

Trevor   I give up . . . I give up . . .

Andy   What did she send you to do?

Mary   Check . . . check up?

Trevor   On what?

Mary   On you . . . the flat. Just to make sure everything's all right and that your father isn't here.

Trevor   Dad's not comin' here!

Mary   Is he not?

Trevor   No.

Mary (*to* **Andy**)   Your mother thought your brother had invited your father to the party . . .

Trevor   Well she's wrong.

Mary   Your mum will be pleased. It's all very exciting. I've been invited, did you know? Of course I'll only stay for the one drink, then I'll make myself scarce . . . You'll understand if I come in these clothes, I haven't got time to change. I'm so looking forward to it . . . It's such a long time since I've been to a party . . .

Andy   You used to go to loads of parties . . .

Mary   Times change, love . . .

Andy   Mary, you had it all – clothes, jewellery, houses, money in the bank. How the fuck did you let it go?

Mary (*holds up the Bacardi bottle*)   Once this starts hitting the back of your throat, nothing else matters. All you think about is where the next one is coming from. You don't care what you're like, where you are or who you're with. For a girl in my game, you can't afford to be like that. Every fucking thing went, everything I had worked so hard for, and I didn't notice, until one morning I woke up in hospital and no home to go to. That wasn't so bad . . . what really hurt was that I didn't have anything left to sell . . .

Andy   You should've got out while you were ahead . . . I'll never let that happen to me.

Trevor   Why didn't you go back home, to your family?

Mary   No, couldn't do that . . .

Trevor   But why?

Mary   Shame for the shame . . .

Trevor   That's the same bloody thing that Dad says . . . What kind of families is it you come from that won't forgive a few mistakes . . .

Mary   It's not them . . . it's us . . . we're the ones who feel the shame . . . because we knew better than all our families and friends we left behind . . . we were the big shots . . . going to conquer the big city . . . We really knew a lot, didn't we, look at us now . . . How can we go back? . . . Well I can't stand about here all day chatting, I've got to get back to bingo. Your mother'll be worrying about me and she's got enough to worry about . . .

Andy   We were just off . . .

Trevor   I'm stayin', Andy.

Andy   Please yourself.

Mary   But what about the party?

Andy   I'm coming back . . . See you about, Trev . . .

Trevor   Yeah, right . . .

Mary   Bye . . .

Andy *leaves.*

Mary   Makes you feel like weeping . . .

Trevor He'll be back . . . We want his arrival to be a complete surprise to Mum, you understand that.

Mary It will be, she hasn't seen him for over a year . . .

Trevor What I mean is that we don't want Mum to know he's been already. You won't say anythin'?

Mary To who?

Trevor To Mum . . . She mustn't know . . .

Mary Don't worry, son, I know how to keep my mouth shut. I'll keep mum. (*She giggles.*) Sorry. I'll tell your mother everything is all right and your father hasn't been . . .

Trevor Hasn't been and is not coming.

Mary Good . . . good . . .

Trevor *almost pushes* **Mary** *out of the door.*

Trevor (*off*) Leave the latch up . . . I might want to get some fags . . .

Mary (*off*) Shall I bring you some?

Trevor (*off*) No thank you, Mary. Bye, Mary!

Mary (*off*) Bye, love.

Trevor *re-enters, puts a record on: 'Hickory Hollers Tramp'. He sits at the table, takes a cigarette butt from the ashtray, lights it. Pours himself a very large Bacardi, no Coke. Downs it in one. Shivers. About to take another one when there's a loud firm knock at the door.* **Trevor** *places the glass on the table. As he gets up, he blows out the candles.*

Blackout.

Scene Two

Darkness. The overhead light is switched on. **Rose** *and* **Mary** *enter in coats, with handbags.* **Rose** *is tired; she yawns as she takes her coat off.* **Mary** *on the other hand is bubbling with excitement and surprised to find the room empty.*

Mary Oh. . . !

Rose Oh? Wha'd'you mean 'Oh'?

Mary Trevor . . . he must have gone for cigarettes.

Rose Bloody good job. We'll have a little bit of peace. (*She shouts.*) Trevor! (*She limps over to her bedroom door, tries the handle. Satisfied the door is still locked, she limps over to the living-room door.*) Now listen, Mare, not a word . . .

Mary You can trust me.

Rose (*at the living-room door, quick peep in the passage, calls*)   Trevor . . . (*She waits. No reply. She firmly closes the door.*) Not a word to anyone, d'you understand?

Mary   Not a dicky-bird, Rose.

Rose   No one . . . no one at all.

Mary   Right.

Rose   You got that, Mare?

Mary   Yes, Rose.

Rose   Not even the kids.

Mary   Rose, I know how to keep my mouth shut (*She winks.*)

Rose   Why are you winking?

Mary   I'm keeping mum. (*She starts giggling.*)

Rose   What's the bloody matter with you, Mare?

Mary   Nothin' . . . nothin'. (*She laughs.*)

Rose   Wha's so bloody funny?

Mary   Nothing, Rose, honest. (*Trying very hard and succeeding in keeping a straight face.*) I'm sorry, Rose . . . sorry.

Rose   You haven't been at the whisky?

Mary   No!

Rose   You know how you go all silly when you drink whisky . . .

Mary   I haven't been at the whisky, Rose. I swear.

Rose   It's bad enough you drinkin', never mind about mixin' your drinks . . .

Mary   I haven't had a drink for over an hour.

Rose   Then what were you doin' running backwards and forwards to the toilet during the second session?

Mary   Excitement, Rose, it's been a very exciting day and there's more to come . . .

Rose   Don't remind me . . .

Mary   What a day . . . Now you'll be able to pay off some of your debts . . .

Rose   Do what?

Mary   I said you'll be able to relieve yourself of some of your debts.

Rose   Don't be daft!

Mary   You won. Rose, you won!

Rose   Shudd up, Mary. I told you I don't want anyone to know.

Mary   There's nobody here yet . . .

Rose   Least of all my Trevor . . . otherwise I'll have 'im up here bumming off me . . .

Mary You'll treat him though?

Rose I'll treat him to the back of my hand.

Mary Rose.

Rose I'll buy little Trev a siren suit.

Mary I don't want to be funny, Rose, but don't you think little Trev's a bit old for a siren suit? I mean, I know mothers don't like to let go, but . . .

Rose Not him . . . little Trev . . . the baby . . .

Mary Isn't, you know, little Trev Trevor and your Trevor is big Trevor and the baby's baby Trevor?

Rose Big Trevor is not my Trevor, you should know that, Mary. My Trevor is middle Trevor, 'just Trevor', and little Trev is his son, my grandson, the baby: 'Little Trev'!

Mary Now I get you. It's little Trev, the baby, that you're getting the siren suit for.

Rose Exactly. I wouldn't give his bloody father anythin'. That boy is no good with money . . . he spends it.

Mary On what?

Rose How should I know? On somethin' bloody stupid, no doubt. I can't make the boy out.

Mary It's nice to have a bit of money about you. Two hundred and thirty pounds!

Rose I thought you said you could keep your mouth shut!

Mary (*hand to mouth*) I'm sorry, Rose.

Rose It's best kept quiet. Don't want the Social finding out, do we?

Mary No, Rose. (*Whispering.*) You were due for a change of luck . . .

Rose What? Can't hear yer?

Mary I said you was due a bit of luck . . .

Rose About bloody time.

Mary Your luck's changed in a big way, Rose.

Rose Don't make me laugh. Two hundred pound. Money doesn't go far these days. About all I can say is that I'll have enough for bingo tomorrow . . .

Mary Not only that, Rose, your son's free . . .

Rose Yeah, and now the worry starts . . . Where has he been, he's not here . . . he hasn't been all day. I mean he usually comes here first. I'll bet he's in some kind of trouble.

Mary Oh no, Rose, you don't have to worry about that. No, Rose, not at all.

Rose Don't I?

Mary He wouldn't get into trouble on his first day out . . .

Rose You don't know him like I do . . .

Mary No, he's all right. He'll be here.

Rose   What makes you so sure?

Mary   Who, me? I can feel in . . . in my bones . . . I just know it that strange kind of way. D'you wanna drink, Rose, cheer you up, eh?

Rose   Na, Mare, you have one.

Mary   (*after a pause*)   Not for me . . .

Rose   You don't want a drink – what's the matter, you sick?

Mary   No . . . I'm too excited.

Rose   Don't start all that again . . .

Mary   I want to keep a clear head. Got so much to remember, don't want my tongue loosened, do I.

Rose   What's going on, Mary?

Mary   Nothing, Rose . . . nothing. I just want to keep my mouth shut, that's all.

The sitting-room door slowly opens and a pale-looking **Trevor** *ambles in.*

Mary   (*knowingly*)   Been to get cigarettes then, love?

Trevor   No.

Mary   Oh.

Rose   Where the bloody hell have you been?

Trevor   In the toilet.

Rose   What the hell were you doing in there?

Trevor   Number two's. I'm sorry for using the toilet without your permission . . . but I knew you wouldn't appreciate me doing it on the carpet.

Rose   Don't be vulgar . . .

Trevor   I learnt it at one of the many children's homes I was in: number one is . . .

Rose   You been listening?

Trevor   To what?

Rose   Nothing.

Trevor   You have any luck?

Rose   Na . . . (*Nudges* **Mary**.)

Mary   Na . . .

Rose   Waiting on one number for a full house . . .

Mary   Eighty-nine . . .

Rose   What?

Mary   The number. For the full house.

Rose   Oh that . . . yes.

Mary (*winking furiously at* **Trevor**)   He . . . er, hasn't been then?

Trevor   Who?

Rose   You know damn well who she means . . .

Mary   Andy. . . ?

Trevor   Oh him, he's been and gone . . .

Mary   And is coming back. . . ?

Rose   What d'you mean been and gone.

Trevor   He came. He went.

Rose   He wouldn't go without seeing me.

Mary   No . . .

Trevor   He did . . .

Mary   I don't understand . . . Perhaps he is busy . . .

Rose   Too busy to see me . . .

Trevor   You were at bingo . . . wasn't she, Aunty Mary?

Mary   He'll be back . . .

Rose   He should've waited . . .

Trevor   What for?

Rose   I'm his mother.

Trevor   Oh yeah, I was forgettin'.

Rose   I haven't seen him in over a year . . .

Trevor   Is that his fault?

Rose   I didn't tell him to go to prison did I? Anyway, he always comes to see me . . .

Mary   Always . . .

Trevor   He did. You weren't here.

Rose   I was only at the bingo . . .

Mary   Just down the road . . .

Rose   You should've told him to wait.

Trevor Oh I see, it's my fault now, is it? If you wanted to see him so badly, you should've stayed in!

Rose I've been in all day . . .

Mary We've only been out to the bingo . . .

Trevor Morning, afternoon and night!

Rose So?

Trevor So you weren't in all day, were you?

Rose Mind your own bloody business . . . I don't live my life to suit you.

Trevor That's pretty obvious.

Rose Don't you start your backchat with me . . .

Trevor He left you some money . . .

Mary Oh Rose, this is your lucky day . . .

Rose *shoots her a look that could kill, as she gathers up the money and starts to count it.*

Trevor Lucky day . . .

Mary Well . . . you know . . . her son being released . . . him giving her some money . . . having her family around her . . .

Trevor What family . . .

Mary I'd say she was very lucky, but no luck at bingo though, eh Rose?

Rose No . . .

Mary Trevor, what's happening?

Trevor You tell me, Aunty Mary, you tell me . . .

Rose (*having finished counting the money*) Twenty pounds . . . he's a good boy.

Mary Looks after his mother well.

Rose (*to* **Trevor**) Which is more than I can say for you (*She stuffs the money into her bra.*)

Trevor Don't you care where he got it?

Rose 'Course I care, I don't want him getting into trouble . . . straight away . . .

Trevor Don't you think, by taking money he's probably stolen, you're encouraging him?

Rose Who the bloody hell d'you think you are – Perry Mason?

Trevor Well?

Rose No. I couldn't encourage him to do anything, he does as he pleases. If I don't take the money, he'll only throw it away on something silly . . .

Trevor Like bingo!

Rose You shut your mouth. I don't know what you're getting so high and mighty about. I've never seen you refusing money he's been dishing out.

Trevor I didn't want to hurt his feelings . . .

Rose A likely story . . . Always the fuckin' angel, aren't yer, tryin' to be the goody-goody . . . butter wouldn't melt in your gob, would it. I'll tell you somethin', if you weren't here, Andy would've stayed . . .

Mary I'm sure he's coming back, Rose . . .

Trevor Don't try and blame me . . . You don't look too upset that you've missed him.

Rose What do you want me to do? Cry? Pull my hair out? He'll be back.

Trevor He's changed . . .

Rose You don't know what you're talking about. How much can he change? He's still my son, I know him better than you. He'll be back!

Mary Of course he will. He loves his mum . . .

Trevor Does she love us?

Mary What a question . . .

Trevor (*to* **Rose**) Does she?

Rose (*after a pause*) 'Course I do . . . I'm your mother.

Mary There.

Trevor How much?

Rose How much what?

Trevor How much do you love us?

Rose Don't be s'daft . . .

Trevor I wanna know how much. . . ?

Rose As much as a mother should . . .

Trevor I've never felt it . . .

Mary I think I'd better be going . . .

Rose You stay, Mare . . .

Trevor I wanted to feel it, but if I'm honest . . . I'd have to say . . . I never have and never will.

Rose You soppy sod. How d'you want me to love you? With kisses, cuddles and pats on the bum? You're not a child any more . . .

Trevor You never had us when we were children!

Rose That's not my fault. I told you before . . . I tried . . .

Mary The things your mother had to put up with . . .

Trevor Like what?

Mary Those were hard times . . .

Trevor How hard?

Mary Trevor, is everything all right?

Trevor How hard?

Mary Because I don't understand . . .

Trevor How fucking hard?

Rose That's enough of your fucking language.

Mary She did make a home for you . . .

Trevor We were in children's homes for over twelve years. What sort of home is it that takes twelve years to make? A twenty-four-bedroomed mansion in the country? This is a poxy two-bedroomed flat in the East End of London . . . How hard did she try?

Mary It has got central heating . . .

Rose I did my best.

Trevor Your best didn't amount to very much, did it.

Rose I don't want to talk about it.

Trevor You never want to talk about it . . . but I do, and now!

Mary It's getting late and the cats are probably wondering . . . I really should be making my way home.

Rose You stay where you are.

Mary *stops in her tracks.*

Rose (*to* **Trevor**) You . . . you go, you go out into the courtyard, close the door behind you. Then you can chat till your heart's content.

Trevor I want to chat to you . . .

Rose I don't want to chat to you.

Trevor Tell me how hard it was, with your two children locked up in some children's home, while you danced round East London with every black man you laid your eyes on . . .

Mary It wasn't all fun . . . She missed you . . .

Trevor Did she now . . .

Mary She talked about you all the time . . .

Trevor Talk is cheap. Isn't that what you're always telling me, Mother?

Rose I'm not telling you anything.

Trevor Then Mary will, won't you Mare, 'cause I know all about you – had a bit of a reputation when my mum first came up from Cornwall . . .

Mary That was all a long time ago . . .

Rose You don't have to explain anythin' to him . . .

Trevor I don't want her . . . I want you to explain to me . . .

Rose It's none of your business.

Trevor Right. Mary?

Mary I don't really want to get involved.

Trevor You are involved. You've known her longer than I have.

Mary She's a friend . . . a good friend!

Trevor Have a good time, did yer, when Dad went inside and we went in homes . . . You and this good friend of yours over there have a good time . . .

Rose Shut your fucking mouth . . .

A car horn hoots. **Mary** *grabs her bag and makes for the door.*

Mary That'll be my cab . . .

Rose You didn't order a cab . . .

Mary Didn't I? . . . Well, I best go and check, hadn't I, and I must be going. I'm sorry, Rose, I've got to go. Bye.

Rose (*shouts*) Mary!!!

But **Mary** *has gone, the door slamming behind her.*

Trevor You never told me Aunty Mary was a prostitute.

Rose It's not the sort of thing you just come and say, is it.

Trevor You told Andy . . .

Rose He knows about those things.

Trevor And I don't? I am the oldest, Mum.

Pause.

Rose Haven't you got a home to go to?

Trevor Isn't this my home?

Rose This is my home.

Trevor The family home.

Rose My home, and you've no right comin' here and showing me up in front of my friends like that . . .

Trevor Haven't I?

Rose You ought to be ashamed of yourself talking like that.

Trevor I don't bloody care.

Rose Well I bloody do . . . this is my home . . . you've got no . . . Listen . . . I'm tired . . . I'm going to bed . . . you go home and do the same . . .

Trevor I'm not tired . . .

Rose Go home and wake your wife up, then . . . I've got to be up early in the morning . . .

Trevor Bingo. That's all you've got to get up for.

Rose Don't be so bloody cheeky.

Trevor It's a fact. You're a bingo junkie.

Rose I've had enough of you. I'm sick and tired of the sound of your voice . . . just go home . . . get out . . . (*Pause.*) Did you hear what I said?

Trevor Yeah.

Rose Well?

Trevor What?

Rose You trying to be funny?

Trevor You see me laughing?

Rose I want you out of my house . . .

Trevor This isn't a house, it's a flat.

Rose I don't care what you want to bloody call it, it's mine and I want you out.

Trevor (*standing up*) I'm not going.

Rose Don't you stand up to me, my lad . . . You ever raise your hand to me and that'll be your lot, my boy.

Trevor What you goin' to do? I'm a bit too big for you to belt with the strap . . .

Rose I'll . . . I'll do something . . .

Trevor Like what?

Rose I'll call the police . . .

Trevor You'd call the police for your own son?

Rose They'll get you out . . .

Trevor You can always rely on them, can't you, Mum.

Rose I want some peace . . . Why don't you go home?

Trevor Why were we in children's homes all that time?

Rose Ask your father . . .

Trevor I did, this evening, while you were at bingo . . .

Rose Your father came here?

Trevor That's right.

Rose You little . . .

Trevor It's all right, you don't have to panic, he didn't come in. He wouldn't, you see . . . Andy had already gone. He didn't want to see you if Andy wasn't around . . .

Rose I didn't want to fucking see him.

Trevor Well the feeling was mutual, Mum. Anyway, he said that he wanted to have us . . .

Rose He couldn't have had you, he'd been to prison . . .

Trevor Not for twelve years . . .

Rose He wasn't fit to be a . . .

Trevor Why do I get this feeling that you never fuckin' cared?

Rose Don't you swear at me . . .

Trevor Why?

Rose Care . . . what do you know? (*Almost spitting it out.*) You don't know nothing!!! With your council flats and Social Security . . . You try living in one room . . . You try getting money out of the N.A.B., while all the while they're looking down their noses at you because you've got a couple of darkie children . . . All that African talk and nonsense . . . He had some African woman I'd never seen before come in and look at your feet the day you was born, to check that you was his. This black woman lifting you up by the feet and I wasn't allowed to say a word. All of that might be all right in Africa . . . but I ain't no African woman . . . Care . . . I cared so fucking much it hurt . . . Nappies boiling in a bucket on the stove . . . Andy crying his head off . . . you wandering around with a box of matches . . . the electric meter going off and not having a poxy shilling . . . a poxy shilling . . . Couldn't heat the place . . . I couldn't heat the bottles . . . Drained the nappies, damp as they were, put 'em in a bag, your siren suit, everything . . . bunged you two in the pram and I was off . . . to Cornwall I thought . . . but the rain soon woke me up . . . I just knew I couldn't cope . . .

Trevor Big strong Rose couldn't cope?

Rose That's right. I learnt my lesson there and then. Never again would I rely on anythin' from black fucking bastard men.

Trevor (*pause*) I'm a black bastard, Mum.

Rose No you're not, you're half white . . .

Trevor I'm black. Black. D'you understand?

Rose   You're not. I'm your mother and I'm telling you . . .

Trevor   You can't tell me what I am. I know what I am and I'm proud of it.

Rose   You're full of shit.

Trevor   You and me both, Mum. (*He walks towards the door.*)

Rose   Where d'you think you're going?

Trevor   Home.

Rose   I haven't finished with you yet . . .

Trevor   Oh yes you have . . . Bye, Mum. (*He goes out of the living-room door, closing it behind him.*)

Rose   Go on then, piss off . . . None of you are any good. (*Shouts and takes bundle of money from her bra.*) Trevor . . .

The door slams. In a fit of temper **Rose** *takes a bundle of money and throws it. It scatters around the room. Pause. She bends down to pick it up.*

Rose   Ouchh . . . Fuckin' leg.

Lights fade to blackout.

Scrape off the Black

Scrape off the Black was the second play I wrote. It was inspired by David Storey's play *In Celebration*, which was filmed for the American Film Theatre in 1974. I was lucky enough to work as Assistant to the Director, Lindsay Anderson, to whom I shall be for ever grateful for his kindness and encouragement.

I have been asked many times what the title means – all I am prepared to say is that it refers to a slice of burnt toast!

Tunde Ikoli
London, 1994

Tunde Ikoli has been writing plays for twenty years. His work has been produced at the Royal Court, National Theatre, Riverside Studios, Birmingham Rep, Nottingham Playhouse, West Yorkshire Playhouse, The Bush, The Tricycle and the Theatre Royal Stratford East, where he is at present Associate Writer.

Tunde Ikoli has written and directed three films: *Tunde's Film*, *Elphida* and *Smack and Thistle*. Tunde is at present heavily involved in developing young writers in East End schools through the Theatre Royal Stratford East's Education Department.

Talking in Tongues

Winsome Pinnock

Talking in Tongues was premièred at the Royal Court, Theatre Upstairs on 28 August 1991, with the following cast:

Sugar	Cecilia Noble
Leela	Joanne Campbell
Claudette	Pamela Nomvete
Curly	Cecilia Noble
Jeff	Neil Dudgeon
Bentley	Nicholas Monu
Fran	Lizzie McInnerny
Irma	Ella Wilder
Mikie	Nicholas Monu
Kate	Lizzie McInnerny
David	Neil Dudgeon
Diamond	Ella Wilder

Director Hettie Macdonald
Decor Ian McNeil
Lighting Johanna Town
Sound Bryan Bowen

Irma can be played by either a male or female performer.

Prologue

Very bright light. **Leela** *is lying on her tummy on a towel while* **Sugar** *crouches over her.* **Sugar** *pours ointment on to her hands, rubs them together, then starts to massage* **Leela**'s *back.*

Sugar Them used to say them was going down a gully fe go wash clothes, but the way them women leave dragging themself like them have rock tie to them foot, then come back skipping like children make everybody suspec' them have some business a gully that have nothing to do with dirty washing. Sometimes them man would try to follow back a dem, but they would only reach so far before something bad happen: one a them get lost in a bush, grow round him while he was walking; another man get bite up by a snake and haffe quick hop home and bind up him foot, an' a nex' one suck up inna hurricane lie dizzy ina bed for a week. No man ever find them.

There were three of them: Jo-Jo, a big, mighty woman who everybody used to say batter her husband; Dum-Dum, a woman who never speak; and Mary, a good, gentle woman who would give you her last penny even if she was starving. These women were a mystery to me. Every day them like every other woman, cooking and cleaning for them husband, except this one afternoon when them bundle up them clothes and go off by themself. I couldn't wait to grow up to discover the mystery of womanness for meself. I used to sit and stare at them to see if I could see it on them, but I couldn't. So one day I follow them. I was nine years old.

I wait for them to leave, pretending like I wasn't taking any notice a them, then after a few minutes I went after them. Me have to run hard to keep up with them. It look like they was walking slowly, them hip a swing from side to side under them frock, but they was moving further and further away from me, so I run as fast as my little leg would go and still they would be ahead of me. Then they come to a gully I never see before – a huge waterfall falling over great white rock. I hide meself behind a rockstone and watch.

Them take them clothes out a the basket and start to wash them in the water, slapping them against rock, then rub them under the water and slap them against rock, lie them out to dry in the sun. Then they start again, slap clothes against rock, rinse them under running water and lie them out to dry. Slap, rinse, slap slap, rinse dry. Them never say anything to one another, never even look at one another, for musse half an hour or more.

I was so disappointed I could cry. I thought I was going to see a woman fly. I thought woman was a mystery – click her fingers and fire would fly out – but woman was just washing clothes. Woman was washing clothes then going home and cooking food for man. I had tears in my eyes. Me ready fe run till one a them start to hum. It seem like everything stop and listen to that humming, the breeze still, the water hush up. Then the other women join in, singing together like in one voice. You couldn't move when you hear them singing. Then them start to sway. Dum-Dum, the silent woman, was in the middle, she start to sway and rise up on her toes like there was something inside her, pulling her up. The other women start to sway too and rise up, and I tell you I see the spirit rise in them women. Them start to tremble and make little jump till they was jumping around like them didn't know where them was. Then all of a sudden the silent woman stand very still like her body seize up and lift her head to the sky and start to call out. She was shouting – a woman I never hear say a word in my life – was shouting to the sky loud loud and saying words very fast in a language you never hear before. A woman who couldn't even talk, filling the sky with words in a language must be not spoken in a million years, a language that go back before race. She lift her fist and strike out one more time. After, she collapse, but the other women catch her before she fall. She just lie there, like she sleeping, and the other women finish washing her clothes for her. When she wake up they give her something to drink and they all go home like nothing happen. I always wonder what madness them release when they shout out like that. (*Slight pause.*) But all that finish now, them women dead off long time. Me, I just go walk down by the beach, lift weight, jog, take aerobic exercise. No need now to go down to gully, eh?

Act One

This entire act takes place in London. Throughout the act there is the constant sound of party music.

Scene One

A house in London. A room with lots of coats in it. **Claudette**, *a young black woman, enters. She's hurt her foot. She sits down and takes her shoes and tights off, examines her foot.* **Curly** *enters.*

Curly Why did you run off like that?

Claudette My foot.

Curly I thought there was something wrong with you.

Claudette There is. He trod on my toe. He's crushed it. It's hanging off on its cord, look.

Curly Calm down and let Curly have a look at it. It can't be that bad.

Claudette Trust me to get caught in the stampede . . .

Curly A man stands on your toe –

Claudette One minute I see all their heads turn toward me, next thing I know I'm flat on my back with footmarks all over me.

Curly It was an accident.

Claudette It's always the same when a white woman comes in the room.

Curly Don't start, Claudette.

Claudette Our men are straining at the leash like hunting dogs on the scent of the fox. Ow. Careful.

Curly There's only two black men here. That's hardly a pack of hounds, is it? Anyway, Bentley's a good bloke.

Claudette Why do you think they invited us here? Do you think it's to get the party going? We're supposed to be good for a party, aren't we?

Curly Leela invited us.

Claudette So why did they invite Leela?

Curly Because they're friends of Bentley's.

Claudette Hours we've been here and we're the only ones dancing.

Curly The fun won't start till after midnight, then you'll think you're in a madhouse.

Claudette It takes these people a long time to warm up.

Curly Stop complaining. Least you got asked to dance.

Claudette   While he's dancing with me he's looking over my shoulder at her. I might as well be a burst blow-up rubber doll he's dragging around.

Curly   We can always dance with each other.

Claudette   What is it with our men?

Curly   I read a good book about it. I'll lend it to you.

Claudette   I don't give a toss about the science of it. What I want to know is where the next fuck's coming from.

Curly   Sit still or this'll hurt.

Claudette   Careful. One man told me he thought black women were too aggressive.

Curly   I'm not aggressive.

Claudette   Aggressive my arse. Pride. That's what it is.

Curly   People do sometimes fall in love, Claudette.

Claudette   What do they feel when they're holding her? Have you watched their faces when they're holding a white woman? They look as though they're in a seventh heaven. Makes you feel like the invisible woman. It's not as if you can escape from it. She's everywhere you go. And every blown-up picture of her diminishes us.

Curly   For God's sake, Claudette, sit still.

Claudette   It's not as if they want to be your friend. The only time one of them wants your friendship is when she's trying to get her hands on one of our men, and once she's done that they're both off without a backward glance: she never rated us in the first place and he doesn't want to be reminded of the detritus he left behind on his way to the top.

Curly   Stand up.

Claudette *stands.*

Curly   Does it still hurt?

Claudette *practises putting weight on the injured foot.*

Curly   Can you walk on it?

Claudette *walks up and down.*

Claudette   What I really hate is the way they have to get off the tube before you do, as though you were some maid following on behind. Or they'll sit beside you brushing their hair out like Rapunzel, thinking they're making you jealous. Many's the time I've missed my stop because I've had my mouth full of some white woman's hair.

Curly   We're supposed to be welcoming in the New Year, not griping about the one just gone.

Claudette   Touchy.

Curly It's the same old record, Claudette, every time we meet. I don't blame Leela for not coming out with us any more.

Claudette What's she been saying?

Curly Nothing.

Claudette She's been talking to you about me.

Curly I told you. She hasn't said a word. (*Slight pause.*) I used to like Friday nights. It was fun, wasn't it? Giggling at the pictures, getting drunk and having a good bitch. I haven't had a good bitch for ages. Why don't we start Friday nights again?

Claudette Friday nights have been cancelled due to lack of interest. Times I've left messages and neither you or Leela got back to me. God knows what you've been up to, and as for Leela, well you only have to look in her eyes to see she's too far gone for intelligent conversation.

Curly I'm happy for her.

Claudette So am I. I'm also just a bit concerned. Did you see the look in Bentley's eye when he caught sight of the living Barbie doll?

Curly Leave them alone, Claudette. They're doing all right.

Claudette She's flying high as a kite all right. Basking in this aura of cosy coupleness. She hasn't got time for us any more.

Curly You two used to be such good friends.

Claudette If you've been single more than six months, coupled women shun you, as though singleness were some kind of curse.

Curly You'd be the same. I know I would.

Claudette She's high on love all right. I want to be there when she comes crashing down.

Curly You sound as though you might enjoy it.

Claudette I didn't mean it like that.

Curly I wonder about you sometimes. I can't see why you have to be so angry all the time.

Claudette But then you wouldn't, would you?

Curly What does that mean?

Claudette Nothing.

Curly Starting on me now, are you?

Claudette Should I start on you?

Curly What gives you the right to tell people how to live?

Claudette When did I tell anyone how to live?

Curly (*referring to* **Claudette**'s *foot*)   That should be all right now, as long as you don't stand in the way of any rampant male egos. (*Starts to go.*)

Claudette   Where you going, Curly?

Curly   I fancy a dance and a drink.

Claudette   You know how you get after a few drinks.

Curly   What's wrong with forgetting myself for a while?

Claudette   Me, I don't want to forget, I want to remember.

Curly   See you outside then.

Claudette   What's up, Curly?

Curly   Nothing.

Claudette   I've known you long enough to know when something's wrong. Why don't you tell your Auntie Claudette?

Curly   I can't.

Claudette   I'm not such a heartless bitch, am I? Come on, Curls, you know how I feel about my friends. Is it that white guy?

Curly (*nods*)   It finished. (*Slight pause.*) It was just one of those things. Happens to everyone, doesn't it? It was nobody's fault. I mean, we got on well enough. We got on really well. He even took me to meet his parents.

Claudette   He must have liked you, Curls, if he took you to meet his parents.

Curly   Nice people. Very simple life, you know the type. Nice. When we got there, they'd bought me a present. They'd bought me this expensive make-up set. Mirror, brushes, eye-shadows, lipstick, the lot.

Claudette   You don't wear it much, do you?

Curly   Just as well because it was the English rose collection, wasn't it? English rose they were expecting.

Claudette   Guess who's coming to dinner.

Curly   We're all just standing there. He's saying nothing. They're saying nothing. I'm holding the English rose collection, not knowing whether to laugh or cry. Then we had dinner. (*Slight pause.*) You're thinking it serves me right, aren't you? You're thinking I'm always setting myself up to get hurt like this.

Claudette   It's not your fault, Curls.

Curly   You've got to keep trying, haven't you? Why didn't he tell them?

Claudette   You're too good for him.

Curly   It wouldn't have happened to you.

Claudette   Fuck that. Let's dance. I thought we were supposed to be welcoming in the New Year, not whingeing about the old one. Come on, Curls, my feet are itching.

Curly *stands*.

Claudette   Teach them how to dance, eh?

They go.

Scene Two

Jeff *and* **Bentley** *are in the room.* **Jeff** *is holding a bottle and two glasses.*

Jeff (*filling glasses*)   That is what you call a well-cut suit, Bentley.

Bentley   Come on, Jeff.

Jeff   Bet your shoes are Italian, handmade.

Bentley   Come on, man, stop taking the piss.

Jeff   I'll bet you've brought your portable phone with you. Just in case.

Bentley   You've got the wrong man, Jeff. I know when to stop working.

Jeff   Success suits you. That your car outside?

Bentley   Which car?

Jeff   You did drive here, right? Very nice. BMW. When I saw it parked outside I knew straight off it was yours. You've got style, Bentley.

Bentley   What you talking about, style? I don't even know cars. A car's a car to me. I drive a Ford Scorpio. We took a taxi.

Jeff (*raises his glass*)   To Bentley. Congratulations and continued success.

Bentley   Thanks, Jeff.

Jeff   I'm proud of you. When we were at college you said you'd be a partner by the time you were thirty-five.

Bentley   Did I?

Jeff   But then you always had drive.

Bentley   You've got drive.

Jeff   Oh, yes? Who was always being chased up for his essays? Who never attended lectures if he could help it? Nothing's changed, only now I'm not as actively lazy, things just sort of wash over me these days.

Bentley   Don't put yourself down. You always put yourself down.

Jeff   Now you, you worked your arse off for that partnership.

Bentley   Ignorance. If I'd known what hard work it was I'd never have bothered.

Jeff That's what I'm saying. You always had that fight in you. What fight I ever had is gone now, vanished. (*He fills their glasses again.*)

Bentley About that letter . . .

Jeff It's all right about the letter, honest.

Bentley I meant to bring it with me tonight, but we were running late and it went right out of my head.

Jeff I don't need it right this minute, do I? It can wait.

Bentley First thing Monday morning I'll get my secretary to type something up and get it posted.

Jeff That's brilliant. I got Richard to write a reference for me as well.

Bentley How is Richard?

Jeff He's got kids.

Bentley Yeah?

Jeff Two.

Bentley Kids, eh?

Jeff I've got to move on, Bentley. I'm stuck where I am now. I said I was lazy. I'm not lazy.

Bentley That's what I said.

Jeff But my boss, now she's got drive – but she gives me far too much to do. By the end of the day I'm so stressed I can't move. Somehow, God knows how, I manage to get myself home, but I spend the rest of the night in front of the TV. I can barely get up to go to bed. Ask Fran.

Bentley It gets you like that sometimes.

Jeff You get like that?

Bentley We all do.

Jeff I thought it was just me.

Bentley It's normal.

Jeff We're thinking about leaving London.

Bentley Are you?

Jeff Well, I am. Fran won't leave without a fight. She loves it, she's happy with her work, but I can't breathe here. I don't feel at home. Of course it's home, I was born here, but it doesn't feel like a home, more like a place you rest at overnight on your way to somewhere else.

Bentley It's something you've got to think about carefully. You might end up feeling even more stuck than you are now.

Jeff I know you're right, but what else can I do? We want kids. I do. I don't want them to grow up here.

Bentley I'm sorry you're feeling down.

Jeff Forget it, it's nothing.

Pause. The record changes.

Jeff Do you remember this?

Bentley (*trying to remember*) A blonde.

Jeff *shakes his head.*

Bentley Dark hair. Of course I remember.

Jeff Ginger hair.

Bentley Oh yes, yes.

Slight pause. They both laugh.

Jeff Sometimes I think about when we were at college, don't you?

Bentley Hardly at all, life moves on, Jeff.

Jeff Just sometimes, because it was – we were free then, weren't we?

Bentley Yes, I suppose we were. Can you still dance to this?

Jeff Ginger bush.

They both laugh. **Leela** *and* **Fran** *enter.*

Leela Here they are. They're in here.

Fran There you are. We thought you'd gone off. What are you laughing at? I don't trust it when men are laughing alone together. It's bound to be some woman they're making fun of. It'd better not be me, that's all.

Jeff We were talking.

Leela About old times.

Fran You get that as well, do you? It's all he ever talks about.

Jeff What's wrong with talking about the past?

Bentley Best years of your life.

Jeff We were a team.

Bentley The two-tone twins.

Leela The what?

Bentley We used to tell women that we were unidentical twins, one of us a throwback baby.

Fran Which one?

Jeff Worked every time.

Bentley The novelty, you see.

Leela You men are such deceivers.

Fran I don't think I'd have been taken in by it. Would you?

Leela I don't know.

Jeff Come on. Twins? Every woman's dream.

Fran It's not like that for women.

Jeff What? Not even the novelty value?

Fran I tell you, it's different for women. Sex is different.

Jeff *snores loudly.*

Leela I'm not sure I believe they really thought you were twins.

Bentley They wanted to believe us because –

Jeff They wanted to have sex with the two-tone twins.

Fran I don't think I want to hear any more of this. Come on, we need you two outside. They've all stopped dancing again. Why don't you get out there and get the thing going again?

Jeff Why don't you get them going? I can't dance.

Fran I thought you were always going to discos when you were at college.

Jeff That was different.

Fran Why?

Bentley We were kids.

Fran And now you're stodgy old men.

Bentley Not exactly.

Fran Looks like it's down to you and me, Leela.

Leela I don't want to. I mean, I can't.

Fran I'll bet that's not true. I'll bet you're a great dancer, isn't she, Bentley?

Bentley She's all right. You dance all right.

Fran See.

Leela Honestly. I'm not very good. I bump into people. It takes all my effort to keep myself upright.

Fran I don't believe you.

Jeff They don't want to dance, Fran. She's so bossy, she thinks everyone should do what she wants.

Fran I love dancing. I love letting go and forgetting myself, don't you?

Leela I never forget my body. That's the trouble.

Jeff Why don't you just go in and dance?

Fran On my own?

Bentley Can't you dance on your own?

Jeff Fran believes in people dancing together. She's romantic that way.

Fran What's wrong with people dancing together properly? People don't dance together any more and when they do it's always this sex thing. I'd like to have been around in the tea dance era when you had to know all the different steps. Don't you think it would be a good thing to know all the rules of the dance? It would be a sexual thing, of course, dancing close to each other and everything, but then the music would end and there'd be no mess, no emotional complication or guilt, just on to the next dance.

Jeff Do us a favour, Bentley – dance with her.

Bentley I'd love to dance with you.

Jeff There you go.

Bentley Later on.

Fran Oh.

Leela Why don't you dance with her?

Bentley I don't feel like it just now.

Fran Well, that's put me in my place, hasn't it?

Jeff I remember you liked dancing at college.

Fran He doesn't want to dance. No one wants to dance. Fine. I think I'll go and get myself another drink.

Jeff Fran –

Fran I'm trying to make things good and all you can do is just stand there and leave everything to me. As per usual. You're not even trying. It wasn't my idea to have a stupid fucking party in the first place. (*She goes.*)

Bentley Did I upset her?

Leela She seemed upset.

Bentley I wouldn't want to upset her.

Jeff I better get out there. She's right. What's the point in having a party if everyone goes off for chats in other rooms. Let's all go, shall we? All you have to do is shake one leg then shake the other and you're dancing, aren't you? (*He goes.*)

Leela Why don't you dance with her?

Bentley I don't want to dance.

Leela You like to dance.

Bentley I said I don't feel like it.

Leela You're always telling me to relax and enjoy myself.

Bentley I am enjoying myself.

Leela Does she frighten you?

Bentley Why would she frighten me?

Leela Women like that frighten me. They're a strange couple.

Bentley How, strange?

Leela They don't hide anything. Don't you think they're strange?

Bentley No.

Leela I can't imagine you being friends with him.

Bentley We were good friends.

Leela Still, people change. What time shall we leave?

Bentley We only just got here.

Leela It looks as though it's going to be one of those parties. We could go on somewhere else.

Bentley You brought your friends with you, you can't just abandon them. At least stay till midnight.

Leela I don't feel very well, flu or something. It's the weather, the way it keeps changing. It's a kind of phobia, my fear of parties, like claustrophobia. I'd love to be able to enjoy myself like other people. But I just get nervous. When I'm in a room and I don't know anyone . . . even my friends seem like strangers.

Bentley (*gentle*) We'll leave just after midnight.

Leela All right.

Bentley So let's go out and shake a leg.

Leela I wanted to ask you something.

Bentley What?

Slight pause.

Leela Nothing.

Bentley Okay.

Leela All of a sudden I feel like dancing.

Bentley Fran'll be pleased.

Leela Yes, she will, won't she?

Scene Three

Leela, **Claudette** *and* **Curly** *are hiding under coats.*

Curly We'll miss the countdown.

Claudette Who cares? This party is so dry. I can't stand the thought of watching those people trying to enjoy themselves.

Curly We should have brought a bottle up with us. I'll go and get a bottle, shall I? You've got to toast the New Year in, haven't you?

Leela I've never liked parties. People get so desperate at parties, don't they?

Curly You like parties. We used to go to a party every Saturday when we were younger.

Leela I never liked those either. I only went because there was nothing else to do. What else do you do on a Saturday night when you're sixteen?

Curly I thought you enjoyed them. We were the bees knees, weren't we? I loved getting dolled up, trotting around on high heels – we wore high heels!

Leela Getting stuck with your nose up the armpit of some bloke you never fancied.

Claudette Or doing something stupid like this just so that you had something to tell your mates on Monday morning.

Curly I'll get those drinks, shall I?

Leela We don't need drinks.

Curly It's bad luck to be without a drink when the clock strikes twelve. What do you fancy? I don't suppose we'll have much choice, anyway. I'll just get what I can find.

Claudette Don't let anyone see you coming up, Curls. Before you know it they'll be up here getting us to join them in the bloody conga.

Curly *goes.*

Claudette What a lot of coats. I'll dream coats. (*Picks one up, tries it on.*) Suit me?

Leela It's not your colour.

Claudette How much do you think a coat like this costs?

Leela Enough.

Claudette You and Bentley know some smart people.

Leela Take it off, Claudette.

Claudette I think I'll keep it on. It suits me.

Leela Do what you like.

Claudette   You can't slouch in a coat like this. You've got to walk upright, haven't you? Did you have a nice Christmas?

Leela   All right. You?

Claudette   What did you do?

Leela   We stayed at home.

Claudette   Just the two of you?

Leela   We wanted it quiet.

Claudette   That's nice. Exchanged presents in the morning?

Leela   Yes.

Claudette   What did he get you?

Leela   I can't remember.

Claudette   It was only last week.

Leela   A chain – a necklace, some perfume.

Claudette   What kind of perfume?

Leela   Claudette –

Claudette   I tried to get in touch with you, left messages on your answering machine.

Leela   Yes, thanks, it was good to hear from you. The song 'Jingle Bells'' – it made me laugh.

Claudette   I thought you might ring me back.

Leela   I meant to. I was busy. I write the message down on a bit of paper and it gets lost.

Claudette   Things have been happening. I needed to talk.

Leela   I'm here now.

Claudette   It passed.

Leela   People have to get on with their lives.

Claudette   Their men.

Leela   I don't have to apologise, Claudette.

Claudette   I was always around for you.

Leela   Curly lives near you.

Claudette   Curly doesn't know me. You know me inside out.

Pause. They hear the countdown to the New Year, then cheers, whistles and people singing.

Claudette   Watching's becoming a habit with me. I can't walk down a street at night without stopping to look through someone's window. I'm becoming obsessed. Honestly, I don't care whether they're in there or not. I stop in the middle of the road to listen to couples quarrelling and listen in on people's conversations in restaurants. The other day I was listening to this couple arguing about whether she ought to go away or not. I must have been staring at them without realising it. He turns to me and says 'Do you mind?' It's becoming embarrassing.

Leela Poor Claudette.

Claudette I can cope.

There's a knock on the door. **Claudette** *puts her fingers to her lips. They both sit still.*

Curly (*off*) Quick, it's me. Curly.

Claudette *goes to the door and lets* **Curly** *in, helping her with bottles and cups.*

Curly They're going mad down there. Streamers everywhere. I got caught up in the conga. Did I miss anything?

Claudette You didn't miss anything.

Leela We were talking about Christmas.

Curly I'd rather put Christmas behind me, wouldn't you? All I could find was Babycham.

Claudette Which cheapskate brought Babycham to a party?

Curly We used to have a lot of laughs, though, didn't we? We were always giggling, remember? We didn't even need a reason, just laughed for the sake of laughing. I reckon we should all make a New Year's resolution to see more of each other.

Claudette I'm all for that.

Leela Me too.

Curly Let's drink to it.

They raise their cups. There's the sound of someone approaching.

Man (*off*) I don't understand what's wrong with you.

Woman (*off, bitter laugh*) You wouldn't, would you?

Claudette Under the coats.

They hide under the coats.

Curly It's just like being back at school.

Leela *and* **Claudette** Sssh.

Silence. **Fran** *and* **Bentley** *enter.* **Bentley** *tries to hold* **Fran**, *but she moves away and locks the door.*

Fran I can see why you chose her. She has a certain charm, a certain passive charm.

Bentley Come on, Fran.

Fran Though I'd always pictured you with someone a bit more dynamic. A real go-getter. Like you.

Bentley *tries to take her hand. She pulls it away.*

Fran No. (*Slight pause.*) Do you want to end it?

Bentley Why would I want to end it?

Fran You might be bored.

Bentley No. Are you?

Fran What do you think?

Bentley *kisses* **Fran**. *They lie on the floor.* **Fran** *traces her finger along* **Bentley***'s face. He strokes her shoulders, removes her panties. They make love. It's tender, noiseless, furtive. They look at each other all the time. Afterwards, they lie still. Then* **Fran** *sits up on her elbows.* **Bentley** *stands, adjusting his clothes.*

Bentley Happy New Year.

They laugh.

Fran Close your eyes.

Bentley What for?

Fran Go on. Don't you trust me?

Bentley *closes his eyes. A moment passes.* **Bentley** *opens his eyes again.*

Bentley What?

Fran I just wanted to look at you.

Bentley Crazy woman. (*He kisses* **Fran***'s cheek.*)

Fran Let's make love again.

Bentley What if someone comes in?

Fran Good. Let them come in.

Bentley Crazy.

Fran She's your guilty conscience, isn't she?

Bentley What?

Fran This is hardly politically correct, is it?

Bentley Come on. Let's get dressed.

Fran I am dressed. Is it?

Bentley Politics doesn't come into it.

Fran Politics comes into everything.

Bentley Even fucking?

Fran Especially fucking.

Bentley Get dressed.

Fran I agree politics shouldn't come into it. Whatever happened to *amor omnia vincit* and all that stuff?

Bentley What do you want me to do?

Fran A little honesty would be nice.

Bentley I'm always straight with you.

Fran I'd leave Jeff tomorrow, you know that. We're finished anyway.

Bentley It's not that easy, Fran. You know that.

Fran Tell me, do all black men let their heads rule their hearts?

Bentley Every evening she comes home she needs to talk. I mean really talk. She never does, though. She just potters around, makes pleasant conversation: 'had a nice day at the office dear?' Underneath it all you can hear this, like a grating sound, you can hear what she really wants to say struggling to get out. But she won't let it out.

Fran Let what out?

Bentley You wouldn't understand.

Fran I see. It's a black thing.

Bentley No. (*Slight pause.*) Yes. She's fighting to make something of herself. I know how hard that is even though I do believe that it's up to the individual to rise above all the shit. That's all that matters. Work hard and you can achieve anything. You're judged by what you do these days, aren't you? Not that she doesn't work hard. Do a good job and no one can touch you. (*Slight pause.*) So the small talk goes on and on. Worse thing is you stop listening and she knows you've stopped listening and she can't help resenting that. So there's that between you. Sometimes you – I can't bring myself to look at her, say I've got a lot of work to do. So it gets worse. You can't rest. You're so busy trying . . . to cope with it, deal with it. To be decent. You can't rest. I owe it to her . . . find the right time . . . explain . . . or . . . (*He shrugs hopelessly.*)

Fran (*rolls over on to her tummy*) I don't want to make trouble, but I don't want to be hemmed in. I want to be free. I think people should be free.

Bentley (*takes her hands, pulls her up*) And we will be. Soon.

They go. After a short while **Leela**, **Claudette** *and* **Curly** *come out from underneath the coats. Silence.*

Curly Sorry, Leela.

Leela What for? It's not your fault.

Claudette The bastard.

Curly Claudette.

Claudette Fucking bastard.

Claudette What do you want us to do?

Leela I want us to go downstairs, that's all.

Claudette Let's go downstairs then.

Leela I'll follow you down.

Claudette We'll wait for you.

Slight pause. **Curly** *nudges* **Claudette**.

Claudette All right.

Curly *and* **Claudette** *go.*

Scene Four

Later. **Curly** *and* **Jeff** *are in the room, getting dressed.*

Curly Of course, I knew the minute I set eyes on them together. It takes an outsider, doesn't it? It could have gone on for years and you and Leela wouldn't have guessed. It was watching them dance together that confirmed it. You could see it even in the dark. They fit together perfectly. None of the usual little bumps and knocks that embarrass people dancing together for the first time. And the way they didn't make small talk, not even look at each other, as though they'd give something away if they did. Elementary, my dear Watson. It won't last.

Jeff *yawns.*

Curly Tired? I'm not surprised. You're a bad boy. And to think they used to kill the bearer of bad news.

Jeff You've got a good body.

Curly What?

Jeff Your body, it's . . .

Curly I suppose they had to. To restore the balance of power. It was bad enough that the messenger knew all his master's secrets, but can you imagine him struggling to keep a straight face as he told his tale? Overstepping the mark. Aren't you getting dressed?

Jeff I am dressed.

Curly You'd look a picture if anyone were to burst in here, wouldn't you?

Jeff *stands up and tucks his shirt in.* **Curly** *takes out a small eye-shadow box and applies make-up.*

Jeff You don't need that. You've got a lovely face.

Curly I don't usually bother but, well, it's a party, isn't it? I suppose we'd better get out of here, hadn't we?

Jeff What about the wine? Let's have some wine.

Curly I don't feel like it. (*Slight pause.*) You have some. (*Puts eye-shadow away.*) I'll see you downstairs then.

Jeff *holds* **Curly** *by the shoulders, then strokes her face, her hair.*

Jeff Why did you tell me?

Curly Don't you want to know?

Jeff No.

Curly You should know the truth.

Jeff Why?

Curly If you don't know what's going on, you're living in a fantasy, aren't you? Perhaps you'd prefer that.

Jeff Perhaps I would. (*Gulps wine.*)

Curly Steady.

Jeff Why did you tell me?

Curly Because I thought you should know.

Jeff Why?

Curly You'd have found out sooner or later, bumped into them in the street or something.

Jeff I wouldn't have let them see me.

Curly You are in a bad way. But that's life, isn't it? It happens. You shouldn't take it so hard. These days lots of people I know have open relationships.

Jeff Do you remember that perfume ad where the woman's running through the street at night?

Curly Which perfume ad?

Jeff It's very striking. There aren't any words. Just this image of a woman running. She just keeps running but doesn't arrive anywhere.

Curly They're like art films these days.

Jeff You're left wondering what she's running to.

Curly Or, more to the point, what she's running away from.

Jeff I'll call you a cab, then, shall I?

Curly Oh.

Jeff We got a number here somewhere. (*Slight pause.*) I'm sorry.

Curly Yes, I'd better be off.

Jeff I'll call you a cab then?

Curly Thanks.

Jeff *goes out.* **Curly** *takes a gulp of wine, stands.* **Jeff** *comes back.*

Jeff It's on its way.

Curly Thanks.

Jeff You don't mind leaving, do you?

Curly 'Course not. Why should I mind? I'm a big girl.

Jeff I don't want you to take offence.

Curly   Honestly, no offence taken.

Jeff   I can see that you have.

Curly   Because you want me to.

Jeff   Listen . . . tonight . . . it was nothing . . . I mean, it was something, it was good, I enjoyed it I mean, but it wasn't . . .

Curly   What?

Jeff   You know.

Curly   Yes, I know.

Jeff   Not that it wasn't, you know.

Curly   Don't go on about it. I know.

Jeff   Stay if you want to. You can stay.

Curly   You just called a cab.

Jeff   I can cancel it.

Curly   You said you wanted me to go.

Jeff   I didn't say that.

Curly   It's what you meant.

Jeff   Look, stay. Why don't you stay?

Curly   Do you want me to?

Jeff   Stay if you want to.

Curly   But you want me to go?

Jeff   I want you to stay. I'll cancel the cab.

Curly   You said it was on its way.

Jeff   I'll call them. They'll put a call through to him and say not to bother.

Curly   They'll charge you.

Jeff   So let them charge me. (*He gets up and puts the cork back in the bottle as much because it gives him something to do in this uncomfortable atmosphere as anything else.*) Why don't you have some wine?

Curly *takes the bottle.*

Jeff   What happened was just between us. You and me. No one else comes into it.

Curly   Why would I think they did?

Jeff   Just in case you did.

Curly   I didn't.

Jeff   Good. I'll cancel that cab. (*Slight pause.*) Just between us, eh?

Scene Five

Lights change. Alone, **Leela** *pours herself a drink, then another and another. She starts to sob quietly, rocking herself. Sound of gentle laughter. Lights up on* **Irma***, who's sitting on the floor in a corner of the room, cross-legged. She's wearing a multicoloured jump suit and trainers, large gold earrings and has a bald head. As* **Leela** *sobs, she laughs softly. As* **Leela***'s crying gets louder, she can't control her laughter and has to hold her stomach. Hearing her,* **Leela** *looks up and her sobs subside. She walks towards* **Irma***.*

Irma (*wiping her eyes*) I'm sorry. I hope you're not offended. I laugh at everything.

Leela *stares at* **Irma**.

Irma You know, it's rude to stare. It's a power thing, an expression of hostility. Though I myself have never had a problem with people looking at me. It's being ignored I can't stand.

Leela Have we met?

Irma I doubt it. I just got here. I'm always late. My friends get used to it. (*Holds her hand out.*) Irma.

Leela (*taking* **Irma***'s hand*) Leela.

Irma You were crying. It always ends in tears. Either that or the china gets broken. (*Pause.*) You don't say much, do you? Not that it matters. I can talk the hind legs off an armchair. (*Pause.*) I was born in south London thirty years ago. My birth was the occasion of great trauma for my mother who, prior to going into labour, had witnessed the strange couplings of common or garden slugs on her kitchen floor at midnight. It wasn't the bizarreness of their copulation that struck her but the realisation that each partner had both projectile and receptacle – she was very fastidious – which, in effect, made the sex act redundant as a particularly flexible slug could impregnate itself. That such a phenomenon existed on God's earth – she was also very superstitious – undermined the very tenets by which she'd thus far kept her life together. She felt cheated. If God had seen fit to bestow this gift upon human beings then she would not have had to undergo the ritual Friday Night Fuck, a particularly vigorous, not to mention careless, session of which had resulted in my conception. She was overwhelmed by the depth of her anger, and the shock of it propelled her into labour. The doctors didn't know how to tell her at first. It doesn't happen very often, but sometimes a child is born with both receptacle and projectile nestling between its legs. I was such a child and the doctors told my mother that she had to make a choice, or I would be plagued by severe mental confusion and distress for the rest of my life. Of course she didn't know which way to turn. In the end she settled on getting rid of the male appendage, not least because she held the things in contempt but also because she felt that black men were too often in the limelight, and that a woman might quietly get things done while those who undermined her were looking the other way. However, she hadn't reckoned with the fact that she had already become attached to me and found me perfect the way I was. So even while the surgeon was sharpening his knives my mother had wrapped me in an old shawl, woven by her own grandmother, and taken me home. I hope I'm not boring you.

Leela No. (*Blinks and sways on her feet.*)

Irma You're drunk.

Leela Am I?

Irma You don't know whether you're coming or going, do you? I've an itch. Would you mind?

Leela Where?

Irma My head. Go on. Don't be scared.

Leela *touches* **Irma**'s *head nervously.*

Irma Give it a good rub, go on. It happened while I was undergoing one of those torturous hair treatments – you know the kind where they put some foul-smelling cream on your head and tell you to shout when it starts to burn. Only when you shout out they can't hear you because they're off on their tea break. So by the time they come back they've got to call the firemen out to administer the final rinse. Not that I'm complaining. I've always been in the vanguard of fashion. You watch. In the future all black women will sport bald heads. And those who haven't had their hair ruined by hairdresser chemicals will go bald in sympathy with those who have.

Leela (*smiles*) That's a lovely thought.

Irma It is, isn't it?

Leela I wouldn't have the guts to shave all my hair off. It wouldn't suit me.

Irma Oh, I don't know.

Leela *looks away.*

Irma Why were you crying? Distance. That's what I'd do. I'd go away. Of course our mothers had religion.

Leela For all the good it's done them.

Irma I wouldn't knock it.

Leela It frightened me watching my mother surrendering to the spirit every Sunday afternoon. When she fell to the ground you'd pull back her eyelid and it was like looking into the eyes of the dead. That total surrendering up of the will frightens me.

Irma You're not telling me you watched that and didn't yourself feel a tingling in your extremities?

Leela Mass hysteria.

Irma Never felt the spirit stirring inside you?

Leela Sometimes I felt I wanted to get up and whirl around the room with them, yes.

Irma Why didn't you?

Leela It would have been dishonest. Deep down I didn't feel anything. I wish I did.

Irma The point is that our mothers found a way of releasing the pain, they never let themselves become victims of it.

Pause.

Leela I've always felt really self-conscious about the way I speak. No one else seems to notice it. At least they've never said anything, but, well, words are sometimes like lumps of cold porridge sticking in my mouth. I always have to think before saying anything in case I get things wrong. I mispronounce words. Or sometimes when there's a choice of two words that sound similar I'll use the wrong one. Not all the time. Sometimes I forget and surprise myself with my eloquence, the precision of my grammar. It's because this isn't my first language, you see. Not that I do have any real first language, but sometimes I imagine that there must have been, at some time. You can feel that sometimes, can't you? If you don't feel you belong to a language then you're only half alive aren't you, because you haven't the words to bring yourself into existence. You might as well be invisible. Other people seem very real. Like you, now, at this moment, seem very real to me. Sometimes it feels as though there's something stuck down here (*Holds her tummy.*) and I want to stick my fingers down my throat and spew it all up. (*Slight pause.*) We've only just met and I'm telling you everything.

Irma There's nothing wrong with that.

Leela I've got to find my friends.

Irma Distance.

Leela It's not that easy.

Irma Did I say it was?

Leela They'll be wondering what happened to me. (*She goes.*)

Scene Six

A room. **Fran** *picks up a coat and is about to leave the room when she's stopped by* **Jeff***, who hides a bottle behind his back.*

Jeff People leaving already?

Fran It is very late.

Jeff We haven't spoken to each other all evening. I've been ignoring you.

Fran You know what it's like when you're playing hostess, you don't notice things like that.

Jeff *takes the bottle and two paper cups from behind his back.*

Fran That's nice.

Jeff Thought you might like something to drink.

Fran I think I've had too much to drink. Don't look at me like that.

Jeff Can't I even look at you?

Fran You're looking right through me, I don't like it.

Jeff Sorry.

Fran I must look a mess, anyway. Can you remember which is Karen's coat?

Jeff The green one.

Fran   You're good at things like that.

Jeff   I wish they'd all go home.

Fran   Didn't you enjoy yourself?

Jeff   I just wish now that they'd all go home and leave us alone. We haven't been alone together for a long time.

Fran   Don't be silly. We're alone all the time. Get fed up of each other.

Jeff   Are you?

Fran   Sometimes. Everyone gets like that. You get ratty with me all the time.

Jeff   The first time I saw you I thought you looked like the girl in that perfume ad.

Fran   Which perfume ad?

Jeff   The one where she's running through the street in her bare feet.

Fran (*laughing*)   Oh, that one. She's running through the street in her bare feet and her knickers, in the pouring rain. I don't look a bit like her. Men.

Jeff   I think you do. (*He is staring.*)

Fran   I'd better give Karen her coat.

Jeff   She's still saying goodbye to people. She'll wait. Have a drink. (*He fills the cups.*)

Fran   I'll be sick if I drink any more.

Jeff   Go on.

Fran *takes a cup.* **Jeff** *looks out of a window.*

Jeff   Black night. Black black night. I love night-time.

Fran   You used to be scared of the dark.

Jeff   Still am. (*Drinks.*)

Fran   You'll be ill.

Jeff   I won't be ill.

Fran   You know what you're like.

Jeff   For God's sake, I can drink.

Fran   I'm not clearing up after you, that's all.

Jeff   I fixed your radio.

Fran   I thought it was beyond repair. What was wrong with it?

Jeff   Nothing much.

Fran   I didn't know you could do things like that.

Jeff   My dad used to say that you should always keep something in reserve.

Fran   Full of good advice, your dad.

Jeff   I think we should go away.

Fran   Oh.

Jeff   We need a holiday. We could go to the Lakes.

Fran   Why this sudden desire to get away?

Jeff   I just fancy getting out of London.

Fran   Is something wrong?

Jeff   Breathe the fresh air.

Fran   You love London.

Jeff   Why don't we both take some time off work and just take off?

Fran   I don't want to go to the Lake District.

Jeff   Why not?

Fran   Because it's all pensioners and babies and rain.

Jeff   All right, pick somewhere else.

Fran   I've got too much work to do.

Jeff   You'll feel better for getting away.

Fran   You always do that. I don't need you to tell me what will make me feel better.

Jeff   I'm not trying to tell you what to do.

Fran   What was all that about then? Let's go to the Lakes. You always do that. I don't have to go with you. We're not joined at the hip. Why don't you go on your own?

Jeff   I just thought it would be nice.

Fran   I've said I don't want to go.

Jeff   All right. I don't want to fight.

Fran   If I wanted to go away, I'd say.

Jeff   All right. All right.

Fran   Look, I don't want to go away. If there's some reason why you want to go away, if there's something bothering you, then we can talk about that here.

Jeff   Like what? What could be bothering me?

Fran   You tell me.

Jeff   There's nothing. Honest. It was just an idea.

Pause while **Fran** *looks for coat and finds it.*

Fran   You used to get angry about things, but it's all gone. You've fallen asleep. You don't care what's going on in the world, can't see beyond your own front doorstep, can you? Wake up, Jeff. (*Slight pause.*) Sorry. I didn't mean that. (*Slight pause.*)

Jeff You're right. Even my parents had something to fight for. Their one dream was to own their own home. It kept them going, the thought that one day they'd get out. They worked themselves into the ground to achieve that dream. Okay, it's not the most admirable of dreams, but it was something to believe in, wasn't it? And they achieved it. All right, so they're still in the same council flat, but at least they own it.

Fran Karen'll think I've run away with her coat. Thanks for the drink.

Jeff Fran?

Fran Yes?

Jeff I fixed your radio.

Fran Yes, you said.

Jeff It's still very fragile, so you've got to be careful with it, make sure you don't drop it or bang it or anything.

Fran Okay. (*Slight pause.*) I don't listen to it any more anyway. (*She goes.*)

Scene Seven

For the first time in this act there is no music. **Leela** *sits on the floor.* **Curly**, *ill, has her head in* **Leela**'s *lap.* **Jeff**, **Bentley** *and* **Claudette** *are standing.* **Fran** *enters with coats.*

Fran Taxis will be here in a minute.

Jeff Everybody hated Othello because he was black.

Claudette In which sense do you mean black? In the biblical sense?

Jeff I'm not talking platitudes now, about darkness within, original sin and all that shit. It's about putting yourself in the other man's shoes, isn't it? I mean, look at the world through Othello's eyes: surrounded by racists, neurotic about his age and appearance, worried about losing his job, his hair. No wonder he ran off with Desdemona.

Claudette I thought they were supposed to be in love with each other.

Jeff He ran off with Desdemona in order to fit into the white world and she ran away with him in order to escape from it. I suppose you could call that a sort of love, if you define love as a mutual need to fulfil each other's fantasies: he wanted to be white and she wanted to be black, or to have conferred on her what she saw as blackness, a certain mystique – all those references to voodoo. In other words, his difference turned her on.

Claudette Why would he need to fit in?

Jeff Everybody needs to fit in.

Claudette Not Othello.

Jeff He needed to fit in more than most.

Claudette Why? Why would he need to fit in? He was the boss. The one who hired and fired, told them what to do, wrote references for them. They had to fit in with him, more like.

Fran Does anybody want another drink?

Leela (*cradling* **Curly**'s *head*) I think we've all had enough, don't you?

Claudette Fitting in. That's crap.

Curly *groans*.

Bentley You all right, Curly? (*To* **Leela**.) She all right?

Leela Her tummy's upset, that's all.

Claudette (*to* **Jeff**) Did you give her something?

Jeff Why would I . . . ?

Claudette To eat, I mean. It must have been something she ate. I'm always telling her to be careful about what she puts in her mouth. Of course, she never listens.

Leela (*to* **Curly**) Are you going to be sick, Curls?

Curly No.

Leela Tell me if you want to be, won't you?

Fran *and* **Bentley** *are standing over* **Curly**, *looking down at her*.

Fran She looks in a bad way. Do you think she wants a coffee?

Bentley (*reaching his hand out to* **Curly**'s *forehead*) Has she got a temperature?

Leela Don't touch her. Can't you see she's hot enough as it is? The poor girl's ill. She can't breathe with you standing over her. Can't you see you're stifling her?

Bentley Sorry.

Bentley *and* **Fran** *are more cautious, standing back a bit*.

Fran Shall I get her an aspirin or something?

Leela She'll be all right.

Bentley Go on, let Fran get her something.

Fran It's no trouble.

Leela I said she doesn't want an aspirin. If she wants one of your aspirins I'll ask you to get her one, won't I?

Bentley Leela –

Leela What? (*Slight pause*.) What?

Bentley Too much to drink.

Leela That's what you think.

Curly *groans*.

Leela Sssh. That's what he thinks.

Fran   I'll get that coffee. Make myself useful.

Claudette   Of course, I reckon that what really got Iago's goat, what really made him jealous, was the size of Othello's penis. Are you telling me they didn't get drunk occasionally in the officer's mess and have spunk-shooting contests? Believe me, they got drunk one evening and Iago offered to do the honours with the old tape measure. Big mistake. He spent the rest of the evening crying into his beer.

Jeff   No, no. That's quite valid. It's just another way of looking at it, isn't it? Of course, you could look at it another way . . .

Fran   Shut up, Jeff.

Jeff   Why? We're just having a harmless post-party discussion. What the hell's wrong with that?

Fran   You're talking shit, that's what's wrong with it.

Jeff   Of course we're talking shit, we're pissed, aren't we? Though, in our defence, it has to be said that the argument has had its moments of subtlety. You've missed the finer points, that's all.

Fran   I don't want to hear any more points – fine, coarse or otherwise.

Jeff   What's bothering you, Fran?

Fran   Nothing's bothering me.

Jeff   I want to know what's wrong.

Fran   (*to the others*)   Your taxis will be here soon.

Bentley   (*to* **Leela**)   Are you all right?

Claudette   Why shouldn't she be all right?

Bentley   You're acting weird.

Jeff   Must be the full moon, Bentley. You know what women are like.

Claudette   Go on, tell him what's wrong with you.

Fran   We're all drunk. I'll get that coffee.

Bentley   Eh, Leela?

Claudette   I'll tell you what's wrong with her.

Bentley   I was talking to Leela, not the fucking ventriloquist's dummy.

Leela   Leave her alone.

Bentley   I asked you a question, Leela.

Leela (*shrugging him off*) How dare you? After touching her, how dare you come and put your hands on me?

Fran God.

Claudette *Amor. Omnia. Vincit.*

Pause. Sound of car horn honking.

Jeff It's all right, Fran. I've been stupid. Now we can talk.

Fran (*to* **Bentley**) So they know. It's good. It's good they know.

Bentley (*to* **Leela**) We've got to talk.

Claudette Bit late for that now.

Bentley I'm sorry, Leela.

Claudette You'll be more than sorry in a minute.

Bentley I sincerely didn't want it to be like this.

Claudette Because, like all men, you wanted the best of both worlds, didn't you? To have your cake and eat eat eat.

Leela For God's sake, Claudette, I can speak for myself.

Claudette Why don't you, then? Go on, speak.

Pause. Sound of taxi horn honking outside.

Jeff You've got your coats, have you? Right, thank you all very much for coming. Happy New Year.

Claudette Charming.

Jeff Not that I'm rushing you or anything but, you know, the party's got to end sometime and now me and Fran want to be alone together.

Fran Stop it.

Jeff Don't we?

Bentley Cool it, Jeff.

Jeff That's funny, after everything you've . . . Are you telling me, in my own house, you come into my house . . .

Bentley I know how you must feel.

Claudette Hark at Mr Sensitive.

Jeff You don't know. Nobody knows. This is my house, Bentley. Get out of my house.

Front doorbell rings.

Bentley Come on, let's go home.

Fran You can't leave now.

Jeff Why didn't we talk? If you'd told me what you wanted . . .

Fran You could never be what I wanted. Bentley –

Claudette   I'm not getting into any taxi with you. You go if you want to, Leela, but I'm going to try for another cab.

Bentley   Coming, Leela?

Leela   No.

Bentley   All right. (*Slight pause.*) All right.

Persistent ringing at front doorbell.

Fran   I think we should go. We might as well go. We can't stay here. (*Shouting through door.*) We're coming! Hold on! I'm going, anyway. You can stay if you want. (*To* **Jeff**.) My things . . . I'll call round for them . . . sometime.

Jeff *is on his knees.*

Fran   Stop it, Jeff.

Jeff   I don't want you to go.

Fran   Get up, you look stupid. (*She goes to the door.*) I'm going anyway, Bentley.

Bentley *walks over to* **Fran**, *and they go.*

Claudette (*as they leave*)   That's right, why don't you just fuck off with your white woman? I hope you'll be very happy together. Leela's too good for you, but you've been so brainwashed you can't see it. Go on, run away. You'll get a shock when you wake up in the morning and the face staring back at you in the mirror is still a black one. She can't make you white, black boy.

Pause. Sound of door slamming shut and car driving away. Pause.

Claudette   That's that then?

Silence. **Jeff** *pulls the string on a party popper. Streamers fly out. He zips up his jacket and leaves.*

Claudette   How're you feeling?

Leela (*after a short while*)   Frozen.

Claudette   We let them off too easily.

Curly *sits up, holding her stomach.*

Claudette   Aye aye. First sign of life she's shown. Slept right through it, didn't you, Curls?

Curly   I feel sick.

Claudette   That doesn't surprise me. Do you know what she's been up to?

Leela   We'd better walk down to the cab office.

Claudette   You've got to admire Curly's indomitable faith in mankind, haven't you?

Leela   Leave her alone, Claudette. This has got nothing to do with Curly.

Curly (*sitting up*)   No, let her carry on. After all, it's just Claudette, isn't it, that's the way she is. Besides, she's right. She is right, though, isn't she? Claudette always is. I deserve her contempt. (*Stands*) After all, she's so high and mighty squeaky clean. (*To* **Claudette**.) Life would be so much simpler if we were all like you. We wouldn't have to question ourselves . . . we'd always be right. We could all feel good about ourselves all the time because we'd be so pure, like little girls who can't risk dirty puddles because they're wearing white socks. The shouting's got to stop some time. Why can't we just live together, why can't we just have some peace? (*She turns, is sick, and then leaves the room.*)

Leela   I'd better see she's all right.

Claudette   She'll be all right. She'll have forgotten half of this in the morning. Curly always does. (*Slight pause.*) What does she know?

Leela   Curly's not stupid.

Claudette   Curly's got no self-respect.

Leela   Fuck self-respect, at least she's honest with herself.

Claudette   What does she know? I'm shaking, look. (*She touches* **Leela**'s *shoulder.*)

Leela   I can feel you're shaking.

Claudette   Why am I shaking? I can't stop. I hate what that bastard's done to you. (*Almost laughing at herself.*) Look, I'm nearly in tears, I'm so angry.

Leela   Poor Claudette.

Claudette (*surprised*)   What?

Leela   Poor poor Claudette.

Act Two

This entire act takes place in Jamaica.

Scene One

A beach. Dusk. **Leela** *is drying herself with a towel while* **Claudette** *stands, drink in hand, watching her.*

Leela I was scared at first. Then one of them made a clicking noise in its throat and gave me a sort of gentle nudge. We swam out together. I've never swum out so far.

Claudette You don't want to swim too far out. You know what they say about dolphins.

Leela I've never even seen a dolphin before. Not in the wild. The water's so clear. It's another world. (*Smiles.*) Like a wildlife film.

Claudette Fucking Jacques Cousteau.

Leela You should come with me.

Claudette I do all the communing with nature I want right here on the beach.

Leela I'd get bored sitting around on a beach all day long. You haven't moved from this spot since we got here.

Claudette Two weeks' time and you'll be back in that office and I'll be back on the road: rain by the bucketful and sexual austerity. I intend to rest, eat, drink, soak up as much sun as I can stand and fuck everything that moves. Yesterday I had three men dancing attendance on me. All the rich young American women on the beach and they're swarming around me. You should have seen Mikie's face.

Leela Jealous, was he?

Claudette Serves him right for chatting up the tourists. He was all over me. Fetching me this, bringing me that. If I didn't fancy him I'd've found it nauseating. As it was . . .

Leela You kissed and made up.

Claudette We made love on the beach. The sea nibbled my toes and the sky seemed so low you could pluck the moon out and eat it like a ripe mango.

Mikie *enters.*

Claudette Talk of the devil.

Mikie I can't stay on this side of the beach too long. That damn Diamond been on my tail all the morning, say I have to walk up and down selling peanuts.

Claudette Who buys them? Nobody wants to eat peanuts on a beach.

Mikie   You tell Diamond. Diamond think that people would buy anything if you force it on them long enough. That woman get crazier every day.

Claudette   You've got to admire her.

Mikie   I don't have much time. I have to talk quick.

Claudette   What is it?

Mikie   Tonight.

Claudette   You can't make it.

Mikie *nods.*

Claudette   Why, Mikie?

Mikie   Sugar.

Leela   I think I'd better go.

Mikie   I'm in big trouble . . . Sugar believe in one man, one woman.

Claudette   Why did you tell her, stupid?

Mikie   I ain't tell her nothing. She say she can smell it on me. That woman have nose like a dog. After I bath and everything.

Claudette   I suppose we're both in trouble.

Mikie   Not you. She won't say anything to you. Diamond wouldn't allow her to mess with the tourists. Is me she beating up on. I got to stay in for the next few nights.

Claudette   Why? She doesn't own you. Mikie, we're only here for two more weeks, this week's almost finished.

Mikie   Maybe, but it's better to keep Sugar sweet. You don't know how much grief she can give a man.

Claudette   I can imagine. Under that obsequious demeanour she looks like a spitfire.

Mikie   Spitfire. Thas Sugar. Spitfire. Yes. Sugar really know how to hit a man where it hurt.

Claudette   So I won't be seeing you for a few nights.

Mikie *shakes his head.*

Claudette   I'll just have to find someone else to take me out on the sea.

Mikie   Two nights. That's all I need to keep Sugar sweet, just two nights. Wait for me for two nights.

They kiss.

Mikie   Pull you shirt down.

Claudette   Why?

Mikie You can't see that old American watching you? Watching like a man ain't eaten for months. A so them does like to watch we woman. Sugar always telling me how American invite her to them room. But Sugar know how to cuss them. Is Diamond fault for setting Sugar on the beach to give massage to tourist. Chuh. Two nights.

Claudette Make sure it is just two nights.

Mikie *goes.*

Leela Be careful, Claudette.

Claudette Aren't I always?

Leela I was thinking about Sugar.

Claudette Sugar doesn't own him. Nobody owns Mikie. Look along the beach, Leel. Everybody knows what the score is. You don't begrudge me a little holiday fling, do you? We all use each other. Everyone goes home happy. No one gets hurt. (*She stretches out lazily.*) Even the sea smells of sex. Forget the dolphins, Leel. Dougie is besotted with you. I tell you, the man's in love. He keeps talking about you. He'll be at Diamond's barbecue.

Leela Which one's Dougie?

Claudette Mikie's friend.

Leela The one who takes his teeth out in the middle of a conversation?

Claudette Life and soul of the party, our Dougie.

Leela I think I'll stick with the dolphins.

Claudette I wouldn't mind if you were enjoying yourself.

Leela I am enjoying myself.

Claudette We don't even get to see each other during the day. You're either off swimming or walking before I've even opened my eyes.

Leela You should come with me.

Claudette I can't think what you get out of it. It's not as if you meet anyone.

Leela I don't want to meet anyone.

Claudette I worry about you.

Leela Don't you wonder what lies beyond the beach? It's more beautiful than I imagined. You can be alone yet not alone. There's a vastness about the place. It doesn't seem like an island at all. The people . . . they seem so at ease with themselves. They have that confidence that comes from belonging. Everyone's got a story to tell. I could listen to them all day. London seems like a figment of my imagination.

Claudette (*gets up, pours wine into a glass for* **Leela**)   Now you're talking. Young women like us should be free. We shouldn't walk around with our heads bowed, apologising for ourselves. We should walk tall. We're young, healthy, beautiful girls. We were born to live like this, Leel. Sod the angst, the wretchedness –

Leela   and the rain and the boredom –

Claudette   To two girls from London –

Leela   two black girls –

Claudette   To hot days and balmy, passionate nights –

Leela   To dolphins –

Claudette   and boys who flex their biceps on the beach just for us –

Leela   To mosquito bites –

Claudette   love bites –

Leela   long walks, coconut milk and mango. To the magnificent silence of the sea –

Claudette   and things that go bump in the night. (*Slight pause.*) To Freedom.

They clink glasses.

Scene Two

Kate *and* **David** *are on the beach.* **David** *is scratching his legs.*

Kate   Scratching makes it worse.

David   How come you haven't been bitten?

Kate   They like foreign blood.

David   By foreign you mean. . . ?

Kate   Tourists.

David   Oh, of course. You're a bona fide exile now, right? Sorry, I forgot.

Kate   I thought you were going scuba-diving.

David   See me scuba-diving? That was Mikie's idea. He's got it into his head that I'm some sort of action man. He keeps suggesting water-skiing and wind gliding. Perhaps he's trying to kill me. He's promised to take me on a guided rum tour of the island.

Kate   He's a nice guy.

David He hasn't got a chip on his shoulder like some of the others. Like that waitress, Sugar. She deliberately keeps getting my order wrong – brings me rum punch when I ask for Coke, chicken when I ask for fish.

Kate Do you blame her? All you tourists care about is sex and cocktails.

David What's wrong with that?

Kate You deserve all the contempt you get.

David It's a long way from home.

Kate Thank God.

David How long are you planning on staying here?

Kate God, it's the Spanish Inquisition again. I don't know how long I'll be staying out here.

David Part of the new lifestyle, eh? Take each day as it comes?

Kate Something like that.

David Isn't everyone looking for their island in the sun? I mean, gardening on a tropical island.

Kate It's a living. I fit in here.

David You?

Kate Okay, so they think I'm a bit strange, but they leave me alone. You sound just like Dad.

David I don't.

Kate You do.

David Sorry.

Kate Wouldn't you stay?

David I don't know. Though I can see why you might want to. (*Slight pause*.) Poor Mum and Dad. Pretty unfortunate to have produced two drop-outs.

Kate You want me to conform so that you can go off and do what you like.

David Yes, why not?

Kate I paid my dues to conformity, David. Now it's your turn. Did they send you out to come and get me?

David No. It was my decision.

Kate Bet they did. You always were a sneak.

David I just wanted to see you were all right. I couldn't live in that strange vacuum of belonging neither here nor there. Wanting here when you're there and there when you're here.

Kate I hardly ever want there.

David Don't you get homesick?

Kate Never. The great thing is feeling yourself disappearing. A little part of you dissolves every day, but you hang on to those things that distinguish you: an accent, the way you walk. You don't give in to the lazy hip-swaying that the other women have. You walk very straight, very fast. People think I'm mad. But the best times are when I feel myself stateless, colourless as a jellyfish.

David Do you think you'll stay here for the rest of your life?

Kate How can I know that?

David Oh yes, sorry, I forgot, nowadays you live moment by moment.

Kate And right at this moment it suits me. It suits me fine.

Scene Three

The beach. Dusk. **David** *and* **Kate** *at one table and* **Leela** *and* **Claudette** *at another. They've just eaten.* **Diamond** *is cutting up tissue-paper to make paper flowers. While* **Diamond** *talks,* **Mikie** *wipes down the tables while* **Sugar** *sets down drinks. Music plays from a radio cassette.*

Diamond I got fed up. I was working my arse out – excuse the French – working my fingers to the bone for those people. I was on my feet for hours in some filthy café. Treated like a dog, worse than a dog. And for what? I had to get out. Back there I was nothing. Here I'm a lady. You can live like a lady here.

David Was it that bad?

Diamond I just couldn't stand it any more. If I had an education, now, like these girls, it would have been fine.

Claudette I wouldn't count on it.

Diamond But as it was . . . I had to get out.

David That's a shame.

Diamond I don't feel bad about it. It was my life. And now this is my life. I don't regret a bit of it.

David (*takes a sip of his drink*) I asked for banana, this is strawberry.

Diamond Mikie, go and tell Sugar to change this.

David Please, don't bother, strawberry's fine.

Diamond That girl must have something on her mind make her forget things so. Look at me. If you let me I would talk all night.

David We wouldn't mind, would we?

Diamond You don't want to listen to me rambling on. I only came out here to try to move you people further down the beach. I'm worried about you all stuck up this side of the beach every evening.

Leela It's more private down here.

Diamond But you missing all the fun. Tell them what they missing, Mikie.

Mikie Jerk pork, jerk chicken. Lobster.

Diamond Cool drinks, swimming in the midnight sea.

Mikie My friend Dougie blowing fire and dancing limbo under a flaming stick. He's very good. Teach himself at home outa book. Nearly burn up him grandmother.

Diamond Get away with you. He think that funny.

Mikie She only get a little burn on she hand, you can't even see it.

Diamond Well, is up to you all what you do, but try to come down. I know sure you would enjoy yourself. See you later. (*She goes.*)

David Diamond's one of those people you could listen to all day.

Mikie If you let her she would talk all day, all night, all year. Diamond have a lot of stories.

Claudette Did you see that? All the beautiful flowers and she was making paper ones.

Mikie She use them as table decorations. She learn it at night school in England.

Claudette I'm glad her time wasn't entirely wasted, then.

Sugar *enters, wearing a cardigan. She's embarrassed talking in front of the hotel guests.*

Sugar Mikie, Mikie. I going barbecue now.

Mikie See you later.

Sugar You coming?

Mikie I follow you later. Diamond want me to stay here a little.

Sugar *wants to say something, but with the others there she can't.*

Sugar All right, see you later. (*She turns and goes.*)

Mikie Sugar, wait one minute. Sugar. (*He goes after her.*)

Pause.

Leela (*fanning herself*) You'd think it'd cool down in the evening.

David I've found that the coolest time is early morning.

Leela You want to strip off, don't you? But then you'd have no protection at all against the heat.

David The other day – (*Nervous laughter.*) I'm embarrassed to say. But the other day I just rolled in the dew, wet my back, my torso, buried my face in the wet grass.

Leela. Yesterday it was so hot I got in the shower with my dress on and let it dry, sticking to me like paper and the dye running off down my legs like blood.

David   It's cooler in the early morning.

Leela   We'll miss it when we get back to England and it's raining. It is hot.

Mikie *enters.*

Mikie   English people always talk about the weather. You go anywhere in the island and find English people, that's what they talking about.

Kate   That's because it's the only thing that unites us. Even in the blazing sun every day, they're talking about the weather.

Mikie *picks a stick up from the ground. While he talks, he makes* **Kate** *and* **David** *stand and each take an end of the stick.*

Mikie   Limbo have a tradition, you know. When people dead, limbo mark the crossing from this world into the other world. The gates of heaven rolling down, people running across quick before the gates of heaven fall on them, then the space between heaven and earth getting smaller and smaller, people so desperate they limboing under the gates so that they can escape from this world.

David   What happened to those people who didn't make it?

Claudette   That's not the point of the story.

Mikie *limbos under the stick. The others – not Claudette – cheer.*

Mikie (*to* **Kate**)   Now you.

Kate   Me?

Mikie   Go on.

Mikie *takes end of stick.* **Kate** *tentatively limbos under stick. She does it.* **Mikie** *and* **David** *cheer. Then it's* **David***'s turn. The stick goes lower and lower. They all take turns until it's too low and* **David** *falls over. Then they all stand dusting themselves off and laughing. The ice broken.*

Scene between **Claudette** *and* **Leela** *overlaps.* **Leela** *watches* **Mikie** *and the others fooling around, smiling.* **Claudette***'s not so pleased.*

Claudette   I'm going to that barbecue. Coming?

Leela   In a minute.

Leela *watches,* **Claudette** *won't.*

Claudette   I hate it when he plays the nigger minstrel.

Leela   He's just having a laugh, Claud.

Claudette   They can't enjoy themselves unless they've taken drugs or drink or got some black to entertain them.

Leela   You're jealous, you want him to yourself.

Claudette   I'm not that stupid. I'm not that stupid, Leel. Me and Mikie speak the same language. When he's kissing me under the stars and telling me he loves me, I know exactly what he means. I say yes darling, yes, and guide his hand up between my legs. It's a cattle market. You sell, I buy. All relationships are some sort of business transaction.

Leela   You weren't always this hard.

Claudette   If I'm a hard bitch it's because I've found that it's the only way to survive.

Leela   Nothing's black and white the way you say.

Claudette   Look at you, aren't they black and white for you? Wandering around the island barefoot like some nun who's just been visited by the Virgin Mary, pretending you can transcend pain through beauty. Mikie and his friends laugh at you. They call you the mad woman of the roadside. Nothing's black and white. What about you and Bentley?

Leela   I'm going to join in.

Claudette   Yes, making fools of ourselves always was a way of evading the issue. Don't expect me to join in, will you? See you at the barbecue. (*She goes.*)

The limbo over, the others collapse into loungers, laughing.

Mikie   You all staying here all night?

Kate   I fancy a quiet night on the beach. We've had a hectic day.

David   We drove right round the island.

Kate   Not quite round the island.

Mikie   You don't want to eat Diamond jerk pork? After I kill that pig with my own hands? Yes. I bring that pig up like it was my own. We was good friends. I used to tell it all my troubles.

Kate   Before you killed it? Poor pig.

Leela   I couldn't kill something I'd reared.

Mikie   Why? Is just a pig.

Kate   You see, that's the difference between men and women. A woman could never see it as just a pig.

Leela   Certainly not if it was a pig you'd told all your troubles to.

David   Pigs bleed a lot, don't they?

Kate   David.

Mikie   Yes, it have a lot of blood. I think that that pig did know when I come in with scraps for it that something was wrong. I didn't talk to it, just throw down the food and watch it eat. Then quiet quiet I get up behind it. You get up behind it, straddle it and hang on. It start to buck like bull then. So you got to hold on tighter. You holding on so tight, you can feel the pig, inside and out, churning about, you can feel fear churning around inside it, trying to throw you off. You have to keep away from it face because pig does like to bite. Pig ready to fight. It would kill you if it could. You holding on tight so that you can smell the pig smell on you stink, feel something beating between you like one animal. Then you feel for the knife, but the knife slip off over him skin in the pig sweat, so you have to get a grip on youself, focus, then slip the knife in. You can feel the last of the life rumbling against you leg. (*Slight pause.*) It have a lot of blood. You soak up with blood.

David   You can almost smell the blood, can't you?

Leela   I feel sick.

Mikie   Why you feel sick?

Leela   I'm going to walk by the sea, get some sea air.

David   We'll come with you. Coming, Kate?

Kate   Not just yet.

David   We promised Diamond we'd go.

Mikie   No rush. Diamond barbecue go on all night.

Kate   You go. I'll catch up with you.

Leela   Coming, Mikie?

Mikie   Later. I better put these things away.

Leela *and* **David** *exit.* **Mikie** *and* **Kate** *are alone.* **Mikie** *smiles.*

Kate   Is your pig story true?

Mikie   It have to be true? You soak up with blood. All over you chest, you hands, it drying on you, sticky. But you don't want to wash youself off, you want to smell that blood on you, let it dry on you. You smell like a animal.

Kate *laughs.*

Kate   I've never met such a cynical people.

Mikie   Who cares as long as we do it with a smile?

Kate   I suppose that story makes the tourists swoon.

Mikie   Some of them even faint.

Kate   I feel a bit faint myself and I've heard it before, or at least something very similar.

Mikie   It's a true story.

Kate   Who were you telling it for?

Mikie   You still here.

Kate   I suppose I should be flattered.

Mikie   You telling me you not flattered?

Kate   I'm not a tourist, Mikie. I've heard that story before.

Mikie   So if I was to invite you to come out with me on my boat, to take in the ocean air . . .

Kate   I'd know exactly what you were talking about.

Mikie   You wouldn't come?

Kate   What is it that you boys who hang out on the beach want? Money? Another notch on your limbo stick?

Mikie   Maybe all those things and more.

Kate   You've probably got a bet on with your friends, haven't you?

Mikie   Now you flattering yourself.

Kate   I'm not one of these foreign women who lie on a beach all day lusting after local boys. You see it in their faces. Young women, there's something aged about them. Harpies ready to tear the flesh off any young man who comes near them. I'm no harpy.

Mikie   And I'm no beach boy. (*He kisses his teeth.*) You think you giving off some sort of sweet odour to mad a man? What make you think you special? You know how many woman like you down on that beach?

Kate   Plenty more fish washed up gasping on the shore, eh?

Mikie   Plenty more ripe mango fallen off the trees, yes. Maybe I shoulda tell you my snake story.

Kate   At least it sounds more original.

Mikie   We have a lot of snakes round here. In the hills. When the sun get too hot they slide down so that they can be cooled by the sea breeze. Sometimes you wake up in the morning and the beach black with snakes. Many people wake up in the middle a the night, find snake wrap round them like rope.

Kate   There aren't any snakes round here.

Mikie   How you know?

Kate   You're making it up.

Mikie   That's what you think.

Kate (*tremor in her voice*)   I don't believe you.

Mikie *hisses at her like a snake.*

Mikie   You scared a snake?

Kate   Always have been.

Mikie   Some people terrified a snakes. (*He pours* **Kate** *a glass of water.*)

Kate   Thanks. (*Drinks.*)

Mikie   So you scared a snakes. Everybody scared a something.

Kate   I'm sure there's not much that frightens you.

Mikie   I'm scared a many things.

Kate   Like what?

Mikie If I tell you, you could use it against me. (*Slight pause.*) It's strange: a woman on her own in a foreign country.

Kate It isn't strange to me.

Mikie I think you're a brave woman.

Kate Not brave. Stupid maybe.

Mikie You must be lonely.

Kate I don't want to talk about this.

Claudette *enters, watches.*

Mikie I would miss my family, friends.

Kate Well, I don't.

Mikie Why don't you want to come out with me on my boat?

Kate Because . . . I didn't say I didn't want to.

Mikie So you coming?

Kate Why not? It's a lovely night. Why not?

Mikie I didn't think you would come out with me.

Kate It has to be on my terms. I know what you are, Mikie, and I don't want any games.

Mikie What you see is what you get.

Claudette *moves upstage.*

Claudette The water's lovely. Of course, I've only got as far as dipping a toe in.

Mikie *and* **Kate** *are embarrassed.*

Mikie Kate want to come out on the boat with me.

Claudette You're going out on the boat?

Mikie Yes.

Claudette I thought Sugar was expecting you.

Mikie Sugar will wait.

Claudette What a good idea. Out on the boat. I hope it isn't too cold.

Kate Why don't you come with us?

Claudette Ask Mikie, I'm terrible on boats.

Kate All right. See you later.

Claudette Later.

Mikie *and* **Kate** *leave.* **Claudette** *sits, pours herself a drink.*

Scene Four

Claudette *and* **Leela** *on the beach.* **Kate**, *asleep, close by.* **Claudette** *gets up, chooses a tape and switches on cassette player, pours herself another drink.*

Leela   Alcohol won't cool you down. This is the hottest it's been at night since we got here. There's usually a fresh breeze off the sea.

Claudette *makes swaying movements to the music.*

Leela   So clammy. I'm sticking to myself. And that smell. Can you smell it? The rawness of the sea and something filthy behind it. Funny how it all seems so big and endless in the daytime but at night closes in on itself.

Claudette *takes* **Leela**'s *arm, pulls her up and dances with her.* **Leela** *places her head on* **Claudette**'s *shoulder, her eyes closed.* **Claudette** *starts to dance faster.*

Leela   You're going too fast for the music. Claudette. (*Giggles.*) Stop it, Claud. Stop it.

Claudette *swings her out. She collapses. They both laugh hard.*

Claudette   Your face.

Leela   Your face.

They laugh.

Leela   Sssssh. (*Points at* **Kate**.) Asleep.

Claudette   Asleep.

Leela *and* **Claudette**   Ssssssh!

Claudette   Poor love's shagged out.

Leela   She's had a rough night.

Claudette   It gets pretty rocky on that boat. You need a strong stomach.

Leela   And an even stronger back.

Claudette   Do you know where they went tonight?

Leela   No.

Claudette   He took her to a cave on the other side of the island. There's a rock pool in it that looks like dirty water during the day. At night it comes alive with all kinds of tropical fish darting about in it like sparks. It's called the Cave of Ghosts because at night the wind whistles through it like a dead man's whisper. It's so frightening you're glad to feel arms around you. (*Slight pause. Referring to* **Kate**.) Travel halfway across the world and they're still there acting like they own the place.

Leela   I didn't think it could get any hotter.

Claudette *pours herself another drink and plays with sticks or stones on the ground.*

Leela   Alcohol just makes it worse.

Claudette   Come halfway round the world –

Claudette *buries her head in her hands, weeping silently.* **Leela** *goes to her, puts her arm around her.*

Claudette It's like there's no escape. You can't run away, it follows you. You can't be yourself because you've always got to be ready to defend yourself. I hate, Leel. I can't stop hating. I hate her. I hate her because she's never been my friend, because she thinks there are two different kinds of woman and that I'm the inferior kind, because she takes comfort in the fact that at least she's not bottom of the pile and delights in my oppression. Because she's constantly betrayed me.

In frustration **Claudette** *throws something at* **Kate** *who stirs. They watch her anxiously. She doesn't wake up.* **Claudette** *smiles.*

Claudette Stupid. Why don't you shut me up? You should shut me up.

Leela She's dead to the world.

Claudette Dead meat. (*Referring to* **Kate**.) Reminds me of a little girl who used to live next door to us. She'd walk past you with her nose in the air, and if she did deign to play with you she'd have to be the one bossing everybody around. It makes me sick to think about the power she had over me. I'd have done anything she told me to. I envied her power. I used to pose in front of my mum's dressing-table with a yellow polo-neck on my head. I'd swish it around, practise flicking my hair back like she used to.

Leela God. Why didn't anyone tell us we were all right?

Claudette I soon grew out of it, though. One day me and my brother lay in wait. We gave her such a beating. (*Laughs.*) Beat her black.

Leela (*laughs*) Beat her black.

Claudette Its make-up's run. You'd think it'd take more care with its appearance, wouldn't you?

Leela Doesn't seem to be bothered with things like that, does she?

Claudette *rummages around in her bag and takes out a lipstick. She goes to* **Kate** *and gently colours* **Kate**'*s lips, quickly moving away every time* **Kate** *stirs.*

Leela (*laughing*) Claudette. You smudged it.

Claudette (*laughs*) My hand's shaking.

Leela You've got the DT's. Give it to me, let me do it.

Claudette *hands* **Leela** *the lipstick.* **Leela** *draws a line across* **Kate**'*s forehead.* **Claudette** *looks* **Kate** *over.*

Claudette Great improvement, I must say, but the hair –

Leela Mmmm. The hair.

Claudette *picks up scissors* **Diamond** *had been using earlier. She opens and closes them.*

Claudette Snip snip.

Leela *watches* **Claudette**.

Claudette (*approaches* **Kate**) Snip snip. (*She tries to cut* **Kate**'*s plait.*) The scissor's stuck.

Leela Stop it, Claud. She'll wake up. Leave it.

Claudette I can't. They're stuck, Leela.

Leela *gets up, takes over. She gently tugs at the plait and, with some difficulty, cuts through it. It falls away in her hands.*

Leela (*shakes it in* **Claudette***'s face*) It's alive.

Claudette Look at those dark roots. She's a fake.

Leela I knew there was something phony about her.

Claudette She slept right through it.

Leela She's had a very tiring night.

Claudette It looks much better short.

Leela Did her a favour, then, didn't we?

Claudette Did her a favour all right.

The mood has changed.

Leela I haven't had such a laugh since . . . What shall I do with this?

Claudette Keep it as a souvenir. Snip snip.

They try to laugh but can't.

Leela Snip.

Claudette Snip.

Leela We'd better clear up.

Claudette No we won't. They pay people to do that. Bed.

Leela (*drops plait*) Bed.

Claudette *and* **Leela** *exit.* **Kate** *stirs, then wakes up, rubbing her eyes as if unsure of where she is. She stands up, then bends down to put her shoes on. When she does so she notices the plait on the ground. She stands stock-still and then slowly backs away. She tries to cry out, but nothing comes. She stands stock-still.*

Diamond *and* **Sugar** *enter.*

Diamond Don't tell me, you haven't gone to bed yet. You English girls. Bet you don't behave like this in your own country, but as soon as you land out here you go mad. It must be the sudden exposure to the sun or something. I don't know. All I do know is that I've got to clean up after you.

Kate (*barely whispers*) Diamond. (*Calls out louder.*) Diamond.

Diamond What is it?

Kate Snake.

Diamond What?

Kate *points at the plait.*

Diamond My God. Don't move. Sugar.

Diamond *indicates the 'limbo' stick.* **Sugar** *picks it up and passes it to* **Diamond**. **Kate** *stands stock-still, trying to control her nerves.* **Diamond** *prods the 'snake'; it doesn't move. She prods again, then straightens up, reaches down and picks it up.*

Diamond   I knew it could never be real. That would be the first time in all the time I live here –

Sugar *laughs.* **Kate** *collapses into a sun lounger, all fear and shock being released. She starts to sob.*

Diamond   I wonder what they would call a snake like this.

Diamond *puts the 'snake' in* **Kate**'s *face.* **Kate** *feels her cropped head. As realisation dawns, she cries out.*

Diamond   Who would do a thing like this? Mikie! Poor girl. Somebody must see something. Mikie!

David *and* **Mikie** *enter.*

David   What's going on? Kate?

Diamond   She have a little shock, that's all. She thought she saw a snake.

David   Snake?

Diamond   This was her snake. (*Holds up her plait.*) Somebody from round here playing a trick while she slept.

On seeing the plait, **Sugar** *bursts into a fit of giggles.*

David   Some trick. (*Puts his arm around* **Kate**.) Are you all right? (*Seeing* **Kate**'s *face.*) God. (*Takes tissue out of his pocket, wipes* **Kate**'s *face.*) What the fuck's been happening?

Diamond   I sorry this have to happen. These people really too jealous. Why can't they just accept the way things are? Her hair will grow again. (*To* **Mikie**.) Go and get her some hot, sweet tea.

David   Don't bother. (*Lifting* **Kate** *up.*) Come on, let's get you inside.

Diamond   You want me to bring you anything?

David   I hope you're going to do something about this.

Diamond   What can I do?

David   Anything. Call the police.

Diamond   Written up on every door in the hotel is a sign which says that the management accept no liability for loss or damage to personal items. I think hair can count as a personal item. Something sweet you, Sugar?

Sugar   The way you swinging that rat tail. It look so funny, Miss Diamond.

Diamond   You think this funny, Sugar?

Sugar   Stop it, Miss Diamond, you going kill me.

Diamond   Anybody would think is you do it.

David   That wouldn't surprise me.

Diamond (*to* **David**.) Go inside. We'll bring you the tea.

David   I don't care how many disclaimers you put up on hotel doors. This amounts to assault. Either you do something about this or we get in touch with the British Embassy and it's trouble for you.

Diamond   No need for all that. We already have enough excitement round here for one day. (*Turning to* **Sugar**.) Get your things and go, Sugar. I don't need people like you working for me.

Mikie   Sugar never do anything. She have alibi. She was with me all night.

Sugar   You think I do that, Miss Diamond?

Diamond   Don't argue with me, Sugar.

Mikie   Miss Diamond, Sugar never . . .

Diamond   You want to lose your job as well?

Mikie   No, Miss Diamond.

Diamond   Well then. Round here we all live together good, have a good time. I don't need people like you to spoil things. We all live good together round here.

Scene Five

Very late, the same day. The beach. **Mikie** *and* **David** *are playing cards and drinking beer.*

David   They could have done anything to her. She was asleep.

Mikie   All I know is, it wasn't Sugar. Sugar wouldn't do a thing like that.

David   I suppose Diamond was a bit hasty sacking her like that. I can't believe she did it either. That's the awful thing, though, Mikie – not knowing who it was. I don't like to think that it was someone from the hotel, but it's even worse to think that it was someone from outside. You don't have any idea who might have done it?

Mikie   Nope.

David   Would you tell me if you had? Certainly in England black people don't tell white people anything. Even your best friend won't tell you his secrets. Why?

Mikie *deals the cards.*

David   She'll be upset, of course, but she won't go home. Too stubborn.

Mikie   Mmmmm.

David   Diamond's right, it'll grow again. But how can people do this to each other? It's not every day you wake up to find your hair's been chopped off.

Mikie *laughs.*

David   Are you laughing at me, Mikie?

Mikie *pulls himself together.*

David   What are you laughing at?

Mikie   Snake.

David   I suppose that it could seem quite funny, though I must say it doesn't make me laugh.

Mikie *hisses like a snake, then laughs.*

David (*puts his cards down*)   Rummy. Another game?

Mikie (*getting up*)   Time for bed.

David   Go on. Another game. I can't sleep, Mikie. I don't feel like sleeping. Go on, stay. You haven't even finished your drink. Finish your drink. (*He deals the cards.*) You wonder what they were thinking while they were doing it. Then you start to wonder what's wrong with these people. Is it some sort of grudge, Mikie? You tell me. You're a man of the world, or should I say a man of the island. Ever been abroad, Mikie?

Mikie *shakes his head.*

David   Don't you want to?

Mikie   I happy here. One day I might go America.

David   You should keep in touch. You're welcome to stay if you find yourself in our part of the world. I doubt if I'll be coming back here. Holiday's fucked anyway. (*Puts his cards down on the table.*) I can't concentrate.

Mikie   See you in the morning.

David   Don't go, Mikie man. I don't know anyone else here. You're the only one I know. (*Shuffles cards.*) Another game. Something else. I know. Come on. (*Puts his arm on the table.*) See if I can beat you. Come on, you're a strong guy.

Mikie   Go to bed, man. You can't stay up all night.

David   I told you, I can't sleep. Come on, put your arm on the table.

Mikie *reluctantly sits and puts his arm on the table. They grip hands.* **David** *wins.*

David   Come on, Mikie man, you weren't even trying. Come on. (*Takes money out of his pocket, throws it on the table.*) Winner takes all.

They wrestle again. **David** *wins.*

David   What's the matter? Isn't that enough incentive for you? That's a surprise. Everybody else here has been quick enough to take our money from us. You've got to tip them for every blasted little thing they do for you. You drop something on the floor and someone picks it up for you, they stand there holding out their hands for you to give them something. I mean, do I look like the world bank? (*Puts some more money on the table.*) That enough? That better? That should get your blood pulsing, shouldn't it. Come on.

They wrestle. **David** *wins.*

David   Looks like I've won all my own money back.

Before **David** *can pick up his winnings,* **Mikie** *takes some notes out of his pocket and throws them on the table. He takes* **David**'s *hand. They wrestle.* **Mikie** *is bending* **David**'s *hand back.*

Mikie You see, now, at this time a night, I not on duty. You see, now, I don't have to smile. You see, now, I don't have to pretend that you have something special about you. You see, what happen out here in the daytime, it's a game, just a game, understand?

David *doesn't reply.*

Mikie Understand?

David *nods.* **Mikie** *bends* **David***'s arm down on to the table and wins the game.*

Scene Six

Very early morning. **Sugar** *sits, hugging her knees, staring out to sea.* **Leela** *enters barefoot, her dress torn, mud on her feet.*

Leela Sugar.

Sugar *looks up and, seeing* **Leela***, looks away.*

Leela You can't sleep either. (*No answer.*) My head . . . The sea looks very beautiful. What a night.

Pause.

Sugar You have mud all over you foot.

Leela I've been walking.

Sugar At this time a night? Boy, unno tourist . . .

Leela I've walked round the whole island. Virtually.

Sugar You better wash that off in the sea. (*Slight pause.*) Why you don't wear shoes?

Leela It's not always practical, is it, to wear shoes.

Sugar I always wear shoes.

Pause.

Leela She'll give you your job back. I'll talk to her, shall I?

Sugar I don't want her filthy job. I tired a people treating me like shit. I tired a fucking tourist.

Leela It won't be easy finding another job.

Sugar I know how to get by.

Leela I feel responsible.

Sugar. How could you be responsible? (*Slight pause*.) Diamond must think I have feelings for these people make me want to do a thing like that. I don't feel no way about those people. They coulda dead for all I care.

Leela I know you didn't do it, Sugar.

Sugar How you know?

Leela (*after a short pause*) I did it. (*Slight pause*.) Me and my friend, we had too much to drink . . . things got a bit out of hand . . .

Sugar (*laughing*) You? That too sweet boy. I don't understand you people at all. Mikie right. He say you all sick, say unno come out here because you broken people. (*Laughs*.) Too sweet boy. What you want from me? You come here looking for . . . You tell me what you looking for. Unno tourist think you belong here. But you come out and you don't know where to put youself: one minute you talking sisterhood, the next minute you treating us like dirt. You just the same as all the other tourists them.

Leela Where else can we go?

Sugar I ain't got nothing for you. I can't give you what you looking for because I ain't got it meself. What happen to unno make you so broken?

Leela (*as she speaks she becomes more emotional and starts to tremble through this speech*) Broken, yes. Invisible people. We look all right on the outside, but take our clothes off and you'll find nothing underneath, just thin air. That's what happens to people who have no language – they disappear. Only your feelings tell you that you exist, so you cling on to them even if they're not nice. And they're not nice. I'm angry, Sugar. I can't stop hating. I hate the world that tries to stifle me. I'm angry with myself for not being strong enough to hit out at it. I want revenge. I want to lash out . . .

Leela's *speech becomes a garble as she struggles to get the words out, her body trembling out of her control. She's breathing very quickly. She starts to mutter under her breath.* **Sugar** *stands and watches, not quite sure what to do.* **Leela**'s *muttering becomes louder and she starts to talk in tongues.* **Sugar** *is bewildered at first, then frightened as* **Leela** *releases all the rage and anger that she has repressed for so long.*

Soon the outburst subsides. **Sugar** *gets behind the exhausted* **Leela** *and holds her by the waist.* **Leela** *is still in a trance, but her utterances have subsided into a muttering again. Her body is quite limp, supported by* **Sugar**, *who rocks her from side to side like a baby.*

Sugar That's right, you relax, you cool down. You rest now. You safe. Safe now. Sssssssh. Sssssssh. Rest. Rest.

Scene Seven

On the beach. **Leela** *and* **Claudette** *at a table drinking,* **Kate** *on stage left at a table on her own, wearing sunglasses.*

Claudette Dougie says everyone'll be there. His little brother's playing. Why don't you come with me?

Leela I can't stand football.

Claudette I suppose you'll be going on another of your walks?

Leela Maybe.

Claudette He's taking me out on his friend's boat.

Leela Oh yes?

Claudette (*defensive*) Our last night, Leel.

Leela What time's he picking you up?

Claudette Seven. I'd better get ready. Will you be all right on your own?

Leela 'Course I will.

Claudette You can always come with us. He asked me if you wanted to come.

Leela Did he?

Claudette I said you probably wouldn't want to.

Leela It's nearly seven now.

Claudette Will you be all right on your own?

Leela Of course I will.

Claudette Well, you know where to find me.

Leela Have fun.

Claudette *goes.* **Kate** *takes off her sunglasses, goes over to* **Leela**'s *table.*

Kate Can I have some of your water?

Leela Help yourself.

Kate The new girl keeps getting things wrong. I ask her for Coca-Cola and she brings rum punch. (*Slight pause.*) It's getting cooler.

Leela It's always cool in the evening. It's the daytime I find unbearable.

Kate My brother couldn't stand the heat.

Leela It is hot.

Kate Not to mention the mosquito bites, though you haven't been bitten.

Leela Time for my walk.

Kate You're going then?

Leela I always walk around this time.

Kate   I know some good walks. Some are so scary you can't go on your own. Rickety little pathways. Look down, you'd have a heart attack. I could show you. Let me put my shoes on.

Leela   Actually . . .

Kate   You don't want to?

Leela   Not right now. Next time.

Kate   It's a deal, next time you're here I'll show you.

Leela   Sounds like my kind of walk. I've got used to walking here. I'm not so frightened of the pitfalls now. It's the way you displace the weight of your body, isn't it? You've got to be in touch with your body. It soon gets used to sudden challenges. That sounds like my kind of walk.

Kate   The next time you're here then.

Leela   It's a deal.

Talking in Tongues

I grew up with the statement 'the personal is political', and I was interested in exploring whether relationships can, in fact, be politicised. Claudette is a fanatic when it comes to expounding her particular brand of racial politics, which are based on a form of separatism, the belief that interracial relationships are a betrayal of the community and, more seriously, a betrayal of the black woman which is connected to her historical degradation. However, Claudette's fanaticism is an attempt to avoid her own pain and longing caused by the traditional double oppression (both within and outside their communities) that some black women experience. This inability to separate the personal from the political means that the ordinary complexities and contradictions of the sexual relationship between Fran and Bentley spill out into the public arena and take on a political significance that is probably unwarranted.

I was interested in the effect that racism has on all our lives – brutalising and reductive – and in the notion of revenge. Do the brutalities of the past demand that we fight fire with fire, which leads to a vicious circle of violence, or should we be seeking other ways to heal the wounds that we have inherited as a result of historical trauma? When Leela talks in tongues it is a scream of rage against the non-communication between the different cultures and the continued repression of the voice of one culture by another. Some critics thought the play pessimistic; I don't. Racism is a fact of life, but it doesn't mean that we can't (or don't) reach out to each other from across the cultural divide. However, we can't do that if we deny the reality of our feelings, whether they be anger or guilt. We can't do it by denying our own individual capacity to wound. When Leela becomes the perpetrator of a 'violent' act herself, she has learnt a lesson, the pain and absurdity of which cannot be expressed in words.

I have always loved the biblical story of talking in tongues. The idea that the whole world once shared the same language appeals to a certain sentimental idealism. In that story the separation of peoples is caused by a fall from grace, the ultimate punishment an inability to understand one another. Like the myth of the separation of men and women who were once one animal, this story suggests that we are potentially more alike than we know and that, while we will never again speak the same language, one of our quests is to find our way back to each other.

Winsome Pinnock
London, 1994

Winsome Pinnock was born in London in 1961. She studied for a degree in English and Drama at Goldsmiths' College and an M.A. at Birkbeck College, both London University. Her theatre writing credits include *The Wind of Change* (Half Moon Theatre, education tour, 1987), *Leave Taking* (Liverpool Playhouse Studio, 1988; Lyric Hammersmith Studio, 1990; Belgrade Theatre, Coventry, 1992), *Picture Palace* (Women's Theatre Group, 1988), *A Hero's Welcome* (produced by Women's Playhouse Trust at the Royal Court Theatre Upstairs, 1989), *A Rock in Water* (Royal Court Young People's Theatre at the Theatre Upstairs, 1989), *Talking in Tongues* (Royal Court Theatre Upstairs, 1991). Awards include the Thames Television best play of the year for *Talking in Tongues* (1991), runner-up Susan Smith Blackburn Award and the George Devine Award (1991). Her television credits include contributions to serials including *Chalk Face* (BBC2) and *South of the Border* (BBC1), and the screenplay *Bitter Harvest*

(1992, co-written with Charles Pattinson for BBC2). She is currently completing a play for the Royal Court Theatre to be produced in 1995. She is at present writer-in-residence for Clean Break Theatre Company. *Leave Taking* is to be revived by the National Theatre's Education Department in January 1995.

A Jamaican Airman Foresees His Death

Fred D'Aguiar

For Kathleen & Godfrey Cadogan

Characters

Alvin Williams
Granny
Bruce
Gerry
Tim
Woman
Man
Kojo
Civilian
Air Force Man
Army Man
Street Vendor
Squadron Leader
Four Scotsmen
Kathleen Campbell
Priest
Pilot
Politician
John Campbell
Mary Campbell

A Jamaican Airman Foresees His Death was premièred at the Royal Court, Theatre Upstairs on 9 April 1991, with the following cast:

Kojo/Kathleen's Father	Jeffrey Chiswick
Bruce/Army Officer	Sidney Cole
Tim/Business	Maynard Eziashi
Granny/Vendor/	
Kathleen's Mother	Maureen Hibbert
Gerry/Airforce Officer	Fraser James
Alvin	Clarence Smith
Kathleen	Geraldine Somerville

Director Hettie Macdonald
Decor Aldona Cunningham
Lighting Johanna Town
Musical director Geraldine Connor-Crawford
Sound Bryan Bowen

Act One

Scene One

Alvin dreams the testimonies of his **Grandmother** *and his three friends* **Bruce**, **Gerry** *and* **Tim**, *including those of a* **Woman** *and a* **Man** *who are witnesses of some kind. The* **Man** *is an English flight lieutenant. The* **Woman** *is Scots and lives in the locality of the base. They are speaking to each other as much as to* **Alvin**, *quarrelling and debating, eulogising as well as thinking aloud.*

Alvin Granny, is you? Granny! You want me name the books. Just say which. Old or new? Pick a psalm. Granny! Ask me. Is me. Alvin. Your one grandson. Granny! You never dead and bury without me there. Them lie. Granny, answer me.

Granny When he was himself, before all this business, he looked like the image of his grandfather. Unlike his grandfather, I used to tell myself, he would live long. I swore on his grandfather's grave. I do everything to make sure his grandson at least lived beyond his fifty years.

Woman He killed those four boys.

Bruce Kill what? I knew Alvin since we this high. We showed each other the first hairs on our balls.

Gerry Dreamer. Al dreamed enough for all of we put together.

Tim Every word a pearl, every sentence a necklace, every gesture of his hanging this necklace in my head . . .

Woman What in hell's name was he shooting at?

Granny I tried to warn Alvin about my dream, but when he get a notion in his head, it burn inside him till it burn out, or burn him up.

Alvin Granny. Don't go!

Man It's all round the base that he didn't like those men. They searched him once, for a tail.

Woman His life for theirs. Where's the good in protecting him. He doesn't have a conscience.

Bruce If a mosquito sucking his blood, he drop everything to watch it drink till it full, then blow on it soft to coax it off him. Not me, boy. Me, I used to let it drink until it so fat and juicy it could barely lift off, then I splatter it with one almighty slap that leave me stinging and bruised and satisfied. Al, he was something else, he would want to fight me over the death of one piddley mosquito, and is my blood the thing sucking, you know.

Woman An eye for an eye.

Gerry You know when he was having one of his visions; his eyes would glaze over. I would carry on talking for a while until I realise he was looking, not at me, but through me. Ask him where he was that was so interesting, what he was thinking, and you'd get this story, this bubbling thing.

Man How can he be loyal to a country he doesn't know? It's not a deep-down loyalty; not in his blood.

Woman Him and his kind should never have been taken on. It was asking for trouble.

Alvin Kathleen? Kathleen!

Tim My head is a vault full of precious things, things put there by Al. Now he gone, I can't get to them. He was me King James, Kitchener and Garvey all rolled into one.

Bruce Boy, sometimes me and him gone up the road over this thing, fighting till we both fall down exhausted. Imagine, the fella willing to put our friendship on the line for a pest!

Woman Not a cloud in the sky. The enemy had turned for home, their tails between their legs. What in hell's name was he shooting at?

Alvin There was cloud. They fired at me first. I fired back.

Man Up there things happen fast, you've got to have the ability to think, deduce.

Woman He aimed good and proper.

Bruce He was no killer!

Alvin Is you for true? Is you! Kathleen! Wait for me. Don't leave me. Not here. Wait! Kathleen!

Man She was a redhead who lacked propriety.

Alvin Bruce. Come back!

Woman That Campbell girl disgracing her family like that. I don't know what she saw in him.

Gerry, *the* **Woman** *and the* **Man** *speak simultaneously.*

Gerry He'd come to, suddenly. Ask him where he was that was so interesting and you'd get this story, this bubbling thing. It wasn't logical, mind you. More like the flight of a firefly. We used to try and follow them in the dark; dashing to the spot where one lit up only to go out when we got near, us running in all directions, trying to guess which spot it would brighten next; if you lucky, it come on right in front your eye, leaving a glow, that shone even with your eyes shut. Is so Alvin leave you feeling good inside.

Man We called him the lascivious Moor but not to his face. It occurred to someone one day and stuck the way nicknames do.

Woman How she could bring herself to kiss him. Ugh, it makes you shudder just thinking about it.

Man He used to get parcels from his grandmother. Weird things in them. Bits of branches he and his friends cleaned their teeth with! Primitive. A root or something he chewed. Oil which he drank and rubbed on his head and body, of superstitious value more than anything.

Woman Must have cast a spell on her.

Tim Al was the single source for all the things I always wanted. Things scattered in various people and places.

Alvin Tim! Come back! Granny!

Granny I warn Alvin about my dream: he was dead, but living; he looked older than me. I was face to face with my grandson who was older than me. It could only mean one thing. He wasn't in this world and he couldn't leave it: he belonged to the next world but he couldn't enter it. He was in limbo. Getting older than me. Watching and waiting. Living and dead. I want him back, Lord.

Tim

                    word pearl
                    pearl sentence
                    sentence necklace
                    necklace gesture
                    gesture hang
                    hang lantern
                    lantern bright
                    bright spot
                    spot precious
                    precious pearl
                    pearl word

                    head vault
                    vault stone
                    stone planet
                    planet jewel
                    jewel shine
                    shine waves
                    waves sun
                    sun sink
                    sink sea
                    sea vault
                    vault head

Alvin Bruce! I still here. Gerry! Tim! I waiting. Bruce! How long I have to wait? Kathleen! I have the book you give me. I learning it by heart. Kathleen! Granny!

Bruce, **Gerry** and **Tim** *form a circle around* **Alvin**. *He tries to get out by ducking through their legs, breaking their linked arms, or just jumping over them. As his efforts increase, they tighten the circle. The good-naturedness of the game is maintained, but the concentration and effort should be serious. After a final effort* **Alvin** *manages to break out of the circle and they all collapse and laugh until their stomachs hurt.*

Alvin Riddle me, riddle me, riddle?

Bruce, **Gerry** *and* **Tim**   Riddle me, riddle me, riddle.

Alvin   What turns, without turning?

Tim (*incredulous*)   What turns without turning?

Bruce   Earth?

Alvin   No.

Gerry   The eye of a hurricane.

Alvin *shakes his head.*

Tim   My stomach when I sat my common entrance.

Alvin *shakes his head.*

Bruce   British policy towards the colonies.

Gerry   The hairs on the heads of Hitler youth from black to blond.

Bruce   Give up.

Gerry   Fed up.

Tim   I know. Madame Josephine's waist just when I tell she don't move.

Alvin   Give up? (*Slight pause as* **Gerry** *and* **Tim** *concede.*) Milk.

Bruce, **Gerry** *and* **Tim**   Milk?!

Tim   What milk? Cow's milk, goat's milk, coconut milk, soursop milk, woman's milk or the milk Josephine milk from me just when I tell she stop.

Scene Two

Early forties Jamaica. A transistor radio, rum and dominoes.

Alvin *walks to a table on which dominoes are arranged in an upright pattern. He pushes the first domino in the line, which knocks over the second in a chain effect until the whole set collapses. He sits.* **Bruce**, **Gerry** *and* **Tim** *enter and sit at the three empty chairs around the table.* **Alvin** *begins to shuffle the dominoes.*

Tim   What is this, a seance? Shuffle the things, man! No war's going to stop me enjoying my game.

Tim *takes over the mixing of the dominoes. They each pull the nearest seven dominoes towards them and pick them up.* **Alvin**'s *double six begins the game.* **Tim** *is next; he slams his down.* **Bruce** *follows, then* **Gerry**.

Kojo, *a mad creole Jamaican, enters, walking in his usual pattern of four steps forward and two backward, with his head held high and looking straight in front of him. This halts the men's game. They watch him pass* *without a word but with looks of disapproval and negative shakes of their heads, more in sorrow than anger.* **Kojo** *takes some time to cross the stage since he pauses between his four-by-two routine.*

Tim (*sucks his teeth long and loud and resumes his game*)   Madass!

Gerry   More than madass, if you ask me!

Bruce   Damn mad ass!

They flick their index fingers against their thumbs and middle fingers at the same time and laugh.

Alvin   Leave Kojo alone. He's harmless.

Tim   He should be in a strait-jacket.

Gerry   More than that he needs a good shock to his system to wake him up.

Bruce   Four steps forward, two steps backward! How far is he going to get walking like that?

Alvin   According to my maths he is making progress; considered progress.

Tim   You right, at least he moving forward, which is more than I can say for this Island.

Bruce (*shouts*)   Kojo! You want a job as a government adviser! Tell Churchill all the youth on the Island wasting away waiting for his call.

Fingers are flicked again and the game taken up with more enthusiasm. **Alvin** *places his domino quietly on the table,* **Tim** *does the same, followed by* **Gerry**.

Bruce   Come on! What's this, a seance?

Gerry   You see ants?

Alvin   The table full of dust and dust make me sneeze when I slam me domino.

Tim   Look like the boy got big plans!

Gerry   You mean epic; we not figuring in it.

Alvin *again places his domino quietly on the table.*

Bruce   Is what? This table got a silencer on top? Put the dominoes down so I can hear!

Alvin   I warming up.

Gerry   Cha Alvin! Play like you playing, man!

Alvin   Is early days.

Tim (*slams down his domino*)   All you happy now!

Gerry   Ecstatic!

Each speaks as he slams his domino.

Bruce   Take this you bitch! Oh Marcus Garvey!

Alvin   Our Odysseus, riding the sea in the Black Star liner to victory!

Gerry   You mean Ulysses on the Liffey!

Tim   O James Joyce with the tongue of a witch and the brain of a dirty old man, inspire this hand up the skirt of the opposition.

A radio announcement brings the game to a standstill: 'We interrupt this broadcast to bring you a special message from Prime Minister Winston Churchill.' *Enter* **Kojo**. *They protest.*

Gerry   Oh no! Not now, Kojo!

Tim   One word out of you and you dead!

Bruce   Maybe he'll be quiet.

Alvin   Leave him. We can listen to both Churchills.

Kojo *delivers a speech in Churchillian get-up which drowns out Churchill's own.* **Alvin**, **Bruce**, **Gerry** *and* **Tim** *play along.*

Kojo (*as Churchill*)   People of the British Dominions. I speak to you today, at a critical time for the restoration of peace in the world. Help from you the Dominions is pouring in, though unsolicited. We are at a stage when the form of the assistance proffered by you needs to be modified. Frankly, if I see another ship dock at Tilbury with a cargo of coconuts, I shall torpedo it. They're too hard to kick or header. Coconut water is as pure as insulin, I'll grant you that, but by the time it gets to us it's cold piss. Don't think we aren't grateful. We are. Extremely. We are of the opinion that the British Minions are little Britains with privileges almost equal to those in the statute of natives of Great Britain (with the notable exception that you get all the good weather and none of the German bombs breaching our shores). I have composed a little lyric about it; yes, there is time for government and poetry. It's unfinished. (**Kojo** *recites to the backing of the tune of 'Land of Hope and Glory'.*)

> Goering's German Luftwaffe
>   are in the fucking air;
> Goering's German Luftwaffe
>   are shitting everywhere;
>
> They shat on granny's bedroom,
>   they shat on granny's street;
> It seems they shit on all things
>   English that they meet.

With a little help from you, the dominoes, I could finish that rhyme. We are a family. The parent is threatened. She cannot take everything thrown at her without it having some effect on you her children. To this noble end I extend an invitation from this Government to you minions to enlist. I have written these closing lines in anticipation of you rallying to the cry of your mother. (*The tune of 'Land of Hope and Glory' accompanies.*)

> Next time the Luftwaffe come to bomb
>   granny's vegetable patch,
> the boys from the Dominions
>   will be there to take the catch!

Alvin, **Bruce**, **Gerry** *and* **Tim** *are jubilant.*

Bruce   Fe fi fo fum I smell the blood of a German.

Tim   Fe fi fo fum I smell the crotch of an English woman.

Gerry Fe fi fo fum I can smell my first million (*He runs his thumb against his index and middle fingers as he speaks.*)

Alvin Fe fah! Churchill is my White Star Liner out of here. (*Slight pause.*) I going shoot straighter than William Tell.

Bruce A crossbow is no match for a repeater rifle; somebody tell him before it too late.

Gerry Remember primary school when teacher used to talk about war.

Tim The way she went on, no one would have joined up.

Bruce Man, she was anti-war.

Gerry Anti-war! If any of us interrupted she would wash your gall!

Alvin She used to ask you questions and answer them herself.

Gerry Boy, if she could see us now!

Tim *mimics a schoolmistress's voice.* **Alvin**, **Bruce** *and* **Gerry** *play school.*

Tim Children, which of you can tell me what the 1914–18 trials and tribulations about.

Hands shoot up, answers blurt out.

Bruce Me miss!

Gerry I know!

Alvin Teach!

Tim Bruceee!

Bruce You get a gun, paint the bullets silver, label them with the names of the enemy, then collect their scalps for trophies.

Tim Not exactly, Brucee. You should cut off the hands as well, otherwise you get disputes about whether the scalps belong to people or monkeys. Gerry, what's your answer?

Gerry Wellll, you get a big, big gun and stick-up everyone, take away their land and make them work it for you.

Tim Warm; but you too kind giving them a job. Alveee!

Alvin I'd let them keep their arable lands, but tax them for the privilege and take a portion of their produce.

Tim You win the knighthood of most ingenious warmongeror.

They switch back to adults, keeping the same high spirits.

Bruce Was it you, Al, who described a swastika as two zeds crossed over?

Alvin Not me.

Gerry Clever, that . . .

Alvin Come to think of it, it was me.

They bundle him, then, rapping their dominoes together and on the table, they strike up a calypso and take turns to improvise.

Bruce   I going to the place they call England,
I got a licence to kill a German;
Though I know I am Jamaican,
You not seeing me back on this Island.

Alvin   You might end up coming back,
Stone cold dead in a pine box;
Once you cross the equinox
In a uniform, you under attack.

Tim   I only going for the English women,
I don't give a damn which side winning;
Give me a girl and take back my Sten,
I just into one kind of shooting. (*He gyrates his waist as he sings his last line.*)

Gerry   I spy money in the armament race;
I spy an empty factory some place;
I spy the entrepreneural space,
For me a man with plenty ideas.

They are jubilant and self-congratulatory.

Tim   Al boy, you were right about putting in our applications early.

Gerry   What I want to know is, how you know they would want volunteers from the colonies?!

Bruce   This man has Swedish ancestry. One of those Viking long boats heading for Britain must have got blown off course to Africa. He got instincts not open to us thorough-bred children of Garvey.

Tim   Duppy consultant.

Alvin   No, nothing that exciting. My grandmother told me. She said she had a dream; all the men on the Island were walking across the sea, walking on water, no less, including us four, and no one was drowning.

Gerry   Ask her if I can make a million as a door-to-door arms salesman.

Bruce   If you not making it now selling what people can eat, I don't see . . .

Alvin   Look, I better check that we at the top of the list for interviews.

Alvin *exits as* **Gerry** *takes up the calypso tune.*

Gerry   I say it before and I say it again,
Nothing can stop me making a million;
If I catch a bullet in action,
Then I go make my money in heaven.

Granny (*talkin' blues*)   When the fire start to burn and there's no water to out it – you know what it mean? Nowhere to run; no place to hide. No one to turn to if you ungodly. Who going save you now. My dream full of everlasting fire. Flames the rivers, oceans and seven seas can't quench. Cities in this fire; cities and the population of cities. Stone, metal and bone melting in the heat. When nothing left in this fire my grandson spring up. But he not seeing me. He calling for me, I beside him, but he not seeing me. He there in the fire, but it not melting him; it holding him together, soldering him together; keeping him in one piece when he want to melt down like everybody 'cause he don't want to be the last soul left in this God-forsaken world. Fire and brimstone and my one grandson facing it all, alone. What it mean?

Scene Three

Alvin's *enlistment interview by a* **Civilian**, *an* **Air Force Man**, *an* **Army Man** *and* **Kojo** *in place of the absent Navy rep.*

Civilian   You wish to volunteer?

Alvin   Yes sir!

Army   Patriotic.

Air-Force   Very like a patriot.

Army   And honourable.

Air-Force   That too.

Army   Patriotic and honourable.

Air-Force   Honourable and patriotic.

Army   Same difference.

Air-Force   One must first have honour; with honour one is in a position to be a patriot. Therefore, honourable and patriotic.

Civilian   There will be neither honour nor patriotism or vice versa unless we can recruit men.

Army   A man with your muscles would do well in a regiment.

Air-Force   A man of your intelligence would do well in a squadron.

Army   I don't see how you could possibly have assessed the man's intelligence when he hasn't said two words.

Air-Force   By the same token, I fail to see how you can talk about his muscles when he is fully clothed.

Army   I made a quick assessment as he entered the room and took six steps to his seat. I could tell from the briskness in his opening and closing the door, by the lightness of his step and from his firm handshake, that he is at least a boxer.

Air-Force   All right, let's test your hypothesis. Now, Mr Williams, if you will kindly enter the room again.

Alvin *goes out of the room, knocks as before, enters, closes the door behind him and waits.*

Army   See! I am vindicated. There's the briskness of an athlete.

Air-Force   Nonsense. It doesn't take much to open and close a door.

Civilian   Gentlemen . . .

Army   These are military matters. We are assessing Mr Williams as we see fit. Will you walk over to this desk as before.

Air-Force   Light-footed?! I counted seven steps.

Army   The last one was a pigeon-step.

Air-Force   I don't care if it belonged to a caterpillar. You are wrong.

Army   Don't jump the gun, he has yet to shake our hands.

Alvin *offers a limp hand.*

Army   You are not the man who walked in that door a moment ago.

Kojo   More like an Englishman's, that handshake.

Air-Force   We are all Englishmen, Englishmen abroad, but Englishmen all the same.

Civilian   Wrong. We are Jamaicans under British rule.

Army   Separate Jamaica from Britain and what are you left with? A poor, small Island without a voice or guardian.

Civilian   Hardly.

Army   Everything we have, and I mean everything, is given to us by Great Britain. A constitution that is British. Think what that means . . .

Kojo   But at what price?

Army   You don't get anything in this world for nothing.

Air-Force   Great Britain does not owe Jamaica a living!

Kojo   Great Britain does not own the lives of our young men.

Army   It's the least we can do.

Kojo   Ditch the Brits.

Army   We must obey the rule of law.

Kojo   Who in this room had a hand in making that law?

Air-Force   The law doesn't apply any less because we're further from Westminster.

Army   Here here.

Air-Force   A principle's a principle.

Kojo   But it has to mean something to the people to whom it applies.

Civilian   Where is all this going?

Kojo   We're Jamaicans.

Civilian   So?

Kojo   And the wonderful constitution you defend is now being contested, right?

Air-Force   The Fascists want to put theirs in its place.

Army   We are not here to question the Government. We are here to carry out its orders.

Kojo   Sometimes the Government is wrong.

Air-Force *and* **Army**   Anarchist!

Kojo   As Jamaicans we can act as conciliators; as a British-Dominion we are forced to take sides.

Army   As a British Dominion? We are a British Dominion!

Air-Force   We have the monarchy!

Kojo   We have plenty monkeys of we own.

Air-Force   This conversation is stupid.

Kojo   Stupid/he, stupid/she, stupid-all-a-we!

Alvin   It seems to me, sir, unless we have this kind of conversation things will never change.

Army *and* **Air-Force**   You too!

Alvin   Don't get me wrong. I am here to enlist. But I am only here because you and you and you told me again and again that was the honourable and patriotic thing to do for the mother country. I haven't been able to see Jamaica and what it is to be Jamaican without seeing an Englishman and the Union Jack. When I do I'm condemned for being a follower of Marcus Garvey. He's the only one who has held up an alternative. He's shown me it's possible to be something other than British.

Army   What do you think of the Army, Mr Williams?

Alvin   It's a good force, sir, but my special interest is in the Air Force.

Air-Force   Bravo! But you know, young man, everyone wants to fly.

Alvin   I've always wanted to fly.

Kojo   Don't be so concrete.

Air-Force   You've got to do better than that.

Alvin   It's my dream, sir.

Kojo (*mocking*)   It's my dream, sir.

Air-Force   What can you contribute to the Air Force?

Alvin   My youth, my strength and my intelligence.

Kojo (*mocking*)   My youth, my strength and my intelligence.

Air-Force   I mean what can you contribute to the Air Force? You, Mr Williams.

Alvin   When I was a boy, my uncle made me a kite, nearly as tall as me. But when I raised it I was too small to control it. A grown-up had to hold my arms to stop it dragging me away. One day I decided to fly the kite on my own. I was sure if I got the right grip and a sure foothold I could steer it – have fingertip control, like I did with smaller kites. I raised it all right. There was a good breeze and the principle is the same whatever the kite-size. I thought I was on top of it – on top of it and on top of the world. I began to jump up and down. I even called out for everyone to come and see me, Alvin, behind that kite they all thought I'd have to give away. Just then a strong breeze hit the kite. Something pulled me so hard I had to look up. All I saw way up in the sky was this tadpole waving. I thought that small thing can't tug with so much force, it must be the hand of God. I thought, if I could hold on long enough, I'd be hauled up to heaven. And heaven to me was all the things I ever wanted but could never have: shoes, long trousers, black puddjng, pepper-pot and souse every day, a new slate for school. Things I dreamed about. Things I knew I would have when I got to heaven. We used to make long lists. We talked to God, but he never replied. When he did answer some people in church we could never understand what they were saying. I tried running along with the pull, but my legs weren't fast enough. I heard the shouts of let go, let go, but I couldn't let go of heaven. I held on for dear life. When I came round they told me I was dragged into a fence. It took me a long time to believe what the preacher preaching on Sundays and even longer to get round to praying. But I never doubted for a moment that I had to fly. Not to God. But because in my head that kite still up there, waiting for me to pilot it to the ground.

Air-Force   Welcome to the Air Force, Mr Williams.

They take turns to shake his hand.

Army   I knew you had a firm grip, must've been nerves, eh? Box?

Alvin   No, sir.

Kojo   You want to fly? We all want to fly.
　　　God's up there in the sky, not down here.
　　　He's up there 'cause he's a bird;
　　　if he's in man's image he'd be down here
　　　getting his hands dirty with the rest of us.
　　　We want to be birds so badly,
　　　we cage them. We teach them our language,
　　　parrot-fashion, in the hope they'll divulge
　　　how it is you grow hollow bones and feathers,
　　　instead of hairs and skin. We consume their
　　　flesh and bones hoping we can digest their wisdom.
　　　But all we get is the stench of our own earthboundness.
　　　We call our women after them 'cause we believe
　　　they were told the secret, but were sworn to silence,
　　　or deliberately withhold it from us for spite.
　　　We spend our lives making paper airplanes,
　　　kites, balloons, airships, real planes, you name it,
　　　even our wishes when we see a star shoot.
　　　We send them all up there to find out

where the birds hide their bird-making formula.
We cry when we're born 'cause the first thing
we notice is that we've got no wings.
So we bawl. We spent the rest of our lives
trying to get back to that comforting, watery,
blub-blub, blub blub, brilliant dark, in the hope
that a second journey will somehow, anyhow,
sprout wings.
Remember and deliver us, O lord, O John Crow,
O sparrow, O Pterodactyl; deliver us this day
from our daily dread of being land-locked,
sea-locked, from our gravity strait-jacket.
Deliver us to birddom, till birddom come,
thy quill be done, on earth as it is in heaven,
a-bird.

Scene Four

Alvin *meets his* **Granny** *on her Singer pedal sewing-machine.*

Alvin   Granny! I join the Air Force!

She sucks her teeth loud and long.

Alvin   By the time I get to England the war might be won.

Granny   Boy, why I scrimp and save to give you an education for?

Alvin   You know how much I want to fly. Jamaica got no air force, joining up is the only way.

Granny   Bird brain.

Alvin   I'll write to you and send my pay. You can save up and run a little shop; get rid of that machine; it's killing your eyes; retire.

Granny   Retire and do what? Go bird-watching? See my one grandson playing the fool in the air?

Alvin   We going spend the whole time rowing!

Granny   Don't talk to me in that tone! For as God is my witness, I going box you down, twenty-one-year-old or no twenty-one-year-old.

Alvin   I love you, Granny.

Granny   You think you are a bird and your station is the sky?
Lick the thread and feed it through the needle's eye.
When the Germans clip your wings explain how you'll fly?
Lick the thread and feed it through the needle's eye.
Are you an eagle or a hawk prepared to kill and die?

> Lick the thread and feed it through the needle's eye.
> Have you done this just to see your old granny cry?
> Lick the thread and feed it through the needle's eye.
> You hardly smell your sweat, don't fall for the old lie;
> Lick the thread and feed it through the needle's eye.

Alvin I don't understand, you were all for it, remember your dream.

Granny That was the other day. I had another dream, not a good one. You was dead, Alvin, but you was still living. You look older than me, next to you I was a young woman. You was dead but living.

Alvin It was only a dream.

Granny Be careful, son; be careful and God bless you.

Alvin The pay good, the sleeping quarters like one of we best hotels. The food good too.

Granny How good?

Alvin Nowhere near your cooking, but good for what you get.

Granny Well, who go thread my needle for me when you gone overseas?

Alvin Send them to me across the sea.

Granny And how long you think that will take?

Alvin Well, you can send me half a dozen needles and six different colour threads. I could send them all back to you ready to use.

Granny You always taking big thing and making light of it. Always. (*Slight pause before she takes up the thread of his thoughts.*) How much you think freight would charge to transport six needles?

Alvin Depends on the type of needle.

Granny Knitting-needle, flour sack needle, leather needle, button needle.

Scene Five

Alvin, **Bruce**, **Gerry** *and* **Tim** *are dressing in their uniforms. They give imaginary, fantastic and true reasons for joining up, accompanied by a snare drum.*

Bruce I joined up to chase the nazis into the sea.

Alvin I joined up to fly across the sea.

Gerry I joined up to kick Mussolini out of Abyssinia.

Tim I joined up for the boots and uniform.

Gerry I joined up 'cause I'm fed up with being broke.

Tim I joined up to stop everybody asking me, 'Why aren't you joining up?'

Bruce I joined up to learn the killing trade.

Alvin   I joined up to help Jamaica's mother in her hour of need.

Tim   I joined up 'cause Jane said if I did I could have what I want.

Gerry   I joined up 'cause I don't have to join up.

Bruce   I joined up. What else is there to do?

Tim   I joined up for the crew cut.

Alvin   I joined up to stop me losing my head.

Tim   I joined up to help me get it up.

Bruce   I joined up 'cause I can't get it up.

Gerry   I joined up 'cause I got a little one.

Alvin   I joined up 'cause I come too quick.

Gerry   I joined up 'cause I like men.

Bruce   I joined up to see what it's like to kill.

Tim   I joined up to get killed. Maybe we can come to an arrangement.

Alvin   I joined up 'cause I'm double-jointed.

Gerry   I joined up 'cause God told me to.

Bruce   I joined up so I can tell my children and their children and my children's, children's children that I joined up.

Tim   I joined up 'cause I told her a very big lie and have to get away.

Alvin   I joined up so I could join the dots on the dotted line where I signed.

Bruce   I joined up to choose how and when I die.

Gerry   I joined up for the feel of joining up.

Tim   I joined up 'cause you all joined up.

Snare Drum Song

Alvin   Mussolini would look a picture
                                  backing in the sea.
                              So would Brylcreem Hitler
                                  and his blond army.

Bruce   Bloody those blackshirts' collars
                                  and Oswald Mosley's.
                              Britain is my father;
                                  Jamaica my country.

All   Join up, join up, everybody join up.
                                  Join the fight so the killing can stop.

Bruce	I'll learn to blow up armour,
	    drink English tea.
	I want to shoot a Luftwaffe
	    down into the trees.

Tim	Jane said she'd let a volunteer
	    do to her what he pleased.
	Britain is my father;
	    Jamaica his battery.

All	Join up, join up, everybody join up. Join the fight so the killing can stop.

Tim	I swore I wouldn't, not inside her,
	    and she trusted me;
	I have to get away fast and far,
	    she has a big family.

Gerry	It's easy to get lost in a war,
	    fighting overseas.
	Britain is my father;
	    Jamaica mothered me.

All	Join up, join up, everybody join up. Join the fight so the killing can stop.

Scene Six

Alvin *is in his uniform. He meets a* **Street Vendor** *and* **Kojo**. *They taunt him.*

Street Vendor Hey! Uniform boy! Buy something for your sweet girl, no!? Army boy! Is army you in or what? Show me your gun. It big? You can shoot straight? (*She winds her waist as she says this. Pause. To audience.*) Him can shoot straight all right, but him going miss me by miles. I is not such a good-looking target for he. Me have somebody me want you frighten with you gun. Hey! Uniform boy! Them don't pay you? You trade in you tongue for you uniform? Lord! Put shoe on country boy foot and clothes on him back and him think him can walk on water. You shit don't stink? Is not the same cloth they wash and press and give you for uniform that come off leper back! (*To audience.*) Him going kill for him mother country and him mother country don't even know she got he for a son. Next thing you hear him turn him gun on Jamaica for him mother country. Him going shoot him mother here for him other mother over there. Is how much mother you got, uniform boy! You not know? (*To audience.*) Him born twice. Lord have mercy.

Part 2 of **Kojo**'*s sermon and appeal to* **Alvin**, **Bruce**, **Gerry** *and* **Tim**, *who are in uniform.*

Kojo Why do you think an ostrich puts his head in the sand? He went and lost his wings and he still looking for them? No. He's ashamed that he had the one thing worth having in this life and he let it slip out of his clutches. He surrendered his bird-given power to break out of the chains of gravity. The ostrich gave up on life when he gave up on wings. Why be like the ostrich? All you will see is dust and death.

Scene Seven

Part 3 of **Kojo***'s sermon and appeal to* **Alvin**, **Bruce**, **Gerry** *and* **Tim**, *who are in uniform.*

Kojo   We're going about getting wings the wrong way. We won't get there by building some fancy contraption or capsule to convey us in the air. When we've wasted ourselves on technology, we'll still be grounded and mentally no nearer to birddom than the tortoise. We must resolve to become birds. I mean putting our minds into being birds. You, my friends, can start this war for the sky, by taking off those uniforms and putting every cell in your craniums to the task of hollow bones and feathers. Why look up at the sky when you can embrace it? Give up trying to conquer the air. Make it yours! Play with it. Empty yourself and it will flow through you like the blood in your veins. Go to it. Go. Go the mental bird way. Go!

A gibberish from childhood days breaks out.

Bruce   Yo-gah-ou thi-gah-rink Ko-gah-o Jo-gah-o real-gah-ley ma-gah-ad?

Alvin   I-gah-i ah-gah-am co-gah-on-vi-gah-n-ced.

Tim   No-gah-o, he-gah-e fa-gah-ke-i-gah-ng.

Gerry   Wh-gah-at do-gah-es he-gah-e sta-gah-nd to-gah-o ga-gah-ain?

Tim   Free-gah-e-d-gah-om o-gah-f th-gah-e ci-gah-i-t-gah-y.

Bruce   St-gah-ay-i-gah-ng s-gah-ane i-gah-s ha-gah-ard e-gah-e-no-gag-uf.

Alvin   I-gah-i c-gah-an se-gah-e h-gah-is p-gah-ain i-gah-n h-gah-is ey-gah-es.

Tim   K-gah-o Jo-gah-o ne-gah-eds a-gah-a go-gah-od be-gah-at-i-gah-ng t-gah-o b-gah-ring h-gah-im t-gah-o h-gah-is s-gah-en-s-gah-es.

Kojo   You people want a free ticket out of here, but you'll be back when your spirit's broken or when you're in a box. We don't want broken people here, people who have given their best elsewhere. You'll end up in the gutter, there's no space for the broken man here. Men that are whole have enough problems staying whole. Come back broken and you might as well return in a box.

Tim*'s insult.*

Tim   You always complaining, complaining;
             you eat chicken batty or something!

Kojo*'s curse*

Kojo   I am your hired griever, pallbearer and gravedigger.
             Your bone harvester. I go impregnate your sister
             when she screaming for you. I go corner your mother

and do to her what you see in your worst nightmares.
You go need eyes in the back of your head and on the top.
You go need eyes on your foot-bottom if you not
going end up dead. You go end up so, you go be glad
when death come to claim you. You go chastise death,
'What take you so long! Get my ass outta this hell!'

Scene Eight

At sea.

Gerry Hey, this ship rocking me like me mother used to.

Tim It rocking me like I rocked Josephine.

Bruce I not feeling so good.

Alvin Me neither.

Bruce Can't you fellas talk about something else or shut up.

Gerry Like what?

Bruce So long as it got nothing to do with water and boats.

Alvin And motion!

Pause.

Tim This ship on this sea like my sweetheart and me:

Bruce Shut up, Tim.

Tim Left and right, up and down, round and round.

Alvin Tim, please.

Tim Be still, I told her, when lying on mined ground;
More still or you'll trigger the detonator;
Absolutely still before I fall off the world;
Please steady your breathing or I am history;

Gerry I feeling bad as well.

Tim All the while I'm begging, she's answering,
Tim, something big, something bigger than us
Pushing and pulling me so, I can't hold on;

Bruce Don't say it.

Alvin No more.

Gerry Please.

Tim I'm harnessed to two stallions powering
Left and right, up and down, round and round.
This ship on this sea like my sweetheart and me.

Bruce I can't hold on.

Alvin I'm getting close too.

Gerry Tim.

Tim So she moved. So slow, moving without moving,

Bruce *vomits.*

Tim You couldn't see her hips' sway; a slowness
Gathering itself; picking-up, picking-up quick;
Then she bucked and I bucked and we exploded:

Alvin *vomits.*

Tim This ship on this sea like my sweetheart and me,
Left and right, up and down, round and round.

Gerry *vomits.*

Tim Pay up, all of you, I win. (*Sings.*) Mih mother seh to mih, she seh, 'Tim, drink some sea watah before yuh board, if yuh doan want yuh stomach fe end up overboard.'

Gerry I ever tell you fellas I can't swin? Well I telling you now. Is true. I can't. I try learning but the water always dragging me down. Now I sit and I reason this thing through. I too shame to tell you fellas. I say to myself, Gerry, this thing here you and you alone must solve. But when I think water all I see is light, when I think swim all I remember is my daddy throwing me in the shell pond at the back of the house with two words: 'Sink or swim.' I wasn't sure which one I had to do to save my skin, so I picked one at random. Sink. I let my arms and legs turn to stone. And I start sinking like I got a purpose. Like all I want to do is get back to land, any land so long as my feet on something solid. But is stupid 'cause the land under water. I start seeing stars and feeling a burning inside like my lungs on fire. I panicked, I thought 'Drink all that pond water and save yourself, Gerry boy.' Man, I start drinking like I had the biggest thirst in the world to quench. The more I swallow the more there was to swallow. Pretty soon I realise I was dying, right there, so I stop fighting. Daddy fished me out and give me a good beating on top. All the time he lashing me I shouting at him through my crying and upset, 'I do what you tell me!' Whap! 'I do what you tell me!' Whap! 'I do what you tell me!' Whap! Whap! Whap! But this war business is like being thrown in the shell pond again, without time to think. I feel like I breathing in water, like I have fire burning up my insides. I feel like I want to get to land by the most direct route.

Bruce Wake eat sleep dream wake eat sleep dream wake eat sleep dream. This life is one hell of a steam train. No pit-stops and no map of where you going. And a conductor who only interested in stamping your ticket and if you ain't got a ticket he damn well squaring up to you to throw you off that train before you choose to get off. I don't recall boarding no train. I just find myself on it and having to make do. For all I know there is no driver. Wake eat sleep dream wake eat sleep dream . . . just driving itself, heading on tracks it find itself on, with no destination in mind and all of us on board listening to our blood tracking and the engine of our heart firing and the way the whole thing can sometimes rock you body and soul and no way of saying hold on a minute I need time to think about this, I got things to do. No real way of getting off. Not when you choose. No siree. You have to jump off the bastard and it's moving at full pelt. You have to watch the ground rushing past and pick your spot and leap. If you lucky you can raise your head and hear that train leaving you behind. Heading into the future without you because you chose when to get off. Wake eat sleep dream, wake eat sleep dream, wake eat sleep dream . . .

Tim   I saying it once while all you sleeping and I ain't saying it again. I never had no girl. I still green. I is one a them fruits that get pick before it ripe. I know what to do because I hear you chaps talking about what you do. I even repeat it and it sound like I was there doing everything exactly the way you all must have done it since I was using exactly the same words. But I never done it. And now I worried 'cause I might never get the chance. I might get myself killed first. I worried too 'cause if I don't get killed then I got to do it. I used to hear my mother and father. It scared me. Her groans sounded like he was strangling her. His grunts like he putting all his strength into killing her. And he was a big man. They never laughed during it, they went quiet after it, so how was I to know they was enjoying it? I should have looked, seen for myself, 'cause what I put in the place of what I didn't see is ten times worse; ten times worse than anything they could have been doing. Girls scare me. I used to like feeling them up when I was young. All of us used to do it. In the playground we used to circle the prettiest girl and try and get a feel of her thing. One day I got the shock of my life. I don't know what I expected when I got near and I put my hand up her dress. I couldn't find anything. There was nothing there, just a space. I ran off thinking whatever Dad doing to Mum, she can't take. The trouble is I know all that was childish foolishness, but I can't see myself with a woman. Not yet. Maybe it will take a war to get me to do it. Maybe at gunpoint or something.

Act Two

Scene One

A welcoming song at an RAF base in Scotland.

> This air force is the best air force
> is a privileged force
> and the only force
> that can muster the force
> against the Nazis.
>
> This air force is the greatest force
> rules the air with force
> talks indecipherable morse
> you are privileged of course
> to be included.
>
> This air force is the one air force
> that has chosen the course
> of justice and boasts
> that it's second to God who's first
> and none other.
>
> This air force will rid the world of the curse
> that plagues Europe and worse
> threatens Britain and the States
> you Dominions can help us
> in this honourable task.
>
> This air force mothers and fathers us
> is our light and purse
> you marry it but can't divorce
> you walk in the mouth and slide out the arse
> if bull-headed you'll be harder to pass.

Porcelain Pilot **Tim**.

Tim

> I leave Jamaica –
> sun, sapphire sea,
> fruits you can pick
> off the trees –
> sail over two weeks
> over 3000 miles
> over a hostile sea
> for this Island in ice,

to end up cleaning toilets!
I am a pilot, of porcelain.
Is pure germ warfare
all the way
I flush out the stubborn
enemy with my pump-action gun.
I banish bad smells
with good ones.
I'm flying
when the chief
tells me
he can eat off
my toilets
it's so clean.
I'm flying
when I have to remind him
to button his blasted flies.

Gerry: *Chief Cook and Bottle-washer.*

Gerry

Can you cook?
Yes, sir!
English food?
Going by the diet
on the base to date,
sir, yes!
We need a man
in the kitchens.
But, sir –
I know it's a lot
to ask of you, not
everyone can fly.
As cook you will be
an important part
of the team.
Your meals will settle
the stomach and train
the eye of a pilot,
steady the hand
of a gunner
on the trigger,
guide that craft
back to base
and the first
thing they ask for
is not a woman,
but something

from cook to eat.
Yes, sir.

Barber **Bruce**.

Bruce I farm. I crop mobile plots of land.
I am the deliberate bushfire
that kills in order to generate new life.
I used to think a head was round.
I tell you, I never see so many shapes
until I started cutting hair on this base.
Hair on a skull is like clothes on a body:
strip it off and you see all the curves,
creases, bumps and dents. Some heads
are vulgar, they suggest genitals
or excreta. Others take on the shapes
of their owners' trade, in this case
bullet-shapes, bayonets, helmets.

One time I ran my hand over a chap's head;
the point on the back of it cut my hand.
Another time I glanced at a fella's head-top;
what I noticed made me double-take,
then stare hard and long. The harder I looked
the closer it resembled between the legs
of a woman and I knew I was lonely bad.

I see the knots and protuberances.
I cut away to the baby in men.
It get so I can read the fortune of a head.
If I look and I see nothing – no hills,
no knots, or bolts, no tributaries –
then I know I cutting a head with no time left
on this earth. It's like the owner's not there.
When I cut back the long straggly hairs
I'm clearing a wild plot to receive him.

Alvin *is welcomed by the* **Squadron Leader**.

Squadron Leader The desire to fly is the oldest in the world. We are born with one of two
hunches: either we had wings but lost them somewhere along the line or we are destined to
have wings, give or take a few million years. But we are having to fly out of necessity. You
know what they say about necessity. (What do they say about necessity?) We have a specific
intention in mind when we take to the air: to bomb the enemy, or shoot them out of the sky.
This is war. You are a thinking extension of a war machine. When you fly it's to kill. No
Sunday afternoon flying here. Up there is a war zone. You're all the time expecting someone
to throw something at you. It's you, flying to meet the other chap, flying to meet you. No
fulfilment of prehistoric instincts there, just plain bloody hell in the sky. So I want you to stop

polishing the wings of your aircraft with your sleeve every time you pass it and start thinking about the nuts and bolts of how to get there, do the job and get back. Any questions?

Alvin Sir, are we allowed to take prisoners?

Squadron Leader If you can take prisoners at five thousand feet, you deserve them.

Alvin If I run out of ammo, can I ram them?

Squadron Leader If you can catch them, yes.

Alvin Can I load cook's blueberry pie into the gun, sir?

Squadron Leader Why, is it a secret weapon?

Alvin You haven't tasted cook's blueberry pie, sir. Can I take a mascot?

Squadron Leader Depends. The last time I granted that request I found the man trying to coax a shire onto his craft.

Alvin Can you fly with me for on-the-spot consultations?

Squadron Leader I'd love to be with you, but I've got to be here for tea: blueberry pie. Jolly good luck.

Scene Two

Alvin *meets* **Four Scotsmen** *in the dark. At first he tries to run, but they surround him, so he fights.*

Voice 1 Don't hurt him, just get his trousers off.

Voice 2 Turn him round.

Voice 3 Shine the torch here.

Kathleen (*shouts from off-stage*) Oi! Leave him alone!

Voice 2 It's a couple of them, let's go!

Voice 1 Did you see it!

They exit. **Alvin** *dresses fast as* **Kathleen** *enters with two torches.*

Kathleen What do they think they're doing! You all right?

Alvin I've lost a couple of buttons, but I'm fine.

Kathleen If I didn't see it with my own eyes I wouldn't have believed it.

Alvin You saw!

Kathleen Of course.

Alvin Saw what?

Kathleen What just happened to you. What do you think?

Alvin What happened to me?

Kathleen Don't you know?

Alvin I'm not sure. This sort of thing hasn't happened to me before.

Kathleen What did they do?

Alvin You said you saw.

Kathleen I saw three blokes running off, I saw you tidying yourself.

Alvin That's all?

Kathleen I can't see in the dark, you know.

Alvin That's all.

Kathleen If you mean did I see you naked, no, I did not. I trained my torch on your face, nowhere else.

Alvin What do you think they were trying to do?

Kathleen You tell me, you're the one who got jumped.

Alvin They were looking for something.

Kathleen Something belonging to them?

Alvin Some notion of theirs which they think belongs to me.

Kathleen I give up.

Alvin That was a great trick with your voice!

Kathleen Till now I've only had to turn it on in the classroom.

Alvin You must teach me. It might come in useful next time.

Kathleen They can't be from round here. It won't happen again.

Alvin How do you know?

Kathleen Because it's never happened before.

Alvin It didn't feel like the end to me, more like the beginning.

Kathleen Report it. They'll be found, that will put a stop to it.

Alvin If not them, others.

Kathleen I don't understand?

Alvin Thanks for your help.

Kathleen Will you be all right to walk?

Alvin Of course, unless you plan to give me a piggyback.

Kathleen I'm Kathleen.

Alvin Alvin Williams.

He holds out his hand to shake hers. She likes his formality.

Kathleen Where're you from, Alvin?

Alvin Jamaica. An island in the . . .

Kathleen   I know where it is.

Alvin   You do!

Kathleen   What's the point of life if not to know the world you live in.

Alvin   I've had to say where it is a hundred times since arriving.

Kathleen   You like Scotland?

Alvin   I like it. I'm not sure it likes me.

Kathleen   You mean to say you haven't had a taste of Scots hospitality yet.

Alvin   Our roads part here. Thanks again.

He holds out his hand to shake hers. She laughs.

Kathleen   I could show you around if you like.

Alvin   Me?

Kathleen   Unless you have a twin as nice as you.

Alvin   Why me?

Kathleen   Go on, I'm not brave enough to ask twice.

Alvin   All right.

Kathleen   Shake on it.

Kathleen *leaves.* **Alvin** *is alone.*

Alvin   Four men in darkness check if I conceal a tail. I am swinging low.

Scene Three

Bruce   Al!

Gerry   We hear you got jumped.

Tim   Let me dish out some of their own medicine to them.

Alvin   You fellas won't believe it.

Bruce   Nothing amazes me about these people. I come here an engineer and they have me cutting hair.

Tim   You can talk, at least you doing something you can write home about. What do I say? 'Dear Mum, I see the enemy as a germ I have to wipe off the porcelain face of the world.'

Gerry   Tell us, then.

Alvin   They stripped me to see if I had a tail.

Bruce   What!

Tim   You joking.

Pause. They collapse laughing at what they see as **Alvin***'s preposterous revelation. They mimic apes by scrambling around on all fours, scratching their bodies, sniffing and trying to look down each other's trousers to see if their tails are intact.*

Bruce   Where's yours, I appear to have misplaced mine.

Tim   Mine's at the laundry.

Gerry   Mine has withered away like Marx's state.

Pause.

Bruce   And the girl?

Tim   What girl? Where?

Bruce   He met someone.

Alvin   Ammm.

Gerry   Good for you!

Tim   When you taking her out? She got any sisters?

Alvin   I don't know. I'm not sure.

Tim   You don't know! Pom-pom staring the man in he face and he turning up he nose!

Gerry   It been so long the man done forget what he have to do.

Alvin   I'm not sure, this not Jamaica, things different here.

Tim   This is more serious than being searched for a tail. You not sure!

Alvin   I don't know . . .

They improvise this song around **Tim***'s opening line.*

Tim	Don't be such a wanker go on take her out.
Gerry	Don't be such a wanker go on take her out.
Tim	Don't be such a wanker go . . .
Gerry	Don't be such a wanker take . . .
Tim, **Gerry** *and* **Bruce**	Don't be such a wanker go on take her out.
Tim	Don't be such a wanker go on take her out.
Gerry	Don't be such a wanker go on take her out.
Tim	Don't be such a wanker . . .
Gerry	A great big bleeding wanker . . .
Tim, **Gerry** *and* **Bruce**	Don't be such a wanker go on take her out.
Tim	Don't be such a wanker go on take her out.
Gerry	Don't be such a wanker go on take her out.
Tim	Don't be such a wanker . . .
Bruce	A wanker from Jamaica . . .
Tim, **Gerry** *and* **Bruce**	Don't be such a wanker go on take her out.

Tim, **Gerry** *and* **Bruce**   Don't be such a wanker go on take her out.
Don't be such a wanker go on take her out.
Don't be such a wanker . . .
Tim   A wanker and a nigger . . .
Tim, **Gerry** *and* **Bruce**   Don't be such a wanker go on take her out.

Alvin   I'm convinced! I'm convinced!

Scene Four

The blessing, signing and launching of the bombers, in three parts, for **Priest**, **Pilot** *and* **Politician**.

Priest (*to the tune of the hymn 'Onward Christian Soldiers'*)

Fly this aircraft, fly it well,
straight from here to Hitler's hell;
when you're there be sure to tell
what your guns can tell so well.
Tell the Nazis that they smell
worse than all the dead in hell,
worse than any words can tell;
that's why your ammo speaks so well.

Pilot

I signed your bombs with my pet name;
given half the chance I'd sign them again.
I feel neither remorse nor shame
for dropping them and causing pain.
I did it in freedom's name;
anyone in my shoes would do the same.
I don't feel bad about the killing game;
it doesn't cause me stress or strain.

Politician

This is the spirit we like to see,
out to defend our democracy,
from the viral spread of Nazis
and the likes of Mussolini.
The spirit of youth and bravery,
the courage to take on anybody;
a peculiar brand of idiocy
that makes me green with envy.
Tomorrow belongs to them, not me.

Scene Five

Alvin *on the safest place in the world.*

Alvin   I used to think the safest place in the world in a war was somewhere between the roof of the weather and space. Not on a Island in the sun none of the factions care for. Not underground in a bunker like a general. But up here, sitting at the back of an aircraft behind a gun, armed just in case I bumped into someone on the other side. We discharged our bombs on a community we flew over high enough not to care about. They fanned out as they got caught up in the full embrace of gravity, beautiful enough to make me pause before the plane banked for home and I had to hold on for dear life. But the higher we flew the more I was reminded of my mortality, of circumstances beyond my control. I was the ant and there was that giant foot ignorantly blotting out my light a moment before sending me to oblivion. I would have been the first to be clapped by any bullets caught by our plane. Some bastard's cannon-fodder. If like me you saw your friends go up but never return, friends you drank with the night before and sat next to at breakfast, you'd know how it feels to be next in line to replace them as rear-gunner.

Scene Six

Gun Talk.

Bruce Rat-a-tat-tat! Rat-a-tat-tat!
Boy they talking about you.
The men saying you shooting
Like the devil himself.
I hear you shoot a cloud
and just when everyone think
you gone mad an enemy fighter
drop like a coconut from a tree.

Gerry Every bomber wants you as rear-gunner.
All I ever told you was you must hold
your damn fire as long as she hasn't fired.
You doing we proud. The white boys saying
you got a natural feel for the thing.
Tell them give you a feel of their sisters.
They're bound to make you a pilot soon.

Tim The Brits will think you can make plane
dodge bullet just like you make bullet
catch plane. Let's hit town tonight.
I hear they have whisky older than me.
The older the better. The young ones
got no pace and don't like the taste.

Scene Seven

Alvin *meets* **Kathleen**. *Each is hiding something in a hand kept behind their back. They move around nervously to keep facing each other.*

Alvin Kathleen!

Kathleen I'm late?

Alvin No, no, no, no, no! Just glad you turned up.

Kathleen Me too.

Alvin You're glad you turned up?

Kathleen No, well, yes. What I mean is, just as you're glad I turned up, I'm glad you turned up.

Alvin You're glad for both of us.

Kathleen Yes, I suppose I am.

Alvin Or twice as glad as I am.

Kathleen Impossible! Gladness fills you up. If I was twice as glad as you I'd need to be twice as big, otherwise I'd explode. (*Pause.*) I got you a present.

Alvin I got you a present.

Kathleen You first.

Alvin Okay. (*He hands her a bunch of flowers.*)

Kathleen Alvin! How in heaven's name did you manage to get these?

Alvin That's classified.

Kathleen They're lovely . . . Now yours. Close your eyes.

Alvin But Kathleen . . .

Kathleen Do it, do it . . . now use your hands as your eyes.

Alvin Rrrrrr! *I see it feelingly*! Kathleen, I'm no good at this.

Kathleen Guess wild.

Alvin A box of chocolates.

Kathleen Wrong. Box is warm; same sort of material. Something that lights up your world without using electricity, gas or coal.

Alvin This is harder than facing the Sphinx. Wait, wait, wait! A book! A book? I hardly have time to read my gran's bible!

Kathleen You can dip into it. Yeats would turn in his grave, though. Most of the really good ones are short. There's one about you.

Alvin Me!?

Kathleen No, silly, about what you do.

She points out An Irish Airman Foresees His Death. *He reads it aloud.* (*See text of poem on p. 278.*)

Alvin Thanks, Kathleen. No one's given me poetry before.

Kathleen I don't know, your gran's bible comes close.

Alvin That doesn't count.

Slight pause.

Kathleen   You know why I like you?

Alvin *shakes his head.*

Kathleen   You don't abbreviate my name . . . you know, Kathy, Kath, K.

Alvin   Is that the only reason?

Kathleen   I'll tell you another some other time. Can't have you getting too big-headed.

Alvin   I like your beauty – it's solid to look at – and what you give out.

Kathleen   Mmmm. I love your voice. Read something else.

Alvin   Any special request?

Kathleen   'When you are old'.

Alvin   'When you are old and grey . . .'

Kathleen (*interrupting him*)   You didn't say the title; you must say the title.

Alvin   Easy, easy. 'When you are old'. Oh, author too?

Kathleen   Read, read.

They exit as **Alvin** *reads.*

Alvin *returns to a welcome from his friends.* **Tim** *sings the first verse,* **Gerry** *the second and* **Bruce** *the third. Those not singing at any one time should say the shoo-be-do lines. Add to this two disgruntled onlookers.*

Tim	When I give her the number one and I walk her home . . .
Bruce *and* **Gerry**	Shoo-be-do-bam-bay!
Tim	When I give her the number one and I walk her home . . .
Bruce *and* **Gerry**	Shoo-be-do-bam-boi!
Tim	When I give her the number one,
	She said, Darling its just begun!
	Put your lips close to mine and walk me home.
Bruce *and* **Gerry**	Shoo-be-do-bam-bay!
Gerry	When I give her the number two and I walk her home . . .
Bruce *and* **Tim**	Shoo-be-do-bam-bay!
Gerry	When I give her the number two and I walk her home . . .
Bruce *and* **Tim**	Shoo-be-do-bam-boi!
Gerry	When I give her the number two,
	She said, Darling who taught you!
	Put your lips close to mine and walk me home.
Bruce *and* **Tim**	Shoo-be-do-bam-bay!
Bruce	When I give her the number three and I walk her home . . .
Tim *and* **Gerry**	Shoo-be-do-bam-bay!
Bruce	When I give her the number three and I walk her home . . .

Tim *and* **Gerry**	Shoo-be-do-bam-boi!
Bruce	When I give her the number three,
	She said, Darling this is milk and honey!
	Put your lips close to mine and walk me home.
Tim *and* **Gerry**	Shoo-be-do-bam-bay!

Scene Eight

Kathleen's *Mirror Monologue.*

Kathleen   Why am I like this? I feel like a schoolgirl. I'm a big woman. Is this what love is supposed to do? Turn my head, make me giddy, make me feel hot from head to toe, make me sleep light and little, make me think about a man more than I think about myself? I don't care. I can't remember feeling this good. He makes me happy. I never thought I'd be happy. I thought the war would kill off all the men in the land. I thought I'd be left alone with my love; with all the love I have in me, left in me to go sour. God, I feel like bursting. I want to love that man so badly I'm afraid I'll scare him off or smother him. I didn't think I had so much love in me. I'm going to burst out of these clothes. I must have love written all over my face and body. Beware lovebug about to burst. I must smell like love. I hope it's a good smell. It's got to be. God, I must stop showing my teeth all the time. This smile doesn't belong to me. It just opens all over my face. I can't wipe it off. I don't want to wipe it off. Alvin. What have you done to me! Whatever it is I don't want you to stop. There's a war on. And I'm happy, happier than I ever was in peacetime. If it had to take a war to get him here to me, then I'm grateful. God, forgive me. But it's true. Thank you Hitler, thank you Churchill. Forgive me God, you invented love. Alvin love.

Kathleen's *father,* **John***, on* **Kathleen**'s *happiness with* **Alvin***.*

John   He's running his hand through her hair. They're talking to each other, they're so close their breaths are mixing. He puts his arms around her body and kisses her on the lips, using his tongue to prise open her mouth. Maybe her mother and I turn a blind eye; maybe not. Maybe if he wasn't around she'd have more time to notice other men. Maybe. But he's there. He's so close she hasn't got time to think without something to do with him always in it, filling her head until all her thoughts for anything else are squeezed out.

Scene Nine

Kathleen's *parents,* **John** *and* **Mary Campbell***.*

John	She opened the door,
	Let in bad weather;
	Weather off the moor,
	Come here to plunder.
Mary	He sees a prized clam
	He's to prise open;

An unguarded lamb
In an unguarded pen.

John

We raised her, she's ours
To give or take away;
Even at this eleventh hour
There's more to do than pray.

Mary

Is there much we can do,
And us in our winter?
Isn't this world a shoe
Made to fit younger?

John

If we say round is square,
Our daughter must agree –
Or her dreams will be nightmares,
Stings infest her honey.

Mary

She stands at mirrors
For such a long time;
She comes back with flowers;
Her happiness blinds.

John

She wears a blindfold
You knitted on her eyes,
With your tales of a world
Where black is worn with pride.

Mary

Your stories of brave men
Of no specific colour,
Must have been an omen
Taken in by our daughter.

John

You bragged about the continent
Shaped like a man's head,
With pyramids like great tents
Full of treasure and royal dead.

Mary

What I told our Kath
I'd have said to any child;
She must sort out the fact
From the fancy and wild.

John

He's flesh and bones
Like the rest of us:
We need sticks and stones,
A knife for deep thrusts.

Mary

What blade is so sharp
It can cut out his tongue,

	Yet play like a harp So Kath hears our song?
John	A blade that's a flower; A blade that can sing; A blade he'll desire; A blade turned on him.

Scene Ten

Rear-gunner **Alvin Williams** *on his final mission.*

Alvin *They firing! They missed? Return fire! Aim! Fire! We missed them? They're still firing! Aim! Fire!* My first time I freezed up. I could only watch. She lying there, her legs spread-eagled. I wanted to touch her but couldn't. I seized up like a engine. It wasn't anything to do with her, she was lovely. It was me. We'd been kissing for ages. At the time I wanted whatever she had to offer. She tore off her clothes; I mine. We were neck and neck, matching each other garment for garment; my shirt her blouse, my vest her brassière, my trousers her skirt, my socks her stockings (I couldn't do anything in socks, I knew that much), my hat, her hairpin that let her hair fall about her shoulders with a slight shake of her head and her half-smile. We were cruising. My underpants, her panties. Us stark naked. Our shoes kicked off long ago, landing somewhere in the room with thuds. *Where did they come from! God, they missed! Fire back, Alvin! Fire back! Save yourself!* Suddenly, I freeze, like someone throw a switch in my head. All I could do was watch her, lying there, her legs spanning the bed, her hips moving from side to side, a quiet groan escaping her lips and her 'I want you'. She couldn't understand what I was waiting for. And us like two sticks rubbing together for a half-hour before, but now only she on fire, me with this thing between my legs that won't work, that could be anybody's. My first time and me only able to watch. She lying there, reaching for the four cardinal points, I mean wriggling like a heel and resembling a starfish or someone treading water all rolled into one. But I'm nailed to the spot at the end of the bed. *Aim! Fire! Bull's-eye!* So it must have clicked with her that I was good for nothing. So she just went ahead without me. I mean we had been kissing, she was all worked up. So, her hands come down her body, she getting louder and louder: 'I want you!' Her hands working faster and faster. Finally her hips rear up clear of the mattress, her heels digging for a grip like they spurring a horse, the bedclothes riding to the bottom of the bed, the bed springs crying. My hands brought to my ears, her cries still loud as ever, my eyes squeezed tight, stars swimming behind my lids till I scream stop! stop! 'No! Not now!' she says, 'I'm nearly there!' Foolishly, I ask where. 'Everywhere!' she shouts. *I hit them! They going down! Fast!* Her knees brought up and together and she rolling onto her side. *Smoke! Fire!* Her free hand pulling the scattered bedding over her body ever so slowly, her groan low and drawn out. Me tiptoeing out, wanting to tiptoe off the world, my heart filling my head in the sudden quiet. (*Slight pause.*) No, God! Not one of ours! Nooooooo!

Scene Eleven

Alvin *is carrying a letter summoning him to an inquiry.*

Alvin Why a summons?

Bruce   Like is you one fly plane . . .

Gerry   Read map . . .

Tim   And shoot gun.

Alvin   Why can't they ask me what happened? Why do they have to legalise everything, write everything down.

Bruce   You just keep your head clear. They're no clouds down here. Nobody shooting at you for no reason.

Gerry   True. Down here you have time to think.

Tim   And you have us to help you do your thinking.

Bruce   So let's think it through.

Gerry   They say they need the details for the records. If they could map our dreams they would.

Tim   Boy, I glad I chose to be a cleaner.

Gerry   You mean to say, you come all this way to fight for them and all you do is shovel shit and you glad. Cha!

Tim   At least they not hounding me. If I foul up I know I already in shit.

Bruce   Don't listen to him, Al. Is no big deal. You're not the first gunner to shoot down one of our own planes.

Alvin   But a summons?

Bruce   You know these Brits. Bureaucracy is their middle name. They have our fingerprint and they keep records of our fillings.

Gerry   Maybe the procedure's changed.

Tim   I bet the white boys don't get harassed when they make a mistake.

Alvin   Mistake? You must be joking! White people never make mistakes; they have 'errors of judgement' or 'misunderstandings'.

Bruce   Don't take it on, Al.

Gerry   They shot at you. What were you supposed to do, wait and check if they got a pilot's licence before you fire back. Cha!

Alvin   It happened so fast I didn't even see them, I just saw the fire from their guns.

Bruce   Ask any pilot what he would have wanted you to do, ask any navigator, ask any of the other gunners. They'll tell you, keep them alive, and that's exactly what you did, Al. Your job.

Tim   I would have done the same.

Gerry   And me.

Tim   Look, try and put it behind you, Al. Let's splash out. Go to a dance in town, listen to some music.

Gerry   Now that's my idea of records.

Tim   Maybe I can score some flesh. That's strictly off the record.

Bruce (*mimics* **Tim**)   Put it behind you, Al. (*Gets angry.*) How can the man put it behind him when it still in front of him. (*Insults* **Gerry**.) Stupidy dogla!

Tim   You mean doogla!

Gerry (*squares up to* **Bruce**)   Who you calling doogla? You know my mother? What you know about my mother!

Alvin *and* **Tim** *restrain* **Gerry**.

Bruce   Let him go! Everyone knows you got coolie blood in you!

Gerry   At least I ain't all slave mentality!

Alvin   Cool down! (*Slight pause.*) What's wrong? You gone mad. Is me one get summons, not all of you. (*To* **Gerry**.) You're right. (*Slight pause.*) Go out, Bruce. Must all we stop living because I get summons. (*Slight pause.*) Anyway, I'm confined to base until this inquiry, as well as grounded.

Bruce   What! Show me that damn letter! (*Slight pause.*) These blasted, ungrateful, untrusting, insensitive, disgusting, using, nasty people.

Gerry   What do they think you're going to do? Renege on your responsibilities?

Tim   You mean re-nigger.

Alvin   Cool down, fellas! Do this for me, eh. Go out. Don't let them see all of us worked up by this thing. (*Pause.*) Have a Scotch on me!

Bruce, **Gerry** *and* **Tim** *exit*.

Alvin *standing*.

Alvin   You ever feel like you on the outside of something and no matter how hard you try you can't get in? Excluded from it though to all intents and purposes in it? That's how I feel in bonny Scotland. You might well ask, how can you be in a place, under its skin, at the centre of its activity, yet as remote from all that equals its life as if you watching a screen. There are entrances, all right. I see people walk in and out of doors all the time. But when I approach where I think there is an opening: nothing, zilch, kapooch, a wall, no niches, not a brick out of place. Only plants growing out of the concrete. That's how I know there is a way to get a foothold. If those plants can put down roots, so can I. (*Slight pause.*) I live out of a suitcase of memories, unpacking a little at a time so I don't run out too fast. If my suitcase empties before I find a way to stick like those plants to those walls put up everywhere, then look for me in one of the many asylums.

Scene Twelve

John *and* **Mary Campbell** *at home.* **John** *believes he has found* **Alvin**'s *Achilles' heel. As he thanks the gods,* **Mary** *enters.*

John	Thank you gods for what you give to those you guard from the wicked!
Mary	How can you call God's holy name in the plural? Your call is vain.
John	The God I don't worship except in a crisis, I will now worship on a daily basis.
Mary	What's overcome you, John Stanislaus Campbell? You leave in a stew; you return all bubbles?
John	We've no need to wrestle with that mortal danger; he'll not pound his pestle in our daughter's mortar!
Mary	A blade that's so sharp it can cut out his tongue? And play like a harp so Kath hears our song?
John (**Mary** *comes in too*)	A blade that's a flower! A blade that can sing! A blade he'll desire! A blade turned on him!

Scene Thirteen

Bruce You can't see her.

Alvin I must.

Tim I thought I was the only one round here who couldn't resist a piece of action.

Alvin It's not like that.

Tim   Yeah?

Alvin   I love Kathleen.

Bruce   Love is a big word.

Gerry   Bigger than common sense.

Bruce   It's too risky to see her.

Alvin   I have to.

Tim   Listen to the man, Al.

Bruce   People talking, rumours flying all round the base. People watching you.

Alvin   What people?

Bruce   All I can say is security is not always in uniform.

Tim   What do you mean, Bruce?

Bruce   Not everybody who say him is friend is friend.

Gerry   The writing on the wall is clear.

Tim   Soon as it goes up I scrub it down.

Alvin   What are they writing?

Tim   Pure stupidness. I was never sure these chaps could write. Now I know they can't.

Alvin   Write what?

Tim   Gibberish. Wor-gah-se th-gah-an w-gah-e spe-gah-ak.

Alvin   Tell me.

Tim   Well . . . imagine a gorilla with a machine-gun.

Alvin   What?

Gerry   A kind of trigger-happy chimpanzee!

Tim   Warm.

Bruce   Johnny Weissmuller to Cheetah: Umgawa! Meaning, come, go, fetch, stop. Johnny Weissmuller to the native extras: Umgawa! Meaning do, don't, try it and I'll break you and your spears in two and now I'm here find another jungle to live in. Johnny Weissmuller to Alvin: Umgawa! Meaning murderer, guilty, hang.

Tim   Very warm.

Alvin   A psychopathic baboon behind a gun in a bomber!

Tim   Hot!

Gerry   Umgawa!

Tim   Boo-doom!

Pause.

Gerry   A man came up to me and called me a killer.

Alvin You?

Gerry Right in my face. You ever hear anything so barefaced.

Bruce You should-a tell them they got the wrong man.

Alvin That's right, send them to me. Better still, deny all knowledge of me.

Bruce Move, Alvin.

Gerry I just cooking my pie and mash. Come feeding time I dishing it out minding my own business. This guy walk up to me with his empty plate looking for me to dish up some mash and thing for him. He wait till I fill his plate, then he call me a killer. I don't know this dry face man from Adam. Boy, he had his full consignment of mash but I dollop a extra spoon of the stuff right in his mug. Me and him end up on the floor.

Alvin I'm sorry.

Gerry Sorry for what?

Alvin You fellas got your hands full because of me.

Gerry It's not your fault.

Tim I got my scrubbing brush. The one with hard bristles. That brush been everywhere. Next time a man say anything to me about the shooting I swear I going to ram that brush down his friggin' throat. Then I going ask him how come he know you guilty before the inquiry and how come every man with a black face on this base guilty too. And if he don't answer I going to push that shitty brush even further down him till the hard bristles so deep inside him they start to clean out his behind.

Bruce Never mind any of that! The man grounded, he's confined to base, he's facing an inquiry, but he still want to see the damn woman!

Alvin Damn woman? You talking about my Kathleen?

Bruce I'm talking about us! Taking a lot of shit because of you. Now I don't mind that, we go back a long way, but I'll be damned if I'll let you jeopardise your future and ours even more by going off the base.

Tim It look like they fixing to get you hanged, drawn and quartered.

Alvin Don't any of you bother. From now on is me one in this. I'll see her.

Bruce (*slight pause*) We mustn't lose sight of this business. You're not a criminal. A mistake is a mistake. But going off the base is another matter, buddy. Count me out.

Tim Me too. Go and see Kathleen now and you might make things worse.

Alvin This don't concern you fellas, you've made your positions loud and clear. You credit rumour and gossip over the actual inquiry! (*He exits.*)

Bruce (*shouts after* **Alvin**) What's the hurry, let we discuss the thing properly. Why you rushing, rushing, Al, like you is some Russian?

Alvin *prepares to go and meet* **Kathleen***; his friends have failed to talk him out of it. He mimics them fussing over him.*

Alvin (*as* **Tim**)   Wear it so! (*He tilts the hat to the left.*) Enjoy your date with her! Just make sure she don't hatch for you! (*To* **Tim**.) I hope you meet someone you can love and not just laugh at. (*As* **Gerry**.) No, so! (*He tilts the hat to the right.*) How he wears his hat could mean the difference between a sprint and a long-distance race. (*To* **Gerry**.) Dougla! Nothing wrong with that. More curls for her to run her fingers through. I could-a teach you how to swim. (*As* **Bruce**.) Nooo, so! (*He straightens the hat as before.*) Don't crowd him. Men who sprint leave women still warming up. (*To* **Bruce**.) My true friend. (*Sucks his teeth.*) What kind of friends fall at the first hurdle? Drop out the race? Leave me to finish it on my own? Friends I can do without.

Gerry   So much for telling Alvin how we really feel.

Bruce   You had your chance, why didn't you tell him?

Gerry   Because you're the one who's always ruminating.

Tim   Rum-in-a-ting.

Bruce   People talking, we defending. Things look bad. But when were they ever really good? When we signed up? When we reached here? When? Hardly a week pass without one of us in a ruction smashing up a bar because they won't serve us or breaking up a dance because they won't let us in. So what's new with this business over Al? He's in trouble, we're in trouble. That's the score. We been keeping it since we got to this place. From now on Al in this on his own. I ain't fighting his battles for him, when he's not prepared to listen to us.

Tim   Can't we stop talking about it? If he's going he's going! (*Pause.*) Knock, knock?

Gerry   Who's there?

Tim   Ruminating.

Gerry   Ruminating?

Tim   Rum-in-a-thing you call a bottle. Rum ain't for eating, rum for drinking. Rum ain't hating nobody. Rum love everybody who love it.

Bruce   Shut up, man!

Scene Fourteen

Alvin *and* **Kathleen**. *We meet them after they've been together for some time.*

Kathleen   I just want to look into your head to see what's going on.

Alvin   Even I don't know that sometimes. (*He pushes back the lids of his eyes.*) Look in these two windows, you'll see everything.

Kathleen   They're not windows, they're screens. (*Slight pause.*) What do you see?

Alvin *(shuts his eyes)*   A calm plain, no people, little vegetation, a stillness everywhere, except for clouds, drifting . . .

Kathleen   Love me.

Alvin   Yes.

Kathleen   Care for me.

Alvin   More than I care for myself.

Kathleen   Think about me.

Alvin   I can't keep my mind off you. Look in my eyes. Don't you see the pictures of you everywhere, no room for anything else.

Kathleen   Marry me then!

Alvin   You can't rush big things like marriage.

Kathleen   Why wait?

Alvin   I have to be sure.

Kathleen   Of what? Me?

Alvin   Of myself.

Kathleen   But . . .

Alvin   Please, don't misunderstand me. This has to do with me, not you.

Kathleen   You don't think I'm right for you.

Alvin   I couldn't wish for anyone lovelier.

Kathleen   A girl is waiting for you in Jamaica.

Alvin   No. I told you, it's me.

Kathleen   You don't think I'm pure enough.

Alvin   I don't doubt that! I haven't been able to get near you.

Kathleen   It's not for want of trying!

Alvin   I love you.

Kathleen   And I only love you if I give in to you . . .

Alvin   No, but it helps. Joke, joke.

Kathleen   The truest things are said in jest.

Alvin   Is that Yeats?

Kathleen   Has to be earlier, jest is a bit archaic for him.

Alvin   He's not far off being archaic; all those poems about fairies.

Kathleen   I'd love to talk to you about Yeats, but you've changed the subject.

Alvin   Which is?

Kathleen   Why you wouldn't marry me.

Alvin   Boring.

Kathleen   Interesting body, boring subject, eh?

He whispers in her ear. She recoils laughing. They kiss.

Kathleen   Well come on, Biggles, what's this great reason why you can't marry me? Once we're married we can do anything you like.

Alvin   Anything?

Kathleen   Anything!

She whispers in his ear. He feigns shock, then grabs her. They kiss. He manoeuvres his body against hers. She pulls away.

Kathleen   No! Not till we're married.

Alvin   You wind me up and leave me.

Kathleen   How come I'm the one has to do all the controlling around here? There's my future and that of any children I might have.

Slight pause.

Alvin   How do you think they would look?

Kathleen   I don't know . . . redheads with suntans.

Alvin   That doesn't sound very pretty.

Kathleen   You ever seen a redhead with a suntan!

Slight pause.

Kathleen   Alvin, why, why, why can't we marry?

Alvin   I wish I could tell you.

Kathleen   We can't have secrets. You know everything about me, everything.

Alvin   Circumstances wouldn't allow.

Kathleen   You can't have everything your own way, Flight Sergeant Alvin Williams.

Alvin   Don't call me that.

Kathleen   You don't have to say, just nod, yes or no . . .

Alvin   No, I'm not playing.

Pause.

Kathleen What's wrong, love? It won't seem half as bad if you tell me. (*Slight pause.*) I couldn't bear to live without you.

They embrace.

Kathleen You can tell me on your deathbed.

Slight pause.

Alvin So, I'm going to die first.

Kathleen If you're to tell me this secret, yes. We'll have to arrange it so that when you die after telling me your secret I'm frail enough to follow you almost immediately.

Alvin What if you're deaf?

Kathleen I could read your lips or you could write it.

Alvin What if you can't see?

Kathleen You'll have to write it in Braille.

Alvin And if you got no hands?

Kathleen We can devise a code, one for yes, two for no . . .

Scene Fifteen

Bruce, **Gerry** *and* **Tim** *form a circle round an imaginary* **Alvin** *and mimic him trying to break out.*

Bruce Come on, Al! Try harder!

Gerry We not letting you go, not this time!

Tim This circle is for life!

They get tired and break the circle.

Bruce Riddle me, riddle me, riddle?

Gerry *and* **Tim** Riddle me, riddle me, riddle!

Bruce How can an Englishman who weighs one hundred and eighty pounds be heavier than a man from the Caribbean who weighs in at exactly the same one hundred and eighty pounds?

Gerry The air in the Caribbean is light. The air in Britain is heavy. When they stand on the scales of justice in Britain the heavy air works against the West Indian by pressing down the scales in the Englishman's favour. You with me? Now, when they stand on the scales in the Caribbean, the light air lifting the native off those scales but it not touching the Englishman, so the Englishman heavier over there too. The West Indian can't win, at home or abroad.

Tim No man. It's to do with gravity itself. It stands to reason that the gravity over here, where the air grey and where the sky so near, bound to exert more of a pull on the body than the gravity in the Caribbean, where we have plenty light and the sky big and far away. But, and this is a big but, since the British control gravity everywhere, all the Englishman got to say is 'gravity do your thing' and abracadabra, his one hundred and eighty pounds weighs more than the West Indian's one hundred and eighty pounds.

Gerry *and* **Tim** Riddle!

Bruce Take Alvin. He was like any other man when he was in a plane behind a gun. In fact, he was better than most because he could shoot straight. Yet when the man make his first mistake, bap! Dishonourable discharge! They hit him for the same mistake the next man make, but they hitting Al bcause his one hundred and eighty pounds ain't worth as much as the one hundred and eighty pounds of the other fella. (*Slight pause.*) Dishonourable discharge! After everything Alvin did for them? Riddle me that.

Bruce *is upset.* **Tim** *and* **Gerry** *comfort him.*

Scene Sixteen

Kathleen *on the wire.*

Kathleen They say I used to be nice, sweet, agreeable, fun, daddy's girl, mummy's girl, a yes mum yes dad three bags full girl.
I say little bo peep has lost her sheep and has no wish to find them.
They say I'm not the girl they raised.
I say damn right I'm not. That girl is now a woman.
They say Alvin is no good for me.
I say my heart tells a different story.
They say Alvin's grounded for shooting down one of our own aircrafts.
I say I'll believe it when I hear it from Alvin.
They say Alvin's a killer.
I say they are liars. Wolves in sheep's clothing.
They say he should be tried for murder.
I say Alvin is my shepherd, I shall not want.
They say I shouldn't speak the Lord's name in vain. He'll punish me.
I say if their God lays one finger on me He'll have to answer to me and then to Alvin.
They say I should not blaspheme under their roof.
I say nothing.
They say have I lost my tongue.
I say nothing.
They say black sheep.
I say Baa, Baa.

Scene Seventeen

Alvin *summons up his* **Granny** *for a consultation.*

Alvin Granny!

Granny Alvin?

Alvin Granny!

Granny Alvin!

Alvin Granny.

Granny Boy, what do you?

Alvin I need you, Granny, here with me.

Granny I here.

Alvin I need you now.

Granny I here now.

Alvin Granny, what should I do?

Granny What you always do.

Alvin But I can't think. I don't know my left hand from my right. Things aren't what they seem.

Granny Hold up your writing hand.

Alvin *obeys.*

Granny Hold up the hand you bowl cricket ball with?

Alvin *obeys.*

Granny Good. Now hold up the hand that threads my needles.

Alvin *obeys.*

Granny Very good. You see. Start there, Alvin. With small certainties.

Alvin *perks up.*

Alvin Ask me something else.

Granny Like what?

Alvin Anything. (*Slight pause.*) Go on.

Granny Which comes first, dignity or honesty?

Alvin *pauses.*

Granny Answer right away. Which hand do you use to flick your index finger against your thumb and middle finger?

Alvin *holds up his right hand immediately.*

Granny Which comes first, dignity or honesty?

Slight pause.

Alvin Well, if you are honest, completely honest, then dignity will always accompany honesty. It's like a race where if honesty winning, then dignity right there by the side of it. They crossing the winning line together.

Granny You don't need me.

Alvin I do.

Granny Alvin, you never really on your own, not completely, not once you got someone in your heart. (*Pause.*) You got a English girl in your heart!

Alvin Scottish.

Granny She got she own teeth?

Alvin No, I have to chew her meat up for her!

Granny Buy her a bar of Lifebuoy.

Alvin Granny . . . she smells like a rose.

Granny Your heart in good condition.

Alvin Sometimes I feel my heart doesn't belong to me. It's thumping in my chest, but it sounds like somebody else controlling it.

Granny It's always yours. Whoever's in your heart is always with you.

Alvin Then why don't I feel it?

Granny Stop seeing yourself apart from things when in truth you link up with them. When you first learned to write you took a long time to make the jump from writing in capitals to writing in longhand or what you used to call join-up writing. When you did your first sentence of longhand you couldn't understand what the fuss was about. The distance between the two was not real. You imagined it. Is like the distance between dignity and honesty. One shouldn't lead the other. They're on the home straight together, side by side. You, Bruce, Gerry and Tim, and whoever else in your heart, in this thing together, believe me.

Scene Eighteen

Alvin *standing*.

Alvin And the first shall be the last. (*Slight pause.*) If I could fly I would. You see these bumps – (*He points to his nipples.*) – they're evidence that I, we, had wings once. In all of us men and women, these wings shrank, then moved round our back to our chests. These are not nipples, they're the buds of wings. I'm going to develop wings. I exercise all the time. One day I'll fly out of this lock-up. I used to fly. Imagine pelting a stone at someone flying at you while you're flying at them? Sometimes you'd wait and wait to see who or what was coming at you before shooting. But you couldn't wait one second longer. It wasn't just your skin you had to look after, a whole crew depended on you. Wait one second too long and all of you were goners. They fired at me first. They missed. I returned their fire. I didn't miss. (*Slight pause.*) I went and lost, my bonny lass, to rass! Where my cutlass! Let we go and cut some ass! (*Slight pause.*) Barber! Chief Cook and Bottle-washer! Champion Porcelain Cleaner! Kite Flyer and Joker without a Tail! Boy, I could shoot! They called me Rear-gunner William Tell, then Rear-gunner David after they asked me where I learned to shoot so straight and I said throwing stones back home. I was their David with my mechanical slingshot finding the temple of the giant every time. But, in my dreams, my finger always squeezing the trigger, and the face that's always coming at me and ready to shoot me down is mine. Mine! (*He opens his bible at Psalm 55 and reads; clearly he knows it by heart.*)

> I said, O that I had the wings of a dove!
> I would fly away and be at rest –
> I would flee far away
> And stay in the desert;
> I would hurry to my place of shelter,
> Far from the tempest and storm . . .

An Irish Airman Foresees His Death

I know that I shall meet my fate
Somewhere among the clouds above;
Those that I fight I do not hate,
Those that I guard I do not love;
My country is Kiltartan Cross,
My countrymen Kiltartan's poor,
No likely end could bring them loss
Or leave them happier than before.
Nor law, nor duty bade me fight,
Nor public men, nor cheering crowds,
A lonely impulse of delight
Drove to this tumult in the clouds;
I balanced all, brought all to mind,
The years to come seemed waste of breath,
A waste of breath the years behind
In balance with this life, this death.

W. B. Yeats

A Jamaican Airman Foresees His Death

A Chorus Circle

The idea for the play came out of a long and loving relationship with a poem by W. B. Yeats called 'An Irish Airman Foresees His Death'. Yeats's Airman was an aristocrat who had his own private reasons for joining the malaise of the First World War as a Gentleman Pilot: 'A lonely impulse of delight', instead of the usual peer-group pressures, nationalistic drives or ego urges associated with killing on a mass scale over a prolonged period. I was fascinated by the notion of a similar impulse in a Jamaican working-class man when it came to the Second World War. The colonial situation would still prevail for the Jamaican as it did for the Irishman, but both would respond to some private need and goal despite a burgeoning nationalism and an obvious but crucial difference between them of class. It seemed that for the Jamaican it would take a special kind of character who would want to fight as a pilot in a war and argue his case on private, selfish grounds instead of opting for the ready-made and acceptable basis of loyalty to 'the mother country'.

It was clear that the play would have two locations, Jamaica and Scotland – Jamaica since I had to show Alvin at home with his friends and then signing up and leaving the Island for the first time, and Scotland because during World War II West Indians went there to train as pilots.

The style of the play was decided partly by the source for it, that is, a poem, and partly by my own leanings in plays I liked to see and read. It would have to use all the modes of speech – prose, poetry, song, monologue, dialogue, soliloquy and chorus – to tell the story of Alvin, the main character, and his three friends, his grandmother and Scots girlfriend, as well as her parents and the other people on the periphery of their lives. Part of this movement away from the straightforward linear-narrative way of looking back had to do with the thing under scrutiny. The Jamaica of World War II was a colony that had emerged out of a slave society. This experience involved forced migration, settlement and resettlement, and government from abroad. A drama that sought to reflect this complex reality would at least have to find a form with a matching fluidity, with elements of fracture and artificial juxtapositions and impositions, if it was to make a serious claim to explore that past. In other words the nature of the past under scrutiny dictated the approaches to it. A chorus of voices in agreement, debate, disagreement, betrayal, war and peace seemed the best way to approach this past.

The preoccupation was not simply with the huge social forces that shaped the colony. In addition to that, I wanted to assess the damage to the individual in psychological terms when subjected to these forces and impulses. The young Alvin (played magnificently by the talented Clarence Smith) would be forced to reconcile his dreams with the reality in which they refused to fit. His girlfriend Kathleen would be pushed to examine her loyalty to blood ties in light of her own openness towards Alvin in blinding contrast with her parents' fear and hostility. In her head she had to murder their authority over her in order to follow her heart.

Hettie Macdonald's inspired decision to stage the play in the entire space allowed by the Royal Court Theatre Upstairs, with an audience drifting around on foot as the action moved from one segment of the space to another, released previously unseen forces, such as the dramatic power of the individual voice, the relationship between apparently diverse episodes, the deracinated nature of the experience of those in the play and its important interior/psychological component. As a result of this directional approach I was able to write and rewrite to the rehearsals. Many of the play's problems were ironed out on the floor by action and discussion. I found this process most illuminating as each line, each stretch of dialogue, each song was put through the test of the voice and of the dramatic moment embodied by that voice: either it passed that test or it ended up on the cutting-room floor. It was a process of testing the past against the mettle of the present. The entire cast added in no small measure to the depth of the characters they portrayed. There was individual discussion by me with each of the actors and a degree of adjustment in terms of a rewrite or cut. The Set Designer and Lighting Designer were as deeply involved in this process.

Some of the language used approximates to the Creole of Jamaica in the spellings used. This is because the pronounciations are safeguarded in the phonetics and because the English spoken was always on a continuum, with the Standard at one end and the Creole and Scots at the other, and the various characters swinging from one to the next. There is no sense in which the dialects are at war: all are marshalled to articulate the complexity of the characters involved, as well as being a testimony to the ornate relationships borne out of colonialism. For the most part the speech is accented according to the geographical location without any need to alter the spelling from the Standard. If the line is a Creole line it will be clear in the grammar. If the spelling is Creolised that's because some adage or saying is being employed by the character to make a point. I wanted the speech to be as plural as the people and the emotions involved.

Finally, I thank Burt Caesar for seeing this project through from our initial conversations about my idea for a play concerned with West Indians in the war to his championing of a reading of the play at the Court and his dedication in bringing it to the point of production. My biggest thanks are owed to the whole crew involved: nuff respect.

Fred D'Aguiar
March 1994

Fred D'Aguiar has written three collections of poems: *Mama Dot, Airy Hall* and *British Subjects*. He has also written a novel, *The Longest Memory*. They are all published by Chatto except for *British Subjects*, published by Bloodaxe Books.